D1252387

The Human Nature
of Social Discontent

The Human Nature of Social Discontent

Alienation, Anomie, Ambivalence

GARY B. THOM

Rowman & Allanheld
PUBLISHERS

To
Mother, Martha, Marcus
and Moby,
without whose help this author
would have been impossible.

ROWMAN & ALLANHELD

Published in the United States of America in 1984
by Rowman & Allanheld
(A division of Littlefield, Adams & Company)
81 Adams Drive, Totowa, New Jersey 07512

Library of Congress Cataloging in Publication Data

Thom, Gary, 1941–
    The human nature of social discontent.

    Includes bibliographical references and index.
    1. Alienation (Social psychology) 2. Anomy.
3. Ambivalence. I. Title.
HM291.T44   1983   302.5′44   83-3154
ISBN 0-86598-105-1

83 84 85/ 10 9 8 7 6 5 4 3 2 1

Printed in the United States of America

Contents

Acknowledgments

I thank the following individuals for commenting on various portions of the manuscript: Martha Andresen, Francesca Cancian, Pete Clecak, Harry Eckstein, Creel Froman, Bernt Hagtvet, Bill Johnston, Robert Lane, Shawn Rosenberg, Carole Uhlanor, Ken Wexler. Special thanks to Graham Little, who subjected the first few chapters to close scrutiny and did wonders for my confidence in the enterprise.

A number of others provided intellectual inspiration and emotional support, in some cases across considerable space and time. These include Terry Baker, Hagit Borer, James Street Fulton, Bridget Glidden, Derald Glidden, Will Jones, Shulamit Kuhn, Phil Kimball, Kevin Lang, Alice Macy, Carruth McGehee, Charles Miller, Jim Vincent, Christian Werner.

Competent and conscientious secretarial assistance was provided by Dottie Gormick. Helen Wildman, Kathy Alberti, and Cheryl Larsson helped reduce the pains of word processing. Gerald Delahunty, assisted by Brenda Horkins and Blythe Ayne, helped prepare and repair the index. Portions of this work were funded and facilitated by a Faculty Fellowship from the School of Social Science at University of California, Irvine.

My debt to certain seminal social theorists, allies and antipodes alike, is made obvious and explicit in the text.

Introduction

We are, I know not how, double in ourselves, so that
what we believe we disbelieve and we cannot rid ourselves
of what we condemn.

Montaigne

What I have to say in these pages was fathered by a previous book, and there is a slight family resemblance. For this I take paternal responsibility but make no apologies. It is a matter of roots. Growing up in rural East Texas meant enduring long-winded fundamentalist preachers week after week, and night after night when revivalists were in town. Early on I concluded that most preachers have but one sermon: the only meaningful test is how often they put you to sleep with it. What are we to think of preachers who change their subject from week to week, or spice their sermon with the mundane and profane? Might they not change their minds as well? Does not one thing lead to another?

In addition to involuntarily receiving a lifetime's dose of the boring and the profound, I thereby acquired a distrust of radical departures and an abiding interest in radical thought. Such are the impious vagaries of what sociologists persist in calling socialization. One wonders whether the perpetrators of such linguistic misdemeanors were themselves poorly socialized. To anyone free of such hard-won hardness-of-hearing, every sermon speaks simultaneously, if not always clearly or loudly, of opposed truths, irrespective of its inattention to antitheses and antipodes. I propose to examine why this is so, and what difference it makes for self and society.

To be specific: I am concerned here with the two fundamental social discontents—alienation and anomie—their poorly understood relation to one another, their place in social and political theory, and especially their human basis. My thesis is that these are dialectically opposed maladies, grounded not only in social conditions and institutions but also in a fundamental human ambivalence. An emotional, human dialectic underlies and accompanies the better known Marxist clash of social contradictions. This ambivalence is between differentiation and dedifferentiation, dividing and making equal or identical. It is a simultaneously cognitive and emotional. The claim is not that all conceptual or emotional oppositions can be reduced to or assimilated by this pair. It is that this pair is involved and reflected in the formation and observance of any distinction. Furthermore, and this is crucial, it corresponds to the division between the differentiated, differentiating conscious faculties and the undifferentiated, dedifferentiating unconscious: our two basic modes of thought and being.

Seen in this light, ambivalence is both human and universal. To assert its significance does not tie us to specific ambivalences salient to particular historical periods, cultures, social strata, or individuals. It does not wed us to dualistic thought, since distinguishing and opposing are basic to any categorical system. The posing and observing of any and all distinctions, the basic ambivalence this always reflects and promotes—these are the ingredients of the essentially human. By the same token, ambivalence in this sense is irremediably social. Specific ambivalences always constitute the "content" of this basic form or relation. We do not experience ambivalence in its pure form, since we never experience it in a social vacuum. The mind and emotions always find particular contents to chew upon. Particular ambivalences eat at us. Even so, given ambivalences are always accompanied and given emotional weight and tone by that most primitive opposition.

In this way I am led to a model of the psyche in which the distinction between conscious and unconscious is drawn according to the degree of differentiation involved in their respective thought processes. The unconscious, in this view, consists of material too dedifferentiated to be accessible to conscious faculties, which are more or less bound to thinking one thought at a time. This "unrepressed" unconscious is usually contrasted with a view which stresses the repression of unacceptable or painful material, though I argue that this may be a distinction without much difference. In any event the unrepressed unconscious is what Freud referred to as *the* psychic reality.

A series of arguments drawing on diverse sources—symbolic anthropology, comparative religion, Sartre's "psychoanalysis of things," Schrodinger's discussion of the nature of life—converge on the proposition that life may be conveniently and fruitfully associated with the process of differentiation, while death can be expressed as dedifferentiation. The larger conception which comprehends and combines both modes is designated as Life, or Total Life. Thus life in the "relative" sense is associated with the conscious, while death is associated with the unconscious. The self is defined as the symbolic union of the conscious and unconscious: the overcoming of the primitive ambivalence or opposition between the modes of difference and no difference. As such, it appears to reproduce its basic structure in every form it creates or observes, since every form can be expressed as some combination of difference and equality, dividing and making equal or identical. This is true of the most elementary distinction we might make, since any distinction not only establishes difference but also "makes identical" both what it distinguishes and what it distinguishes from. The self seems to model itself after Life, though it may be the other way around as well.

Alienation and anomie emerge from these deliberations as two fundamental, apparently opposite ways of failing to adequately accept or realize this ambivalence in the forms we create or confront, including those conceptual categories which inform our ways of thinking about ourselves. These discontents represent the failure to express our being (the undifferentiated totality which is our unrepressed unconscious) by means of our becoming (the life process of differentiation). The contention is that alienation is or involves excessive or exaggerated separation of the two modes, the absence of contact and communication, whereas anomie is the unmanageable influx or intrusion of less differentiated material into the differentiated conscious functions and faculties. In both cases this denies the self, understood as the union of conscious and unconscious, the identity alive amidst these opposed modes, adequate expression in the forms it creates or must comply with. Rigidity and chaos are the calling cards of alienation and anomie, along with numerous other binary pairs which denote or connote the two modes.

This way of looking at alienation and anomie insists upon both individual and social sources: our fundamental discontents are simultaneously human and social. What is more, given that these conceptions arise out of and are embedded in an epistemological outlook profoundly skeptical of opposites, the suspicion is that our two basic discontents are ultimately one.

These issues are first broached in connection with a critical look at numerous representatives of the contemporary social science of alienation and anomie. This literature manages to be both lifeless and chaotic, reflecting and promoting the very maladies it seeks to illuminate. Partly this is the result of neglecting or distorting seminal treatments of these matters found in Marx and the classical sociologists. Partly it stems from preserving and exploiting weaknesses in classic accounts. And partly it is the result of proceeding as if no theory were necessary, or as if theory will emerge full-blown from allegedly pre-theoretical facts. Afterwards there is a mad scramble to find out what their data and the myriad discontents they uncover have to do with alienation and anomie. Meanwhile the data are mum. One partial exception to this atheoretical and atonal affair is the perspective of Robert Merton. But he thoroughly blunts the cutting edge of Durkheim's account of anomie. I conclude that the lion's share of the deep difficulties in this and many related areas derives from the neglect or sociologization of human ambivalence.

With this in mind I return to those classic sources, to Durkheim on anomie and Marx on alienation. The goal is to separate the two concepts and associated theoretical perspectives in such a way as to make synthesis possible and plausible. I point out that their treatments of these maladies are born of opposed perspectives on man and society, but I try to open the door to a perspective which might accommodate what is essential and worthwhile in both. The key to the door is humanly general ambivalence. On this note I turn to Freud, for whom the concept is central, and to the task of making servicable his interlocking conceptions of ambivalence, the unconscious, and the death instinct.

Rejecting the death instinct, foregoing any attempt to specify the nature of instinctual ambivalence, I am led instead to the psychology and symbolism of life and death, the locus of a basic ambivalence not instinctual but psychological. (Chapters Six and Seven may seem a bit unhinged to readers unfamiliar with literature in this area. Those who wish to obtain an overview of the argument may wish to skip these chapters initially.) The upshot of this excursion is the notion of life as differentiation and death as dedifferentiation. I proceed to show how these perspectives parallel and underpin Nietzsche's doctrine of the will to power, his critique of logic and epistemology, analysis of *ressentiment,* and polemics against Christian asceticism and modern libertinism. In some respects my argument substitutes life and death for the will to power. His dialectical monism becomes a dialectical dualism, but the overriding theme, that opposites as such are false and the belief in opposites pernicious, is much the same.

What is distinctive about the argument is that thought itself is seen as ambivalent, as both dividing and equalizing in nature and intent and effect. The process of equalizing is associated with the unrepressed undifferentiated unconscious. The creation, observance, and dissolution of forms is critically dependent on the interaction of the two modes. Any form can be thought of as establishing a difference, a making distinct, a rendering individual; but the division is always accompanied by an equalization of all those other distinctions and differences. But this is equivalent to rendering them undifferentiated and therefore unconscious. Once we focus on this unconscious material it is no longer unconscious. While it always accompanies the conscious mode, we can never catch or isolate it. Not only does this dramatize the cooperation of the undifferentiated mode in establishing and maintaining boundaries of distinctions and forms, it also suggests its crucial role in rendering boundaries permeable, flexible, movable.

In this light, then, alienation may be seen as lifeless form, and anomie as formless life. The life process of differentiation—the growth, extension, expression, elaboration of the self—depends on dedifferentiation, and thus a larger conception of Life which embraces life as differentiation and death as dedifferentiation, overcoming and relativizing the conflicts and differences in the two modes. To associate death with the unconscious makes death a symbol for all those other aspects of Life any particular conception of life leaves out—all those aspects left out by the repression of opposites, and all distinctions and details save the one we have brought to consciousness.

This brings us finally to Simmel, who injects the notion of ambivalence (though he does not speak of his dualisms this way) into the analysis of all social forms and their contributions to alienation and anomie. Man, for Simmel, is both the fixing of boundaries and the reaching out across these boundaries; this dovetails with the primal distinction or ambivalence I stress. We are not one or the other. What is missing from his account is the link between his dualisms, which in-form our every form, his characterization of man in terms of boundaries and their violation, dividing and equalizing; and the notion of ambivalence. The key to seeing these together is the association of that equalizing activity (which accompanies differentiation in his every analysis of specific forms) with the cognitive activity of the unrepressed, undifferentiated unconscious. Simmel's characterization of man is thus seen to refer directly to our two modes, the difference being that the cognitive act of distinguishing is seen as a simultaneous equalization of all other distinctions, and therefore their rendering unconscious. With this in mind, his notion of Life as contents plus form is reinterpreted in terms of life as dedifferentiated unconscious contents and death as differentiated, conscious form. Together with the analogous reinterpretation of Nietzsche's will to power, this view of Simmel's formal sociology and overriding concerns forges a close link not only with Nietzsche—a connection that has received little attention—but also with Freud—a connection that has received no attention.

What emerges from the argument is a genuinely psycho-social understanding of alienation and anomie, and a larger theoretical perspective which unites the hemiplegic outlooks of Marx and Durkheim. Central to it all is a view of human nature grounded in human ambivalence, and the model of psyche and self which issues from it.

At the risk of special pleading, I suggest that these are ideas whose exposition involves unusual difficulties. The idea of overcoming oppositions insults the very logic with which we seek to lend credence to the idea. An argument dealing with less differentiated, unconscious modes must speak of phenomena and enunciate propositions seemingly irrational and certainly arational, and the difference between the former and the latter is often difficult to discern. After a point, less differentiated phenomena can only be intuited, suggested, expressed metaphorically. The unconscious can be known by its effects on consciousness, but of course this knowledge is quite differentiated. To focus on the less differentiated is to bring it to consciousness and change its mode.

As a rule we pride ourselves on our sharp distinctions, hard data, clarity, precise formulations and calculations, even when we offer little more than tough-minded apologies for the soft-headed. The rest of the time is spent in the vain attempt to connect these allegedly separate matters, to find the unity and continuity and identity waylaid amongst the distinctions we have ourselves insinuated and defended so testily. The enterprise of logic no doubt consists of the pursuit of such unity, along with the erection of formidable barriers to its achievement. Such efforts are themselves differentiating, like the labors of that tribe of specialists in generalizations in which Durkheim naively placed his hope. More meaningful and less differentiated truths are fugitives from the justice we seek to wreak on the world, from the sometimes vengeful, ressentiment-laden logic and language with which we seek to put and keep it in its place.

Moreover, the theory must be applied to the theorist and theorizing; the argument to the way it is argued, to its creation and creator. Otherwise we are merely talking theory. This is a generic difficulty of theories of a scope sufficiently wide to include the theory and theorists themselves, though the frequency with which the difficulty is recognized in social science is embarrassingly low, and serious attempts to grapple with the difficulty are pitifully few. The special difficulty here is that the idea of overcoming opposition requires us to challenge opposites by means of opposites; to call into question the law of non-contradiction by means of arguments which respect and affirm it; to do battle with dualisms and overdrawn distinctions even as we employ them.

We are bound to expressing ourselves in ways that confine and constrict, stuck with the differentiated, tedious, one-thought-at-a-time conscious mode. If in fact consciousness is but a surface, then in a fundamental way man is the superficial animal. This is why he is capable of profundity. That we are bound to the superficial view, or at least to superficial reports on the depths, is in no way denied here, though in a sense it is repeatedly defied. The idea is to explore the origins, significance, consequences, the range of possible relationships between these fundamental modes, and to suggest their intimate relationship to the pathological rigidity of alienation and the pathological chaos of anomie. In the process, everything remains the same, and in its place. On the other hand, the very being we uncover is such that it insists on becoming. So that everything is changed, and nothing sits securely any longer in its appointed place.

Words count for less than we wordy ones think, especially in an argument profoundly skeptical of their limitations and distortions. Logic and language are unreliable and sometimes treacherous guides to their own limitations, and if life is larger than both, than any given structures and forms, then it is life itself which must convince us. The argument must be brought home. A conversion of sorts is required, given a cultural and social setting so prideful of its distinctions and so ill-equipped conceptually and emotionally to challenge them except by denying them outright and altogether. On the other hand, the materials are always at hand: a sudden and fleeting intuition of some unity which logic or language insist that we divide; the sheer wonder of a dedifferentiated image which "makes no sense" but carries a world of meaning and a force of a character and potency unknown to the physical world; the mystery of creative dedifferentiation, somehow guided by conscious faculties which seem for all the world to have gone to sleep; the experience of standing aside and assisting one's work when it begins to speak for itself; the liberating effect of some authority sensed as humanly meaningful; the disciplined spontaneity we achieve on rare occasions.

To dwell in emotional and logical and linguistic oppositions, for once resisting the compulsion to escape by means of yet another distinction bearing even more confusion—to be stunned by the sudden recognition that there is an entire world of good things and good ideas out there struggling vainly to embrace one another—one does not emerge from such experiences unchanged and unscathed, speaking the same tongue or meaning the same things by old terms. A new attitude toward truth itself is called for, and a new appreciation of the seductions of the old. We must be as leary of the pursuit of Truth and the belief in the old God as we are of the modern and social-scientific claim to have dispensed with both. Most of all, we must be vigilant when the world serves up something, as if for us alone, about whose truth and beauty there seems no doubt. To capture and confine that delicate and exquisite bird whose graceful flight and splendid plumage seduces our very soul, to protect it from the beasts outside, is our greatest seduction and misfortune. It will flutter about frantically, destroying its plumage and squandering its power, beating itself to death on the bars of the cage we have so lovingly constructed. Then the lifeless cage will be all we have, and it will be ours. Outside, formless beasts will roam at will a bleak and blackened landscape.

To speak in terms of conversions and sermons, then, is not merely the idiosyncratic reflection of a misspent youth. There was a time when these arguments would have been spontaneously expressed in religious terms, however heretical or devilish their underlying impulse and ultimate impact. Apparently it is God's fate to live on in the form of various secularized versions of the reconciliation of opposites, as expressed most vividly, perhaps, by figures like Nietzsche and Rilke. The confused and abortive attempt to achieve some such reconciliation is surely the basis of human selfhood and striving, including otherwise pointless rituals and writhings, and wild gyrations from self-infinitization to infinite self-denigration. As Nietzsche suggested, when all else fails we will believe in nihilism itself, crushing life with life. As between alienated belief and anomic disbelief, who will know the difference, and what difference will it make?

On this note we come finally to the acid test suggested at the outset: what of that fellow whose snores already cast doubt on this message? Sleep is no barrier, not necessarily. Blessed are the drowsy and inattentive, for their dreams and day-dreams are the royal roads to the undifferentied unconscious, as Freud said. Down that road may appear a vision of ambivalence and its overcoming, of alienation and anomie and their significance for social science, self, and society—more profound than anything accessible to all those so severely confined to pulpits and pews.

Even so, dreamers need the rest of us to interpret and translate, to prevent their becoming lost in the very process of finding themselves, to translate the experience and make specific sense of it. It takes all types. It also takes a sense of what all types share, lest the distinctions we draw make altogether too much difference, and eventually none at all. This is knowledge desperately needed and increasingly scarce. So to serious listeners and dreamers alike, this timeless but timely sermon is addressed.

1

The Social Science of Alienation and Anomie

What from your fathers you received as heir,
Acquire, if you would possess it.

Goethe

To offer yet another interpretation of alienation and anomie at this late date requires a certain amount of cheek. Perhaps the same cheek was instrumental in creating the proliferation of views so characteristic of the intellectual chaos in this area. Each well-meaning attempt to order the confusion has tended to contribute to it. The result is a mixture of confused anarchy and confining order, the two extremes feeding off one another. There is a large lesson in this, part and parcel of a viable theory of these maladies. A satisfactory account of social discontents would fathom and feature this deadly alternation between chaos and rigidity, formless life and lifeless form, anomie and alienation, in social theory and society. To do so it must be grounded in a view of being human in which ambivalence and the attempt to overcome ambivalence are fundamental.

To understand alienation and anomie as opposites, grounded in human ambivalence, is to resist the oversocialization of the individual in the service of a social science less pinched and more human. My effort to do so is indebted to Nietzsche; Simmel, powerfully influenced by Nietzsche; and Freud, whose fundamental contributions Nietzsche and Simmel anticipated to a surprising degree. Marx and Durkheim also figure importantly, particularly since it is questionable whether their classic accounts of alienation and anomie have been substantially improved upon, much less superseded. To wrestle simultaneously and successfully with these titans is a feat beside which Jacob's mastery of the angel looks trivial. Discretion suggests beginning with wrestling partners less formidable: contemporary social-scientific students of alienation and anomie.[1]

The Human Nature of Social Discontent

Let us focus for the moment on alienation. It is difficult to overestimate the degree of disarray in recent treatments of alienation. Most non-Marxist views involve variations on the theme of marginality: separation, distance, exclusion, powerlessness, hostility, disaffection vis à vis dominant social forms and cultural emphases. Most of these "marginal" states combine the idea of being left out or standing apart with the idea of being oppressed or exploited in various ways. Sometimes this marginality is more or less chosen, sometimes not. Usually these are the individual subject's estimates and perceptions of what is the case. To the extent that the two senses of marginality can be sorted out, the idea of standing apart often takes precedence. The underlying political orientation and the proffered solution to alienation tends toward a conformist liberalism or an antinomian hyperliberalism. Both camps offer crude choices: conforming or not conforming, oppression or exclusion. The possibility that alienation may be compatible with or the result of attachment, membership, citizenship, allegiance to authority, conformity to group or institutional requirements is either slighted or carried to the extreme of regarding all social forms, all modes of dependence, attachment, membership, and subjection to authority as alienating. Self-alienation is neglected because a conception of the self is missing.

This failure to deal adequately with the human subject is accompanied by the reluctance to see alienation as an objective social and individual condition. Clearly this is not alienation as Marx understood it. Neglecting the social-structural setting, and thereby the possibility of false consciousness, leads to reliance on self-reported beliefs and feelings in assessing the extent to which the subject is alienated. Analysis of alienating structures and ideological self-conceptions is avoided, or alienation is promiscuously associated with any and all social forms. Both positions are more closely related to liberalism or anarchism than to leftism.

Much the same occurs in anomie research. Standards of health and happiness, notions of what constitutes anomie, are drawn from the cultural milieu of modern liberal societies, particularly that of the middle classes. This makes it difficult to assert that one can subscribe to legitimate means and cultural goals and be anomic *because* of conformity and acquiesence, participation and "belonging." The possibility that the well-adjusted and fully integrated could be composed of mutants and marginals, the isolated and the lonely is slighted, much as students of alienation do not contemplate the possibility that many participants in social institutions might be alienated. Again the root difficulty is the absense of any serious consideration of the specifically human and humanly general. With few exceptions, the standards invoked are those derived and distilled from society as presently conceived and constituted.

This crucial hiatus makes inevitable and intractable the problems encountered in this research and elsewhere in social science and theory. In lieu of an account of ambivalence and its overcoming, it is likely that one of the brilliant one-dimensionalizations of human nature offered by Marx and Durkheim will be hastily rejected, the other carelessly embraced. This in fact is what occurs. Yet somehow both are valid. Thus it is not simply a matter of calling errant moderns back to the classic texts they ignore or distort, but of pulling together partial views of what is fundamentally human, especially those put forward by Marx and Durkheim. It is ambivalence itself which pulls together and illuminates the relation between these classic accounts of fundamental social maladies. Likewise it is ambivalence which makes the task difficult, even frightening. Nevertheless, our understanding of both maladies awaits our simultaneous affirmation of the human qualities of which they are extremes. This is by no means a strictly theoretical enterprise, even for theorists.

Alienation and the Hyperliberalization of Marx

With these introductory remarks in mind, consider some representative alienation research of relatively recent vintage. In an influential survey Melvin Seeman argues that past uses of alienation have included at least five distinct interpretations: powerlessness, meaninglessness, normlessness, isolation, and self-estrangement.[2] In light of these differences he warns that it is a "deadly sin" to seek unity or coherence in the usages of alienation. Dean and many others hail this contribution ("Seeman has restored order to this chaos").[3] Finifter suggests that Seeman's categories serve as a "bridge between philosophical and contemporary empirical work."[4]

Others are dubious, and suggest that Seeman has restored chaos to chaos. Lewis Feuer is among the skeptics.[5] He points out that the formulation of Seeman's different categories in terms of Rotter's expectancies (powerlessness, for example, as low expectancy of control of events) neglects the fact that many people complain about the predictability of the world as well as its unpredictability. Slater, Hardin, Bateson, Wilden, and a host of social critics have complained of precisely what Seeman applauds: our narcissistic, aggressive, anthropocentric stance vis à vis nature and society. Feuer also asserts that Seeman attempts to take the polemical spirit out of concepts which are inherently critical.

Still others suggest that Seeman's admonition to avoid mixing meanings of alienation amounts to advocating that we cleave asunder what must be kept in one piece. Some assert that Seeman's categories are separate dimensions of a multidimensional malady. They are prone to add dimensions, transforming the concept into a kind of sponge. This may be inherent in their method. Finifter incorporates all of Seeman's categories except the troublesome one of "self-estrangement."[6] She derives her chosen dimensions from a factor analysis, and explains that the approach to alienation which emphasizes different dimensions is superior because most dimensions tend to be weakly correlated. Nachmias, with a slight change in the dimensions employed, claims to have "re-established the multidimensional proposition."[7] Exactly when a one-dimensional concept becomes multidimensional, or when the multidimensional concept becomes many concepts, is not altogether clear. Nor do they attend to the problem of naming the dimensions factor analysis yields, the question of what they actually mean.

In any event there is a point at which multidimensionality collapses into one dimension. Dimensions become mere facets. Some focus on one facet or another: for example, Keniston singles out "the explicit rejection of traditional American culture" as the meaning of alienation.[8] Nettler's alienated are similar: they are individuals "who have been estranged from, made unfriendly toward their society and the culture it carries."[9] Alienation involves the "consistent maintenance of unpopular and averse attitudes." Hadja's alienated are friendlier than Nettler's, though equally isolated or excluded. They have a

> sense of uneasiness and discomfort... reflecting exclusion or self-exclusion from social and cultural participation. It is an expression of non-belonging or non-sharing, an uneasy awareness or perception of unwelcome contrast with others.[10]

This rivals Nettler's conception in its grab-bag quality; it is hard to say who is excluded. (Nor, I shall argue, is it clear whether this bag catches alienation, or anomie.) Similarly, Aiken and Hage treat alienation as alienation from or dissatisfaction with social relations.[11] In like manner, Grodzin's alienated feel no sense of belonging to their community or nation. Their personal contacts are neither stable nor satisfactory.[12]

Others (Seeman, in his empirical studies) stress marginality in the sense of powerlessness. Some stipulate that the subjective feeling of powerlessness should be accompanied by the individual's perception or belief that this condition is wrong or unjust. The democratic norms of the society have taught that a share of power is "rightfully his" (Thompson, Horton, Levin, Clark).[13] Clark reduces Seeman's categories to a matter of lack of means (thereby encroaching, as we shall see, on the territory staked out for anomie by Merton). Alienation becomes the "feeling of powerlessness to achieve the role he has determined to be his in specific situations."[14] This is tantamount to defining alienation as any discrepancy between what one wants and what one gets. Finifter effects a similar metamorphosis, claiming that conceptions of alienation converge on the idea of a discrepancy between a set of values and the socially structured opportunities for achievement of these values.[15] In this way Clark and Finifter fling open the door to all manner of megalomania, or endless indiscriminate griping. In the same vein, Kariel advocates the uninhibited expansion of the "political present", confusing his caricature of liberalism with radicalism.[16]

The prize for this sort of generalization by means of attenuation may belong to Amitai Etzioni.[17] In attempting to connect alienation to the literature on human needs he consults an enormous sample of studies. He concludes that the core meaning of alienation consists in the unresponsiveness of the society to the wants of the individual. This approach is not particularly concerned with what the individual was encouraged to want. It may well sponsor wants incompatible with any conceivable society. But even this most catholic conception leaves out a number of alternative definitions.

Coming full circle, consider what alienation (as powerlessness) becomes in the hands of Seeman. He admits that powerlessness has an objective reality and specific institutional referents in the Marxist context, but he redefines it as "the expectancy or probability held by the individual that his own behavior cannot determine the occurrence of the outcomes, or reinforcements, he seeks."[18] As he points out, this departs from the Marxist tradition by removing the critical element from the idea of alienation. The corollary is that individuals generally know their real interests, what moves them. This is a curiously unempirical assumption. It could be argued that whenever there are many who *are* aware of the structural determinants and hidden wellsprings of their actions, socialization and indoctrination have failed. For most people, most of the time, most of culture is unconscious. Posing as more realistic, less value-laden, this approach may be merely less perceptive and more naive.

Similar results obtain when self-alienation undergoes this radical surgery. Interestingly, with respect to the theorists of self-alienation Seeman overcomes his reluctance to delve beneath surface "rhetoric," as if everyone but theoreticians can be trusted to say what they mean. "The basic idea contained in the rhetoric of self-estrangement," he contends, is "the idea of intrinsically meaningful activity":

> One way to state such a meaning is to see alienation as the degree of dependence of the given behavior upon anticipated future rewards, that is, upon rewards that lie outside the activity itself.... [I]n this view, what has been called self-estrangement refers essentially to the inability of the individual to find self-rewarding ... activities that engage him.[19]

Self-alienation is therefore severed from any shared or shareable notion of what is self-rewarding or self-fulfilling. Accordingly, we can treat everyone equally, democratically: overcoming self-alienation differs little from letting go and doing your thing. Few notice that doing your thing in the culture of the middle classes is often the thing to do, that exaggerated individualism and widespread conformity can go hand in hand. To avoid committing a psychology we acquiesce in the vulgar democratization of alienation, ignoring the differences in pleasures and aspirations attained or thwarted. Pushpin or poetry, it comes to the same. Similarly for pains: for all we know, it matters not whether you are exploited or peeved, oppressed or just irritated.

Seeman's categories do not constitute a theory of alienation. There is no principle for determining the categories, what is similar and what is different, other than the fact that various theorists have used the idea of alienation in this way and that. That is, theorists and theories are treated democratically as well. Even as a compendium of past usages, his account is deficient in excluding those analyses which retain Marxist tenets. This is part of the larger problem of detaching concepts from their theoretical context and moorings, and their political implications. The prime example is that *anomie* ("normlessness") is designated as one of the varieties of *alienation* (although he complains that this sense of *alienation* has been overemphasized). These points apply with even greater force to the many less careful compendiums and characterizations.

These accounts of alienation (as unresponsiveness of society, as powerlessness, and so on) are obviously vulnerable to some of the radical antinomian currents of the day, notably the impulse to blame society for just about every ill that ails us. Such a persuasion is neither radical or leftist. It is a variety of neo-utilitarian instrumentalism, carried to new extremes. The long-run effect on the moral and political order is inevitably corrosive, especially to those nonutilitarian aspects of law, contract, and social interaction on which the plausibility of utilitarianism itself depends. As Schacht has observed, to the Hegelian–Marxist idea of alienation as separation modern theorists have added the vague idea of "lessness." The less in question does not refer to some Durkheimian conception of what is normal to societies at given phases of development. Nor is it less by reference to some hypothesized normal or ideal state of man: Marxist, Durkheimian, Freudian, whatever. It is simply less of what liberal culture defines as worthwhile. And the cure for less, our culture tells us, is more.

By the same token, there is predictable confusion between alienation and anomie. Undoubtedly this has to do with the fact that for many of us, modes of oppression and exclusion have become less tangible and obvious. It is conceivable that the confusion also reflects the primitive intuition that anomie and alienation are dialectically related, and that fear of anomie may contribute to alienation, and conversely. But since there is no independent standard by which alienation can be seen as compatible with participation in given social forms, since in most sociological circles it is considered virtuous and progressive to reject any explicit, articulate conception of self-alienation and human nature, alienation is inevitably thought of as being outside the society in some sense, marginal to those forms. Hence the confusion. Unless Durkheim's classic account is rejected altogether, anomie, however formulated, certainly has *something* to do with marginality.

It is tempting to see the practice of defining and assessing alienation by reference to given social forms and relations as a simple matter of rejecting the Marxist view. In part it is. This accounts for the fact that alienation has come to mean much more than it did for Marx, that it is now applied to all manner of separations and attributed to all sorts of causes. But this also explains why alienation has come to mean far less. Critical elements of Marx's conception have been systematically and self-consciously discarded. These include the class struggle, capitalism, commodity fetishism, the division of labor: in short, the proposition that alienation is an all-pervasive social and individual malady which has an objective, systemic existence. The result is a strong dependence on the account the subject manages to give, on the basis of the questions posed. This approach is directly related to the practice of severing alienation from its Marxist roots. Alienation comes to mean almost anything, and practically nothing. It is in many respects a subjective or psychological approach, minus a theory of the subject.

Marx himself is responsible for some of these difficulties. The historicism and sociological relativism sponsored by Marx and Marxists have come to detract from the significance of alienation itself, to contribute to the conservative practice of appealing to society for the standards by which to judge society. This is why the most prominent and significant omission in the literature of alienation is alienation from self. The working assumption is that it is natural to want more and more of more and more, a notion sanctioned and promoted by that utilitarian culture which both Marx and Durkheim pilloried. Seeman's conception of self-alienation resembles a formula for anomie or mayhem. At the same time, it condenses and codifies much of what the society and culture are all about.

Marx's willingness to blame self-alienation exclusively on that "other man" was the fateful step by which he was led to to pin all alienation on a repressive society. In this crucial respect these non-Marxists have followed Marx all too closely. When they take the cultural premises of their own liberal society to extremes, this partakes of Marx's own hyperliberal tendencies. After a brilliant if one-sided beginning, Marx abandoned direct appeals to a conception of human nature divorced from given social forms and facts. Most moderns have followed suit. Admittedly it is far more difficult now to theorize in the vein of the *Economics and Philosophic Manuscripts of 1844*. Maybe we now know too much to dare much. In particular we cannot ignore the very structural perspectives Marx developed so impressively once his philosophical anthropology went underground. Even so, even as it becomes vastly more difficult to think and theorize in such terms, it becomes the more important to try.

Anomie and the Missing French Connection

Surveying the territory occupied by the students of anomie is easier, first of all because the difficulties are similar to those we have already encountered. Admittedly, Durkheim is invoked more often than alienation theorists invoke Marx, but critical elements of his work have been discarded in like fashion. The process is facilitated by discarding or oversimplifying Durkheim's fitful efforts to articulate a view of human nature, and by offering no alternative. Anomie is reduced to a matter of marginality or deviance with respect to given social forms and cultural emphases.

The study of anomie also differs in being a smaller and more homogeneous affair. Many contemporary sociologists are bent on avoiding the embarrassing conservatism in their sociological tradition, and neglect this particular French connection. "The soil on which sociology grew," as Gouldner puts it, "was manured by a pervasive anomie."[20] The gingerly if respectful treatment accorded anomie by many sociologists might reflect the wish to avoid confronting the smelly conservative origins of their discipline. For whatever reason, anomie is definitely the junior concept, certainly as measured by the numbers of those who explicitly concern themselves with it.

On the other hand, anomie (or something reminescent of it) is often included among the alleged manifestations of alienation. Students of anomie have had limited success in defending it from those omnivorous conceptions of alienation which are now applied to all conceivable maladies. Many students, engaged in what appears to be anomie research, claim to be studying alienation. "Dimensions" of alienation such as normlessness, confusion of norms, isolation, social maladjustment, meaninglessness, marginality are closer to Durkheim than to Marx. This confusion may reflect a desire to have it both ways, to liberalize or radicalize but somehow preserve that non-Marxist sociological tradition. (It may also suggest that Durkheimian and Marxist concerns are not really so far apart as generally believed.) Many American sociologists have been trying for some time to get in step with liberal and leftist perspectives, even when they must do so in a functionalist vocabulary. This sometimes produces genuine oddities, as when Marxist-Weberian accounts of alienation are offered in the vocabulary of Parsons, or Freud is combined with Durkheim in such a way as to insure we will want what we should want.

For many such reasons anomie theorists constitute a smaller and more homogeneous tribe. Symbolizing and powerfully contributing to this homogeneity is Robert Merton's interpretation of Durkheim's anomie, which has held sway over much of American sociology for over four decades. Its remarkable dominance explains why the illusion of normal science, cumulative results, and routinized progress is more easily maintained in anomie research. "The near monopoly it has enjoyed," Albert Cohen rightly observes, "testifies to the paucity of original thinking in this field."[21] Perhaps it also reflects fear of the disciplinary or intellectual anarchy that might ensue in the absence of the umbrella effect of Merton's paradigm. Anomie students take their subject seriously, it seems.

Merton's familiar paradigm pictures anomie as the result of a disjunction between American culture, which emphasizes the pursuit of material success as everyone's opportunity and duty, and the social-institutional means to this goal, which systematically restrict the possibilities of success and structure the incidence and the character of deviance.[22] Anomie, this disjunction, produces the pressure and tendency to deviate from cultural goals, the legitimate social means, or both. In his initial formulation, deviant adaptations to anomie included rebellion, retreatism, ritualism, innovation, and conformity. Retreatism refers to those who have given up on both the pursuit of success and the means by which it might be achieved. Innovation accepts the cultural success goals but rejects the legitimate means. Retreatism includes vagabonds, beggars, denizens of skid row, whereas innovation applies to organized crime, business and white collar crime plus the many who operate in the gray area of the law, play boundary games with conventional mores, and cut corners in various ways. Ritualism refers to those who have given up on the chances of material success, but still adhere to the legitimate institutional means, continuing to go through the motions. Finally there are the two most troublesome categories, rebellion and conformity. Rebellion consists of the rejection of both goals and means, and the attempt to affirm and substitute other goals and means. About rebellion he has little to say; within his scheme it is hard to explain. The last category is conformity. Merton includes it "for completeness": he does not consider conformity deviant or pathological.[23]

Merton's treatment of anomie has its share of critics. Discovering some new flaw in it is a traditional sociological pastime. He is roundly criticized for positing cultural homogeneity, the consensus on success goals defined in material terms. This has been challenged by Hyman, Williams, Lane, Parsons, Harris, Horney, and numerous others.[24] Lemert asserts that the notion that our society has a common value hierarchy "strains credulity." Along with several others, he questions Merton's contentions as to the rates of deviation in various social strata, suggesting that existing research "leaves serious doubts that deviant behavior is proportionately more common at lower class levels in the society."[25]

Lemert also suggests that Merton's category of retreatist lumps together a variety of different deviant groups on a superficial and dubious basis: "we find a certain *tour de force* quality in lumping together activities of such vaguely defined people as 'vagabonds,' 'pariahs,' 'vagrants,' and 'autists' with chronic drunkards and drug addicts and, without specifying what the 'activities' are, attributing to them a common 'escapist' motivation which eventuates in 'asocialized individuals.'"[26] This complaint also applies to Merton's other categories of adaptation, and to the rather abstract motivations attributed to each. The point is crucial. Merton, along with most sociologists, does not eliminate psychological assumptions so much as render them simplistic and obscure.

Dubin has observed that Merton's deviant modes of adaptation are not necessarily dysfunctional for society: it depends on whether success or approval follow the deviant act.[27] In addition to overemphasizing cultural homogeneity, Merton's conception of culture is static and one-dimensional. The emergence of alternatives, from either "culture" or "society," is hard to explain. In a related vein, Cohen has accused Merton of offering an atomistic and individualistic theory of deviance.[28] He claims that Merton pictures the individual as completely isolated from immediate social influences, choosing freely among modes of adaptation. Here again a larger difficulty is touched upon. While anomie students are or should be concerned with the social bases of personality, they seem to have followed Merton in neglecting those intermediate associations and relations which the great theorists of pluralism have consistently stressed. Nor is it merely a matter of neglect: Merton's paradigm, and the orientation of many anomie researchers, is far more liberal than pluralist. It might be argued that they have lost touch, not only with the pluralist tradition, but the sociological tradition as well.

Lemert offers a parallel argument, suggesting that Merton gives little weight to the fact that individuals are subject to various kinds of control by social groups to which they belong.[29] This may suggest further impediments to the pursuit of success goals. It likewise suggests possible buffers against the anomie with which Merton is concerned. Similarly, Cohen contends that Merton's anomie does not explain many of the actions of subcultural delinquents. Often their activity is less utilitarian than expressive and symbolic, or derives from role expectations rather than any disjunction of culture and society.[30] These observations question whether success is all of what anyone wants, whether the culture is as homogeneous as Merton suggests, and whether he has one-dimensionalized what makes us go and refuse to go. "Belonging" to a society dominated by success goals might be the cause of anomie, rather than its cure.

Merton's interpretation of anomie by no means emerges unscathed by these criticisms. It seems to have remained intact because an alternative of comparable scope has not been put forward. The same pattern of continued reliance on problematic formulations applies to subjective anomie. One of these has seen repeated use: the Srole scale, which coexists uneasily with Merton's view of anomie.[31] The friction between the two approaches has to do with the distinction between *anomie,* a social phenomenon, and *anomia,* the outlook, the emotions, the psychology of the victims of the sociological state of anomie.

Merton complains that few genuine indicators of *anomie* have been developed and employed. There is some evidence that Srole may have been confused as to what he was measuring. Apparently at the last moment he decided that his scale measures anomia, previously having thought that it measures alienation. (Finifter refers to it as "diffuse alienation.")[32] Even those who employ the scale debate what it means and measures. Meier and Bell, for example, claim it is a measure of despair.[33] The confusion over anomie itself, the neglect of any standard which is not social, which does not spring full blown from the data themselves, gives all such speculation a peculiarly unhinged quality.

Hence the remarkable absence of alternatives to Merton's paradigm and Srole's scale. A few studies take a more expansive view of the malady or attempt to show the relevance of neglected psychological variables, but they receive little attention. This timidity and rank-closing may function to keep anomie from creeping into the lives as well as theories of those who study it. But in another sense Merton has not succeeded in keeping this from happening. His own theory reminds us that the adaptations to anomie are pathological. According to the theory, the theory itself (its conformist cast, its neglect of pluralism and community, its failure to take present and potential alternative goals and means seriously) represents an adaptation to anomie. Merton includes conformity with the other pathological adaptations to anomie only as a special case, for "completeness". This suggests he does not appreciate the full relevance of the theory he himself offers. Nor does he appreciate the extent to which his analysis reflects those cultural values and social strata plagued by anomic striving and maladies of the infinite, precisely those strata singled out by Durkheim as particularly prone to anomie. On the contrary:

> For the historian of social thought it is comforting and perhaps even edifying that the history of anomie has taken the course it has. That history of anomie indicates the slow, hard evolution of a complex sociological idea over a period of some seventy years.[34]

It is doubtful whether Durkheim's original idea of anomie has even survived this "hard evolution." If so, it has been battered beyond recognition. But as justice would have it, anomie itself, in anomie theory and society, appears to be alive and well.

Whatever combination of social influences and personal motivations has weakened the link with Durkheim, it is clear that certain difficulties with Durkheim's account have been exploited in the process of emasculating his classic analysis. (Much the same can be said of Marx and the alienation literature.) Admittedly, Durkheim's analysis of anomie, the maladies of the infinite, and modernity present problems. One key difficulty is whether these "infinite" goals he indicts are products of that original, biologically based egoism described in "Dualism of Human Nature," or whether the culture itself elevates such troublesome goals to the status of legitimate first principles.[35] Durkheim seems to have never resolved the issue, probably because the vigorous affirmation of transhistorical needs would have caused havoc throughout his work.

Another difficulty concerns the distinction Durkheim draws between egoistic and anomic suicide. While Durkheim emphasizes that the two are closely related, later theorists have used his distinction as a means of dissociating anomie and egoism entirely. There is also the problem of determining the psychological correlates of anomie, given a psychology impoverished in accordance with his rules of sociological method. There is the murky relationship between the two standards by which Durkheim sought to distinguish normal and pathological social institutions and cultural beliefs. Societies are compared at similar stages of development, or institutions and behavior patterns are compared within a given society. But Durkheim was not altogether comfortable with a thoroughgoing sociological relativism. This is not only reflected in his dualistic account of human nature, it is implicit in his treatment of such topics as anomie, morality, and authority.

Anomie theorists, following Merton, have eliminated many of these difficulties at the price of severely restricting the concept of anomie. In Merton's version of anomie only one aspect of Durkheim's critical perspective remains: society should meet the expectations it encourages. This tends to transfer attention to the inadequacy of social-institutional means, away from the possible insanity of the cultural consensus, away from "cultural contradictions" and cultural diversity. It overlooks psychological perspectives other than those, like learning theory or rational choice models, which tend to be codifications and elaborations of the logic of dominant cultural emphases, institutional requirements, and associated notions of individual identity. It also neglects the question of the *satisfiability* of cultural goals: what patterns of goals can be achieved simultaneously. Even the question of adequacy of the social institutional means is treated in an individualistic, instrumentalist vein, as though commitments to the work ethic, for example, were not as important in equalizing demands and deliveries as institutional reform, and as though the problem of subordination would no longer exist under a meritocracy. In general, the possibility of taking a critical stance vis à vis cultural goals and institutional means is not merely lost, it is precluded.

As a matter of fact, Merton's personal politics are far from conservative, and he has no particular bias in favor of conformity and integration over innovation and rebellion. But the salient point is that the emergence of alternative goals is not only inexplicable in terms of his typology (and motivational assumptions), it is undervalued by the very structure and categories of his theory. The treatment of rebellion as "deviance" suggests this, as does his belated recognition that it is inappropriate to do so. There is little curiosity concerning the causes of such maladies, what motivates deviant responses, other than the explanation deeply embedded in the structure of the theory itself: those who do not make it are those who cannot. That some might not want to, or that everyone might be ambivalent about doing so, or that the culture itself reflects and promotes that ambivalence, is all but unthinkable in this theoretical setting. Apparently we are supposed to assume that everyone (whether rebels, withdrawals, innovators, retreaters) would like nothing better than to be able to conform to cultural goals as well as legitimate means. Through poor socialization, lack of opportunities or low intelligence they have been forced onto other paths. Naturally they relieve the anxiety of not succeeding, or not employing legitimate means, by romanticizing and rationalizing their failures and trespasses, disreputable activities, outsider status. As for rebels, who openly tout alternatives: they must be hurting most of all. Here this sociological approach sometimes shows its flexibility, flirting with depth psychology. What most people say can be taken more or less at face value, but not so for the rebellious and unsuccessful.

The social order most anomie theorists wish to conserve and reform is the twentieth century liberal order. Typically this involves at least a grudging acceptance of corporate capitalism, large bureaucracies public and private, the main contours of the welfare state, measures intended to enhance equality of rights and opportunity, and increasingly centralized and extensive political authority in pursuit of these goals. Merton's scheme conceivably could be adapted to the Tocquevillian argument for pluralizing goals and means, associations and institutions; Tocqueville's fears for freedom, pluralism, and community when material goals, in tandem with egalitarianism and egoism, are universalized. Yet these concerns play little or no role in his analysis. It is the *means* which must be reformed and expanded, through education, job training, equal opportunity, and affirmative action.

To proceed in this fashion is to ignore the very doubts about liberal society which disturbed the great theorists of anomie, the very concerns around which the non-Marxist sociological tradition took form. Tocqueville, Nietzsche, Toennies, Simmel, and Durkheim pointed to ominous possibilities of self-infinitization implicit in just such conceptions of material success and instrumentalism. They feared the consequences of an equalization of competition which would vastly reduce the percentage of successes among the competitors while vastly increasing the time and difficulty involved in advancement. They pondered the problem of subordination in a society pursuing meritocratic principles in an increasingly democratic-egalitarian setting. They feared that liberal society was in the process of creating expectations that no conceivable society could fulfill. This was the basis of Durkheim's criticism of the socialists for example. On the one hand, socialists seek to free desire and ambition of all constraint. On the other, they propose to satisfy and placate the appetites they thereby encourage and create. Moreover, the classical theorists of anomie suggested that aside from the workability of such a society, aside from the possible disjunction of what is demanded and what is produced, there remains the possibility that such a society might prove intolerably bleak. Aside from an indiscriminate prejudice for belonging over being marginal, this legacy has been largely squandered.

The result of enthusiastically embracing what classical theorists found profoundly disquieting is that anomie theory exhibits surprisingly little concern with pluralism, the communal bases of personality, and those elements of liberalism and market society productive of anomie. These concerns are not obviously compatible with classical liberalism (which would restrict centralization for different reasons), nor the liberal preoccupation with social welfare and socioeconomic advancement. Few take seriously the connections between egalitarian materialism, centralization, and anomic individualism which Tocqueville so masterfully sketched.

In point of fact, many social scientific accounts of alienation and anomie could not be more opposed to social pluralism or "community." To think of alienation in terms of social responsivity in general, to brand an entire society unresponsive, spells trouble or death for group loyalties of any but the most superficial, contractual, instrumental, fleeting sort. Little attention is directed to what association and membership mean in human terms. For this reason, sociological accounts of different social modes lapse into heavy-handed, often aimless description. The same is true for arguments on behalf of the contribution of groups to social rationality, the prevention of the overgrowth of state powers, or the undying affiliative needs for belonging and security. Most significantly, there is no concern for that possible third mode of social relations, somehow synthesizing difference and equality, *Gesellschaft* and *Gemeinschaft*, which was a virtual obsession for the classical sociologists.[36]

Durkheim vacillated in his own commitment to pluralism, partly because he saw it as a potential threat to national unity, partly because the division of labor was supposed to overcome egoism and isolation, and partly because the decline of pluralism seemed to be the mark of modern society, and his sociological relativism gave him no effective means of objecting. But both pluralism and the division of labor were taken seriously as vehicles by which increasing differences could be converted into a new form of social solidarity. And both were seen as potentially divisive and order-threatening. The division of labor was regarded as a major potential source of anomie.

Durkheim's approach to the division of labor is distorted by psychological premises weighted toward differences and handicapped by the sociological hubris that most anyone can be molded to most anything. He thereby understated the problem of social order in a society based increasingly on more and more unique individuals, though he never stopped wrestling with it. Nor did he see the problem in terms of order alone. He explicitly addresses the question of self-fulfillment in connection with specialization and its limits. By contrast, alienation and anomie research proceeds much as liberal political theory does, as though neither the division of labor nor pluralism exists, much less presents unprecedented difficulties. Meanwhile, liberal society makes urgent the "problem of difference" like no society ever has.

Much the same can be said for issues of equality or likeness. The notion that we could make sense of ourselves in terms of sheer differences—as in the "nineteenth century individualism" described by Simmel—Durkheim would have found absurd and repugnant. In a sense the conscience collective, what we share, becomes more important as the proportion of social life to which it applies steadily shrinks. Durkheim took pains to spell out its content for modern differentiated societies, and the conditions for its acceptance. He also took care to identify its enemies, especially the enemies from within liberal society and culture: unmitigated utilitarianism, egoistic individualism, "the cult of the self," "maladies of the infinite." Socialism as well as liberalism was assessed in these terms. While in theoretical contexts he sought to diminish the extent, if not the significance of shared beliefs for modern differentiated societies, his "principles of 1789" and religion of humanity play a decisive role in more political and polemical writings, especially those penned in response to the Dreyfus affair.

Merton's version of the conscience collective is the consensus on success goals. What we share, therefore, is distance and difference. Little is said about those elements of the Puritan ethic which have served liberal society in lieu of external constraint, which have traditionally inhibited the antinomian potential of unmitigated individualism. The cultural goals Merton delineates depend heavily on some such beliefs (work as a calling; abstinence; keeping promises; repression and delay of gratification); that is, on *other* cultural emphases. Otherwise these dominant emphases might breed an entire race of con men, crooks, shysters and sharks: or "innovators," as Merton blandly puts it. No doubt he actually relies on other such sacred tenets and spheres which continue to resist the realm of utilitarian calculation.[37]

In this way we return to the proposition that anomie is quite consistent with participation in some social relations and sharing in certain kinds of beliefs. The conscience collective can be anomic in motivation and impact. All manner of madness can be shared. Belonging, in an anomic society, can amount or lead to isolation and disorientation: witness the fact that some have sought to escape such a society in order to establish communal alternatives. Durkheim's unstinting concern with that anomie generated by widely accepted cultural emphases and perfectly legitimate social institutions is a matter of record. Recent anomie research and theory fails to come to grips with the possibility of an anomic society.

For Durkheim, egoism virtually spelled anomie: thus the close association of egoistic and anomic suicide. Utilitarianism and egoistic individualism were his primary ideological opponents, powerful acids corroding all distinctions and ideals, inimical to a viable and progressive social order. Little of this emphasis survives in most modern treatments of anomie. Egoism in various forms, from Etzioni's unadulterated concern with what society can do for the individual to Merton's consensus of egoistic striving, is applauded, promoted, radicalized. Conformity to these norms is rarely viewed as pathological. Deviance is to be minimized or eliminated rather than learned from. As Merton says, anomie scholarship has come a long way.

Small surprise that anomie and alienation students, having lost touch with Durkheim's anomie and Marx's alienation, find themselves at a loss to specify the relationship of the two maladies. For example, some interpret Srole's anomia scale as measuring alienation. (Finifter thinks it measures "diffuse alienation.") Others regard alienation as the subjective manifestation of anomie.[38] Finifter also suggests that Srole's anomia might measure personal disorganization rather than "active alienation." In another context she suggests that a high score on the scale indicates feelings of "aloneness and helplessness."[39] We have seen that Meier and Bell think that it measures despair, "although alienation appears to be measured in some degree as well."[40]

Seeman classifies normlessness as one of five different conceptions of alienation. Some commentators have referred to Merton's work on alienation, not anomie. (Merton himself has done so.) Scott argues that anomie, anomia, and related concepts are so vague as to be useless. Seeman supports this view by arguing that the idea of normlessness has been thoroughly overextended. In the same spirit, Finifter proceeds as though anything from malaise to moronization might prove to be a dimension of alienation. Clark sees virtually all maladies in terms of powerlessness. Etzioni attempts to reduce past usages of alienation to the idea of the unresponsiveness of society. Kariel stops just short of suggesting we are alienated whenever we do not get whatever we want. Seeman does much the same with his notion of self-alienation. Finifter suggests that the core idea of alienation may be the disparity between what we are encouraged to want and what we obtain. (Merton equates this with anomie.) Finally, Igor Kon argues that it is alienation which has been abused and overextended.[41] Kon doubts whether alienation can be rescued from this tendency to apply it to everything in sight, and asserts that anomie is far and away the more useful concept.

What can be learned from this chaos? For one thing, alienation has a strong tendency to gobble up anomie. This is itself a cultural prejudice: when lost and confused, we are often led to believe we are oppressed, confined. Second, we learn that alienation and anomie are highly correlated. Given the sizeable overlap of their definitions, high correlations are neither surprising nor impressive. But no matter. The entire enterprise might have lost its way, but it is making excellent time. Nietzsche once remarked that the progress of knowledge consists of comparing one error with a previous error. Surely he had something else in mind.

Subterranean Psychology

According to an admirer of Merton, one of his outstanding achievements is to offer an analysis of anomie which divests itself of all Durkheimian speculation concerning natural, egoistic man. Even the egoistic-infinite impulses and aspirations which so troubled Durkheim are socially generated, Merton points out. On the surface his insight seems consistent with Durkheim's general outlook, notably his views on the segregation of psychology and sociology.

But this is indeed a surface view. Together with Durkheimian speculation concerning natural man, the central Freudian (and Nietzschean) doctrine of human ambivalence has been ignored, socialized, or otherwise gutted. It is not that psychology has been dispensed with altogether. The denial or sociologization of ambivalence involves psychological premises of the greatest import. It is rather that psychological premises are not made explicit and are difficult to distinguish from codifications of dominant cultural assumptions and institutional requirements. Significant areas in psychology plays a crucial and largely unacknowledged role include: (1) reliance on the individual subject in assessing alienated or anomic states; (2) quasi-psychological assumptions underlying Merton's categories of response to anomie; (3) neglected psychosocial pathologies (envy, mania, the "malady of infiniteness"); and (4) the bipolarity of culture, as it reflects and promotes individual ambivalence. A brief survey will be helpful.

ALIENATION AND ANOMIE SUBJECTIVIZED

Despite its sometimes militant antipsychological stance, the sociological study of alienation and anomie has certainly been rendered subjective. Alienation theorists deny the social and objective reality of alienation and rely heavily on instruments which purport to capture the individual's view of her or his condition. In like manner, the study of anomie involves heavy reliance on tests and studies of subjective anomie.

This approach is psychological in other respects. It rejects depth psychology, along with phenomena like rationalization, displacement, projection. Informally, however, an exception is made for many deviants, especially those who appeal to alternative goals and means. These appeals are not usually taken at face value. As for anyone taking satisfaction in deviant activities, or positively preferring a different kind of society, this is regarded as no more likely than the possibility that prostitutes may enjoy their work.

RESPONSES TO ANOMIE

Merton's categories of deviance are discussed in terms of social strata particularly vulnerable to specific modes of deviance. The basis of the sociological categories, however, is apparently a quasi-psychological matter. Thus we have those who "retreat," for example. Just as surely, categories like ritualism and innovation are united primarily by unstated motivational assumptions. The overriding assumption is that there are no positive preference or arguments for deviant or rebellious modes. This distorts the motivations of rebels and proto-rebels, blurs the distinction between "don't want to" and "can't," and shortchanges the positive alternatives appealed to in all these ways.

To repeat Cohen's observation: there is a kind of rational–choice bias in the picture Merton gives of the deviant and the choices which confront him. [42] The designation of social forms exclusively in terms of *means* is surely significant in this connection; it reflects the neoutilitarianism which permeates the entire theory. The concern for forms as such, for principles, for process and participation, for the intrinsic desirability of belonging and cooperating and participating, receive little attention. This bias is not always easy to detect. Rational choice and instrumentalist assumptions inevitably seem less psychological, since they are grounded on the psychological premises appropriate to an anomic society. To anyone sufficiently immersed in Merton's cultural consensus, or Parsons's instrumental activism, cultural beliefs and practices will resemble reality, not ideology or psychology.

In some cases psychological premises are not so much buried as belated, offered ad hoc in response to special problems or to criticism. Some time after the publication of his original typology of modes of adaptation to anomie, Merton discussed the anomie of success. This is a different and difficult phenomenon because it seems to call into question the cultural goals themselves. After pointing out how psychoanalysis might explain the depressions and suicides often attendant upon success (in terms of unresolved Oedipal conflicts), he turned to a preferred sociological explanation: the individual who has arrived suddenly realizes there is no resting place and must depart immediately. Derived from Durkheim, this assumes a great deal and explains little. The response it depicts is no more rational, nor explicable in rational terms, than the infamous "sorrow of finitude" Hegel's finite spirit experiences when it encounters anything seemingly other. Only a pathological culture could fail to see both, and the misguided Faustianism latent in both, as pathological.

Why the individual reacts in such ways requires further scrutiny, lest we simply replicate socio–cultural rationalizations in the guise of explanations. Perhaps the whole point of the individual's struggle was a roundabout and self-defeating attempt to earn unconditional acceptance, radically distinguishing oneself in order to be included, and nurtured. Whether or not we insist on tracing these mixed motives all the way back to Mother, the point is that the relevance of ambivalence is rarely considered.

RELATED PSYCHOSOCIAL PATHOLOGIES

Another set of difficulties concerns Merton's neglect of social maladies which do not fit well with his particular combination of the sociological and the subterranean psychological. In particular there is *ressentiment,* which may affect as many different social strata and sheer numbers as his category of 'retreatism'. Merton discusses ressentiment in other contexts, but he does he make a place for it within his typology. Merton distinguishes envy from rebellion and then drops the subject abruptly. One explanation for this cursory treatment is that envy may be so normal it is difficult to detect. Another is that envy as such is often unconscious, and must be located in our exaggerated attempts to deal with or deny or obscure its presence to ourselves and others (denigration or idealization of the envied object, professions of indifference, megolamaniacal attempts to assimilate it, and so on.). Perhaps this reluctance is also due to the fact that envy exposes the ugliness of a culture and society which, to a frightening extent, depends on envy and greed to grease its wheels. (Daniel Bell has called bourgeois society the "institutionalization of envy.") Nor are Marxists in any position to exploit this ugliness, given that so much envy has been mobilized in the service of their cause. The whole idea may be a bourgeois plot to denigrate redistribution and the revolution.

Maybe Merton does not think of ressentiment as a form of deviance. If it *is* deviant, then we must admit that the disjunction of society and culture produces a staggering percentage of these deviants, many of whom are solid citizens from upper strata, in the very thick of things. If *not,* then the consensus on goals, intimately bound up with envy, begins to look less attractive and more pernicious. Moreover, many of the deviants, particularly the "innovators," begin to look less deviant. The inclusion of ressentiment as a major aspect of alienation or anomie would challenge the association of anomie with deviance, since an envious consensus and envious conformists might be ridden with anomie. Similarly with alienation. Likewise it would question, with Tocqueville, whether there are problems with egalitarian materialistic egoism that a more determined focus on means would not cure, however praiseworthy the effort to open up and equalize opportunities.

Envy also suggests the relevance of psychoanalytic concepts grounded in psychic ambivalence, and not merely because Klein and her students have attributed such significance to its various manifestations.[43] It represents a uniquely destructive way of expressing the fundamental ambivalence as between the desire for difference and the desire for equality. The various flights from envy can be equally pathological. On the one hand, there is lynx-eyed fascination with what is superior, fine, creative, distinctive. On the other, there is the effort to crush, to level, to homogenize, to equalize. Moreover, as Nietzsche argued, this attempt to get others down in the hole that you are in is symbiotically, dialectically related to the exaggerated egoistic hedonism of compulsively free-thinking moderns: those for whom difference appears to be all that is desired, all associations and convictions are prisons, and all forms are pernicious. After the veritable orgy of envy under crude communism, we are told, distinctions will no longer be invidious, since only invidious distinctions will be suppressed.

With this we rejoin Durkheim's maladies of infiniteness. Contrary to Durkheim, there is nothing particularly "natural" or instinctual about such maladies, nor the megalomaniacal egoism on which they feed. Certainly they can only be expressed through sociocultural channels, and these must be learned. Certainly there are interactive effects which fuel the fire. But to attribute the phenomena solely to society and socialization is not satisfactory either, as Durkheim seemed to realize. This fails to explain some of its central characteristics. One is its irrationality, its volatility. As with envy, such obviously self-defeating behavior must remain mysterious to those who are prone to attribute all our mistakes to stupidity or ignorance.

A related phenomenon of great significance is the alternation of maladies of infiniteness with opposite maladies of finiteness, the Faustian oscillation between God and worm. The relationship between anomie and alienation suggests the dialectical relationship of manic-megalomanic and depressive states, for example, and the resemblance is not merely that of an analogy. But investigation of these matters has hardly begun, partly because such maladies are generally are not considered pathological.

In sum, these neglected maladies suggest the relevance of psychic ambivalence. They simultaneously call for a closer look at the cultural goals, and at those who accept or reject them.

CULTURAL BIPOLARITY AND INDIVIDUAL AMBIVALENCE

Even those who have vigorously questioned the extent of Merton's consensus on success goals have overlooked the crucial point that the dominant culture itself has contradictions. This oversight results from the neglect of individual ambivalence. "Cultural bipolarity" should be distinguished from cultural diversity, or sub- or countercultural phenomena. It refers to contradictions within the dominant culture and ultimately to the fact that any message is accompanied by its opposite, along with various other linguistic associations. We hear much more of this than we are aware of hearing. All messages are bivalent, and all listeners are ambivalent. The denial of ambivalence lends to attempts to segregate these different cultural emphases (both in theory and society) in different spheres of life. Many go further, insisting on attributing opposed orientations to different individuals and groups. In this way ambivalence, perhaps beginning with their own, is avoided.[44]

Merton misses this vital point even when he addresses it. In commenting on Horney's idea of cultural contradictions interacting with individual ambivalences (success versus love), he passes over precisely what distinguishes her analysis from the strictly sociological view.[45] His own work in this vein offers a further illustration. His idea of *sociological* ambivalence (conflict of roles) not only diverts attention from the inevitably double-edged quality of cultural messages, it leads us to believe that all ambivalences are reducible to role conflicts. When roles (and associated prescriptions and expectations) do not conflict, individuals are not conflicted.

Merton's rejection of human nature and psychological ambivalence by no means stands alone. Like difficulties play havoc with alienation research, as well as more philosophical and Marxist treatments, as I shall show. Even deliberate attempts to incorporate Freudian emphases succumb to similar cultural biases. Talcott Parsons's "motivational" analysis of anomie is a particularly significant example.[46] Parsons appears to grant considerable importance to psychological ambivalence, ambivalence not entirely attributable to present conflicting social directives and expectations. To this end he introduces the concepts of "alienative need dispositions" and "conformative need dispositions." Yet he asserts that once a disturbance has upset the pattern of stable interactions which ego and alter have established, the person who is thereby alienated and rendered deviant will probably be ambivalent toward deviating. Meanwhile, the actor who winds up conforming in the wake of this disturbance may or *may not* be ambivalent toward conforming.

This hemiplegic view of ambivalence pervades Parsonian theory, paralyzing the analysis of conformity as well as rebellion. It is involved in his treatment of the Oedipal crisis, in which everything is settled by the internalization of cultural values as individual superego. It is not simply that Parsons's Freudian man is strangely id-poor, and "affectively neutral." More important, his man is conflict-free, unless and until conflicting roles put him in a bind or quandary or for some reason he fails to conform or perform. In the end Parsons's view is little more psychoanalytic or "motivational" than Merton's. Ambivalence is invoked in order to argue that deviants and rebels are not only dangerous and disruptive, but have no fun.

★   ★   ★   ★   ★

In part the difficulties of the social science of alienation and anomie stem from ignoring or removing the teeth from the very intellectual traditions of alienation and anomie to which lip service is paid. In part they reflect disciplinary commitments which make it difficult to see, much less to ferret out the manifestations of a fundamental human ambivalence. No coherent view of these discontents or their significance can possibly be offered, much less an account of their dialectical interplay and deadly symbiosis. Instead of a sustained and systematic inquiry into the human as well as social significance of those fundamental maladies, we have rigid distinctions, premature fusions, chaotic mixtures. As Marx said to Proudhon: this is not synthesis; it is composite error.

2

Rescuing the Perishing Oppositions

Those who wish to be mediators between two resolute thinkers are marked as mediocre: they lack eyes to see the unparalleled; seeing things as similar and making them the same is the mark of weak eyes.

Nietzsche

The difficulties which plague the social science of alienation and anomie are related to the neglect, dismissal, or misuse of seminal nineteenth century treatments of these and related topics. Hence the failure to distinguish the two concepts, a failure which alternates with putting altogether too much distance between them. Hegel suggests that the aim of philosophy is to abolish indifference. Here I introduce the proposition that alienation and anomie are dialectical opposites, the most intimate, least indifferent relationship of all.

To proceed with one eye on intellectual history is not to deny new uses to old terms, but to affirm that concepts do not come to us from out of the timeless blue. They are accompanied by conceptual systems, linguistic associations, theoretical frameworks; they arrive with nearest conceptual relatives and normative baggage. They have an emotional impact always worth investigating and never safely ignored. They bring with them a human and cultural history. Therefore, to the many researchers measuring this sociological or pyschological state or that, for which there is a less ambiguous and loaded concept than alienation or anomie, the question must be posed: why these concepts, if the associated traditions are being ignored or thrown over? It is a rare student of alienation or anomie who does not want it both ways: rejecting or ignoring the tradition, he soaks it for all it is worth.

Separating the Antagonists

To say that alienation is not anomie amounts to saying that Marx and

Durkheim criticized the ills and evils of capitalist society from markedly different standpoints. Consider the division of labor. To Marx it was not only bound up with the class divisions of bourgeois society, in *itself* it represented a terrible diminution of human powers: the overdevelopment of certain specialized faculties at the expense of the multitude of talents and potentials we are presumed to have. Beginning with *German Ideology* the emphasis on the division of labor began to overshadow the alienation which results from the worker not owning his means of production. Division of labor assumed more importance and was applied more widely and metaphorically, virtually to the point of viewing its abolition as sufficient condition for the inauguration of pure communism. To Durkheim, by sharp contrast, the division of labor meant the possibility of "profound" as opposed to "superficial" individual development. It meant the possibility of a new moral order based on the cult of the individual and the growing interdependence of society.[1] The specialized worker is not normally made to feel that he is being made into a machine or a small part of a man. Instead he feels that he is serving something intelligible and worthwhile.

Or consider the utilitarian-contractarian view of what makes society possible. Both Marx and Durkheim see this as the ideological self-explanation of utilitarian society. It systematizes and summarizes the understanding such a society has of itself, as opposed to explaining how such assumptions could ever produce that (or any other) society. At the heart of utilitarian theory they both saw rampant egoism and the glorification of self-interest. But here again they diverge significantly. Marx complains that utilitarians assume what is useful to the Anglo-Saxon shopkeeper is useful in serving our truly human, species needs. He saw egoism and self-interest, as defined by capitalist market society, as reified activity appearing over and against the individual. Individuals are free, to be sure: free to reproduce the conditions of their bondage. In this way he manages to view a society based on egoism, self-interest, and greed in terms of constraint and coercion. Durkheim saw the same matters quite differently: instead of reification, excessive constraint, and oppression, he tended to see the absence of constraint, anarchy, and anomie.

This contrast extends to numerous issues of central importance and mutual interest. In each case, additional facets of the contrast of anomie and alienation emerge in bold relief. Durkheim's anomie is described as a social state of normlessness, deregulation, rulelessness, a species of anarchy. It suggests the problem of social control and the plight of the individual in a society which lacks controls and constraints.[1] Anomic man, Lukes observes, is the unregulated man in need of rules to live by. He needs limits to his otherwise boundless appetites. These include the secure confines of specialized roles, life circumstances and normative guidelines which confine his choices within relatively narrow bounds and create a comforting backdrop of major choices and issues which have been settled for him. We must be freed from the incessant search for proper conduct.

Alienation, as it emerges from both Marx and Durkheim, is a quite different malady. Oppression, rather than the adequacy of social control, is the concern. Alienation poses the question of legitimacy: "the problem of power defined as domination," as Horton puts it.[2] From this perspective, social order may be quite adequate, yet this may be the problem. By contrast, illegitimate power is not usually associated with anomie. Social control and the integration of otherwise anomic individuals inevitably steal attention from the precise terms on which the individual is brought within the fold and obligated to obey. Marx views society as composed of individual selves, acting collectively, extending themselves through self-activity, objectifying themselves in their environment through the process of externalization. Society is not viewed as a thing, as transcendental, as an entity *sui generis,* as Durkheim insisted sociologists should view it. To see society as objective, external, thinglike is an alienated view of the relationship to man and his productions and surroundings.

Alienation thus refers to obstacles to the productive growth of individuals, and to "forgetting" that concepts, theories, social mores and institutions are human constructions and humanly changeable. For Marx, Lukes observes, "alienation from society is *a priori* alienation from self."[3] The alienated man finds himself in the grip of a system and cannot escape from the specialized activity which is forced upon him. Alienation is a deep-seated systemic malady, in which our social means of mastering nature become our masters.

A deep chasm separates this understanding of alienation from those watered down and expanded versions such as Seeman offers: powerlessness in general, abstracted from any theory of the significance of the condition, severed from the social, objective character of alienation, divorced from its social and human causes. Practically any situation of "powerlessness," the enjoyment of less power than one wants, qualifies as alienation. With relatively minor changes Seeman could have constructed a measure of megalomania.

Marx's immanent conception of man and society forcefully emphasizes the value of freedom from constraint, often in the best liberal tradition. Durkheim's transcendental conception emphasizes the value of moral constraint. Lukes goes so far as to suggest that "alienation is what characterizes precisely those states of the individual and conditions of society which Durkheim sees as the solution to anomie."[4] The point is overstated, but it serves to combat the prevalent understatement of the opposition of the two concepts encountered in the social science of alienation and anomie. When Durkheim sees society as a "reality from which everything that matters to us flows . . . which transcends the individual's consciousness . . . and has all the characteristics of a moral authority that imposes respect," this does approximate Marx's view of alienation. When Marx suggests that it is "above all necessary to avoid postulating society once again as an abstraction confronting the individual," Durkheim would regard this maxim as a reckless prescription for anomie. Or as a symptom of anomie itself, inimical not only to social order and control but also to the possibilities of human freedom and self-realization.

The last point bears emphasis, in view of the conventional stereotype of Durkheim as being interested only in order and constraint. The issue between Marx and Durkheim is not so much the value of human freedom and self-realization as it is a fundamental disagreement over the conditions under which they are promoted. Lukes summarizes this difference: "social constraint is for Marx a denial and for Durkheim a condition of human freedom and self-realization."[5]

"Alienation and anomie do not identify themselves . . . independently of the theories from which they derive."[6] Neither individual mental states or social conditions can serve in this capacity, since "they themselves are to be evaluated for their degree of alienation and anomie."[7] To rely on subjective appraisals is to deny that by its very nature alienation involves and promotes distorted perceptions of the proper relationship of individual and society. To expect a lucid account of his condition from an alienated individual is rather like asking an advanced psychotic to diagnose himself. It is likewise unreasonable to expect that an anomic individual would have a clear view of his condition. The only order victims of anomie may know is disorder. As Durkheim suggests, they "elevate to a rule the lack of rule from which they suffer." The state of anomie may be confused with the human condition, or life, or culture, or even liberation, given sufficient gratuitous cultural support for such interpretations.

Social-scientific treatments of alienation for the most part focus on the individual who in some way or another is left out or does not belong. The usual assumption is that this is a painful and unproductive state related to all sorts of psychic and social disorders, and that it would be altogether better for everyone if they were more securely attached to society by way of friendships, group associations and activities, and institutional involvement. But these assumptions come much closer to the animating spirit of anomie, to Durkheim's assumptions concerning the desirability of social constraint, group attachments, and the spirit of discipline, than to alienation as Marx interpreted it. To be alienated in Marx's sense is not equivalent to being marginal, outcast, at odds with, hostile toward one's society or toward specific social institutions.

Alienation may involve one or more of these states, but the key question for Marx concerns the nature of the connection with society. Is it a dialectical relationship, or is society viewed primarily as an immutable, inhuman facticity? Repairing this rupture is neither a dialectical tour de force performed at the typewriter nor a matter of cutting one's hair, taking regular baths, or jockeying for place in the rush hour. It involves the active appropriation or reappropriation of man's objectifications and externalizations, the entire social world. It is a matter of exercising and espressing a wide range of productive and creative potentials—species powers—whose "self-realization exists as an inner necessity, a need." Lukes points out that all this can

> only take place in a world in which man is free to apply himself to whatever activity he chooses and where his activities and his way of seeing himself and other men are not dictated by a system within which he and they play specified roles.[8]

Some modes of participation will not be conducive to the development of essential human powers: marginal individuals and groups may have something more to tell us than the fact that it hurts to be left out. (Some societies may offer few such opportunities to anyone.) Those leading conventional lives, not disturbing the going order except in approved ways—Sartre's *salauds,* who read their newspapers and fornicate— might well be the alienated ones. The reach of the social scientific theorists encountered earlier extends not far beyond the confines of their corner of the discipline, the outlook of their own middle class strata, and the apotheosis of egoism and self interest which both Marx and Durkheim condemned.

This neglect of assumptions concerning human nature and "normal" social behavior is at least as damaging in the case of the descendants of Durkheim. Durkheim saw human nature in need of limits and discipline: "limitation is a condition of our happiness and moral health." Humans are made for life in a determinate, limited environment. Man, in Durkheim's famous, infamous formulation, is *homo duplex*: he consists of a socially derived self and a biologically based self. The latter self consists of unruly, boundless, anarchistic, greedy, egoistic passions and desires. Only "society as a whole or through the agency of one of its organs, can play a moderating role, can stipulate the point beyond which passions must not go."[9] The contrast with Marx's extravagant optimism concerning the productive and creative potentialities of man (once freed from social roles and fetters) could scarcely be more dramatic.

In this light the full significance of Merton's revision of anomie begins to emerge. Merton deliberately drops the external standard of human nature. Anomie becomes a disjunction between cultural goals and institutional means. The critical focus is now the inadequacy of the institutional means and the presence of inequalities which are not the result of meritocratic competition. Even if Merton were otherwise prone to criticize dominant social institutions and the cultural consensus, he would no longer be justified in doing so. He is no longer entitled to speak, as Durkheim can, of those who raise to the status of a rule the rulelessness from which they suffer. Suffering is one-dimensionalized. What amounts to the same thing: he has largely forgotten that those who manage to conform can suffer for it. Horton suggests that Merton identifies with the very groups and values that Durkheim saw as a prime source of anomie. This seems to be the case, but the problem is deeper. For Merton has difficulty, given the built-in assumptions and oversights of his own paradigm, even raising such questions. Nor can he raise the question of whether the dominant cultural goals are themselves anomic. Yet, as Tocqueville predicted: to maximize the opportunities for achieving success, to perfect the means, would in no way end anomie. Nor would it eliminate the envy Merton finds no place for in his categories.

For Merton, anomie can only be associated with deviance with respect to the society that is and the powers that be. The idea of deviant or anomic societies would require some standard by which to determine from what the society deviates. Apparently conformity is natural and desirable, if only the means for going straight are available. While ritualistic conformity is regarded as a kind of deviance, this is because it is associated with giving up on the competitive struggle, not because it reveals the hidden truth of lifeless repetition at the core of that struggle. Those who conform smoothly and readily, as if they liked it, even to the most ludicrous and chaotic of social standards, are not treated as victims of anomie, however much certain reckless psychologists, aberrant humanists, and renegade social critics may scream pathology.

Alienation as a Defense against Anomie

Peter Berger claims to have synthesized basic aspects of both the

Marxist and Durkheimian outlooks in his account of the "social construction of reality."[10] From Durkheim he derives his view of the nature of social reality as *sui generis,* coercive, external, thinglike. This is modified by the introduction of a dialectical perspective he attributes to Marx, and "an emphasis on the constitution of social reality through subjective meanings derived from Weber."[11] Finally he employs an analysis of the internalization of social reality drawn from the work of George Herbert Mead. Berger repeatedly emphasizes the importance of the Meadian–Marxist synthesis, warning neo-Marxists away from theoretically untenable laisons with psychoanalysis. Psychoanalysis is one of the few major intellectual orientations excluded from this ambitious treatise.

The essentials of the resulting theory can be expressed simply. The first moment, externalization, is Marx's special contribution. Here society is conceived as a human product, as externalized human activity. The second is moment is objectivation, in which society is seen as a reality *sui generis,* an "inexorable facticity." This is the Durkheimian emphasis. Third there is internalization, in which the objectivated world is reabsorbed into consciousness, so that the structure of one's social world determines in large measure the structure of one's mind and personality. This is Mead's (and Parsons's) contribution to a Durkheimian emphasis.

Thus man is seen as both a product and a producer of society, in concert and conflict with other men. By changing the circumstances under which his own growth and creation proceed, "man makes himself." Man produces society through the universal anthropological process of externalization. The result is that objectified human activity comes to confront us as so many facts. In Berger's view this latter insight, Durkheim's great contribution, is also a limitation. Berger claims that Durkheim tended to confuse this moment of a dialectical process with the only possible relationship of individuals to society and social facts. For Berger, then, the task of accounting for the social construction of reality can be reduced to this question: how can meaningful human activity (*Handeln*) produce a world of things (*choses*)?[12]

Using an approach reminiscent of Parsons' analysis of the interaction of ego and alter, Berger considers the way that typifications, those schema and categories in terms of which alter and others are apprehended and dealt with in face to face situations, are built up even in the simplest of interactions. The social structure amounts to the "sum total of such typifications and the patterns of interaction established and maintained by them."[13] Then he moves from the subjective activity of constructing social reality to the objectified reality we so construct. Here Berger relies on the anthropological suppositions of Plessner and Gehlen, drawn from comparative biology, which Berger sees as the extension of the anthropological assumptions brilliantly intuited by Marx and German philosophy. Gehlen's theory of instincts suggests that man's world, or *ambient,* is imperfectly programmed by his own constitution. Man's relationship to his environment is therefore characterized by a relative world-openness. This biologically intrinsic world-openness "is always, and must be, transformed by the social order into a relative world-closedness."[14] "No existing social order can be derived from biological data," he admits, but "the necessity for social order as such stems from man's biological equipment."[15]

Habitualization, in tandom with social typifications and roles, provides the "direction and specialization of activity that is lacking in man's biological equipment, thus relieving the accumulation of tensions that result from undirected drives."[16] In the process of world-building, made necessary because of man's inadequate instinctual guidance, man specializes and channels his drives and provides stability for himself. Institutional requirements and roles come to function much like instincts. Here he is very close to Durkheim. Given the great plasticity Berger attributes to human instincts (most dramatically illustrated by the ethnological evidence concerning sexuality) the possible habits, rules, typifications, institutions, and symbolic universes which could adequately channel instincts are virtually infinite. This is reflected in the myriad ways of being human that anthropologists have discovered at home and abroad.

The conclusion can only be that

> Human-ness is socio-culturally variable. In other words, there is no human nature in the sense of a biologically fixed substratum determining the variability of socio-cultural formations. There is human nature only in the sense of anthropological constants (for example, world- openness and plasticity of instinctual structure) that delimit and permit man's socio-cultural formations . . . . [W]hile it is possible to say that man has a nature, it is more significant to say that man constructs his own nature, or more simply, that man produces himself.[17]

Without externalization and objectivation the reality of everyday life could not be. Without instinctual guidance or its social-institutional substitutes life would be sheer horror. Everyday reality represents a small clearing of lucidity in a formless, dark, always ominous "jungle," full of "lurking irrealities" as conjured up in nightmares, fantasies, and marginal experiences like death and disaster. Or those occasions on which your faithful dog momentarily looks like a cunning wolf, your husband begins to resemble a vampire, or your food seems about to eat you.[18]

So man is biologically bound to build a cultural home, an objective, collective world. Precisely because it is not the only world conceivable, he is prone to cling to it as if it were.

This brings us once again to the question of alienation and anomie, but first we should briefly consider Berger's third moment or perspective on the relation of man and society: man as a social product. Here Berger presses George Herbert Mead into service.[19] Mead's basic postulate is that our self, or the bulk of it, is a reflected self. We first learn of ourselves through the eyes of significant others, typically parents and other early influences. The "other" becomes progressively less personalized, more generalized and abstract as we move out into the larger society, from Mother to family to school to church to economic enterprise to nation. This amounts to the individual's reabsorption of social objectivations (in the form of typifications, expectations, roles, rules, categories, and so forth). In this way society constitutes our very conception of self. Mind, self, and society are "co-emergent." As Berger puts it, "the individual becomes that which he is addressed by others."[20] "Every name implies a nomenclature, which in turn implies a designated social location."[21] In any role in which we are placed, including those which we do not relish at all, we are not only prone to play the role but to become it. It is far easier that way. Berger offers the example of the man who not only plays the role of uncle, but he is an uncle. If socialization has been fairly successful, Berger contends, the man does not wish to be anything else.

Together with Mead and Durkheim, Berger assumes that there remains a part of self which is not the social self. It becomes possible to conceive of our self as having been only partially involved in the action by reflecting on the action afterwards, by reflecting on experience. Why this reflective self is not also socially derived is unclear. "There are always elements of the subjective reality that have not originated in socialization."[22] But the nature of the elements, and why they defy socialization, is never quite clear. It is only a "segment of the self which is objectivated in terms of the socially available typifications."[23] This is the strictly "social self," the "I," which is experienced as "distinct from and even confronting the self in its totality." The latter self is the somewhat mysterious "me."[24]

The claim is that the total self enters into a dialogue and dialectical relation with the social self, affecting and being affected in turn. The individual's identity is "ultimately legitimated by placing it within the context of a symbolic universe."[25] The symbolic universe "puts everything in the right place" for the individual. Its protection and guidance are especially important in dealing with ever present and always dangerous margins, in interpreting marginal experiences. Here "the fundamental terror-assuaging character of the ultimate legitimations of the paramount reality of everyday life is revealed."[26] In Berger's symbolic universe, when lurking irrealities burst forth, everyone heads home for the covers, clutching for the most familiar, reassuring realities they can. Berger dismisses the view that some individuals might find certain irrealities humorous or harmless, or see them as a source of new ideas, or as the necessary and temporary dissolution of a personality or social role or symbolic universe gone rigid and sterile. And apparently the idea of anyone searching out such irrealities, ambiguities, and anomalies is beyond the pale.

> On the level of meanings, the institutional order represents a shield against terror . . . while the horror of aloneness is probably already given in the constitutional sociality of man.[27]

Much as Marx does, Berger defines alienation as a rupture of consciousness such that one's joint authorship of the social world is forgotten. The individual's dialectical relationship with the world is no longer perceived, even though the relationship continues nonetheless. In the stage of reification, *Verdinglichung,* things become the standard of all his reality. The rub is that Berger never really explains why externalization and objectification are humanly necessary, while alienation and reification, though omnipresent, are merely *de facto* aspects of the human condition. Marxists were quick to criticize his account for leaving out specific historical and institutional sources of alienation.

The reason for the different status of externalization and alienation in Berger is easily inferred from his anthropological assumptions, from the psychological functions alienation serves. It is suggested by his constant references to boundaries, margins, the terror of marginal experiences, death, chaos, the desperate need for stability and order. It is further suggested by the opposition he draws between the sacred and the "yawning abyss" of chaos. In short, both individuals and society are constantly threatened by incipient anomie, and the terror that accompanies and exacerbates it.

Berger claims that his perspective is neither essentialist nor psychologistic, but is grounded in the simple facts of human consciousness of mortality and the "biologically given fact of sociality." In the face of terror, no price is too high to pay to put chaos to rest and isolation to an end. The means of doing so is a symbolic universe in which everyone has a place and regards the given social order, social interactions, and social institutions not as infinitely malleable, not as expedient or functional for this or that purpose, but as inevitable parts of the natural order of things. Berger sees alienation, and the escape it provides from the disturbing, unsettling realization that things could be otherwise, as the price most people pay most of the time to escape a far worse malady. That malady is anomie. Alienation as a protection against anomie or flight from it: this is his simple but arresting formulation.[28]

This represents a significant step toward sorting out the relationship of alienation to anomie. Berger's suggestion does not do wholesale violence to the traditions out of which these concepts spring. He preserves the Marxist recognition that neither alienated nor anomic individuals are necessarily the best judges of their state: the alienated did not get that way in order to be easily reminded of their condition, while anomics may be so confused as to think everyone sees things their way. In either case their condition may entail their not knowing their condition. Especially important is the recognition that alienation may be associated at least as much with conformity, passivity, and acquiesence as with deviance, defiance, or self-conscious marginality. As Berger observes, "seeing the socio-world in alienated terms serves to maintain its nomic structures intact."[29] Finally, he not only distinguishes subjective alienation from anomia or anomie (anomy), he sharply distinguishes them: "Subjective alienation is not anomy. On the contrary, such alienation can be a most effective *barrier* against anomy."[30] We must combat the "psychologistic misunderstanding of alienation: to say that a man is alienated is not the same as saying that he is anomic or that he feels hostile."[31]

For all its merit, this stimulating formulation suffers from a neglect of crucial psychoanalytic insights and a myopic misreading of classic sources. To begin with we must ask whether the relationship postulated betweeen anomie and alienation is dialectical. Why can't anomie be regarded as a defense against alienation? Anomie is certainly involved in the destructuring of social and political forms. Presumably it could be therapeutic for social institutions suffering from rigidity, ossification, excessive constraint and coercion: that is, from alienation. No doubt it can serve analogous purposes for the individual. On both counts Berger is silent. Instead he constantly reminds us of the psychological horrors of *anomie*. He has remarkably little to say about the psychological horrors of alienation—nor, for that matter, its other horrors. Berger fears anomie with a deep and abiding passion. For him it is tantamount to falling from grace, or being excommunicated. He attributes this fear to all of us, and in much the same degree.

There is a further difficulty which applies to his characterization of alienation as a "forgetting" of one's actual or potential authorship of the social world. For someone who wishes to avoid a psychologistic or essentialist view of these maladies, Berger certainly delivers a great deal of ammunition to potential critics. Forgetting: as if the alienation were due to an unaccountable human absent-mindedness. As Marxist critics point out, Berger's account of alienation rarely refers to specific, oppressive, historical social institutions, institutions which are capable of being changed, reformed, destroyed, replaced. Berger's response is that his argument depends not on psychology but on the basic "existential" fact of human consciousness of always impending death. As with all such characterizations of the human situation which purport to dispense with human nature, this contains far more psychology than it admits to. Berger does not deem it necessary to ground both anomie and alienation in a theory which affirms the human wishes and fears involved in both. Contrary to Berger's leftist critics, the problem is not that his account is one-sidedly psychological. The problem is a one-sided psychology.

There is little question that Berger's argument depends more on general human propensities than social and economic institutions. Despite disclaimers, he leaves the impression that all social institutions, perhaps for all time, are equally alienating. Alienation is uniform and ubiquitous, since anomie poses a constant threat. We must wonder why all this Marxist paraphernalia and dialectical hoopla has been so enthusiastically imported, if the end result is to rival Durkheim at his most static and conservative.

Berger forgets that people remember as well as forget. He repeatedly fails to notice the ambivalent quality of the many activities which he unfailingly discusses in terms of their conservative, fear-of-terror, wish-for-security-and-familiarity aspects. For example, to say that the development of typifications or the use of language is a nomizing activity prejudges the issue of what psychological ends and social functions are served and involved. The creative use of language involves *un*naming what is supplanted or superceded or thought of in a new way. It may even involve creating a new concept, an activity both denomizing and nomizing. Establishing a new order can be aggressive, expressive, expansive as well as nomizing, expressing conservative personality needs. Establishing a new order of meanings can not only be a means by which we combat anomie, chaos, confusion. It can also be an activity which destroys alienating forms and institutions in the process of creating new ones.

The irony associated with Berger's one-sided synthesis is that Durkheim came considerably closer to such a Janus-faced perspective than did Marx. Durkheim spoke often (albeit rather carelessly) of our liberating dependence on authority: it was his *idée fixe*. Yet Berger turns to Marx for the dialectical understanding missing in Durkheim! Language, the coercive "given" par excellence, can be a vehicle of creativity and self-expression as well as a clumsy tool which crushes truth as it tries to grasp it. Its authority is intimately bound to its liberating effects and vice versa. So with other cultural and social forms: the effect on the individual can combine the sense of submission and dependence with the sense of enhanced power and freedom. Durkheim had the good sense to marvel at this mystery, as did Nietzsche before him. Language and logic establish sharp differences between such terms as liberty and authority. Our liberal political heritage tends to turn such differences into ironclad oppositions. Marx and Marxist thought often do so as well. But all of this may amount to more of an indictment of human limitations than than an indication that opposites cannot coexist. Life may be neither linguistic nor logical.

In Berger's synthesis we see only the ordering aspect of socially constructed realities. In this respect his focus and preoccupation differ little from those of Marx; he simply offers the opposite evaluation. Whether it is his account of religion ("the sacred canopy"), logic, language, roles, habituation, typifications, or entire symbolic universes, Berger seems incapable of conceiving these phenomena in terms of simultaneous differences and opposites—combinations of expression and repression, desires for expression, expansion, power, freedom, autonomy, as well as conservative needs for order, dependence, security. Rather than denying that life can be nomizing and denomizing, form and formlessness, we would do well to notice that logic itself if one of those forms through which life expresses but never exhausts itself.

In this attempt to trap life, however, Berger has company from all over the political and intellectual spectrum. The belief in opposites, Nietzsche declared, is the fundamental faith of the metaphysicians. And metaphysicians are everywhere. Once again: the irony is that even Durkheim, whose emotional make-up and social outlook are generally quite congenial to Berger's own, repeatedly called attention to the strange coincidence of opposites involved in social behavior. It was Marx who thought contradiction and conflict were evils that could be finally eliminated. On the level of individual personality he tended to neglect them altogether, except as continuations of social conflicts. Much like Merton, Marx thoroughly socializes our ambivalences, domesticating them in the process.

The abstract quality of Berger's argument protects it from having to deal with manifestations of social life that are difficult to reduce to their ordering aspects and conservative motivations. Granted, it is possible to imagine arguments which would fit any conceivable activity into this narrow frame. Mountain climbers, climbers of all sorts, may have decided to protect themselves from their consciousness of death and their fear of heights the hard way, by doing over and over again what is excruciating and harrowing. But this is doubtful. It is also doubtful that Bergerian cave men would ever have gotten off their rears in order to spend time fashioning better clubs, or to seek out a better cave. One must often be daring, dynamic, enterprising even if the ultimate goal is always security, peace, order. In Berger's world the only conceivable place for man the producer, inventor, creator, overcomer and overreacher, hell-raiser, mover, seeker, the mountain climber—the sometimes *chooser* of the marginal, alien, the frightful—is in connection with crude, defensive attempts to make the world more secure, safe, orderly, peaceful. To offer this as the whole story of what motivates our restless striving and makes history strains credulity. Bergerian man would have generated a very different history, if any history at all.

All these movers and climbers, inexplicable exceptions to Berger's implied universal truths of human psychology, might be renegades who somehow escaped the socialization process. To the extent that Berger allows for such exceptions, however, he admits the possibility that the socialization process might conflict as well as accord with some of our basic impulses. Berger can not seem to make up his mind about the fragility of the social order. On the one hand, socialization and the closing of world-openness is supposed to be perfectly consistent with our deepest needs: to avoid anomic terror. But if this is so, it is no longer clear why social order is such an obsession. (Recall that only a "reasonably good socialization" suffices to make the uncle believe he is an uncle, to follow a social script for the part of uncles.) Given the attractions of order, the enthusiasm and relief with which we take our places in the society and its symbolic universe, it is difficult to fathom why socially constructed realities are constantly threatened by anomie and chaos.

Yet Berger obviously feels that the socialization process, all the typifications and institutions, legitimizations and elements of the symbolic universe, are eternally vulnerable to corrosion and prone to dissolution. It is as though Berger suspects that some or all of us have other, even opposite purposes in mind. Putting the point more conventionally: there is little room here for a viable and attractive account of freedom, given its inevitable, intimate association with chaos. Its only place in Berger's account is in connection with "dereification." Berger's examples of dereification (the very term suggests the effort to distance the phenomenon itself) suffice to discourage all but the most ardent and fearless advocates of freedom. They feature anarchy, chaos, disaster, upheaval, loneliness, marginality: extreme anomie.

No doubt everyone fears being excluded and abandoned. But maybe everyone also fears oppression, suffocation, being trapped or getting stuck:

> Not to remain stuck to a person—not even the most loved—every person is a prison. . . . [N]ot to remain stuck to a fatherland—not even if it suffers most and needs help most—it is less difficult to sever one's heart from a victorious fatherland. Not to remain stuck to some pity—not even for higher men into whose rare torture and helplessness some accident allowed us to look. Not to remain stuck to a science—even if it should lure us with the most precious finds that seem to have been saved up precisely for us.[32]

Where such impulses and needs come from is impossible for Berger to say. Conceivably they could be derived from the socialization process or the culture, though the notion that we can be socialized to engage in activities which promote anomie presents difficulties for his argument. Berger does not distinguish between social orders predicated upon a great deal of (bounded) disorder and learning when *not* to know one's place, and those in which boundaries are more narrow and rigid, one's place is better defined, and one's role does not include the expectation that the role itself must be subject to criticism and change. Alternatively, some such drives might somehow have escaped the socialization process, or have continued to fight a rear-guard action against it. Berger, in concert with Mead, clearly asserts the presence of a non-socialized self. He even compares Durkheim's *homo duplex* with Bergerian man. Yet he oscillates between neglecting the nonsocial self, the "me," and collapsing the distinction between the "me" and the "I."

In all events it is clear enough to Berger what happens in the socialization process. To be sure, at one point he grants that "the little animal fights back." Fortunately for child, parents, and teachers, "he is fated to lose the battle." How Berger knows when the battle is finally over, or that it ever ends, is a mystery. What it means to lose is not adequately explained either. The child may capitulate to this exercise in spirit-breaking only to fight again, or to hatch fiendish plots. He may continue to do so long past childhood. But Berger holds stubbornly if anxiously to his faith in the powers of socialization, the attractions of being one with our roles. Resistance is "progressively broken in the course of socialization," though it "perpetuates itself as frustration" whenever we desire what society forbids. Though this assessment seems to allow for the possibility of anti-social or disruptive behavior, Berger cannot see past those examples in which the same reality is created for individuals as that which they readily assume. His model is and remains the uncle who quickly, gladly becomes the uncle.

Occasionally he wonders whether socialization is so powerful that it may become an oppressive straight-jacket. He expresses concern over the possible effects of preparing generation after generation of graduate students in sociology for taking their place in the cage of role theory and jingoistic functionalism. But it was those students of sociology, brought up on Parsons and taught by his students, who had learned all about inescapable roles and inexorable socialization, who were among the most over-represented in various kinds of student protest. Underlying such oversights is a failure to notice that *any* talk of social roles and requirements, any socialization message, conjures up the possible violation or defiance of these prescriptions, even as it emphasizes their persuasiveness and power over us.

The upshot is that Berger, despite the promise of his perspective, shares a basic difficulty with the other students of alienation and anomie: there is little room in their picture of man for human ambivalence. Merton removes the teeth from the idea of ambivalence by associating it exclusively with culturally and socially induced conflicts. Berger neglects ambivalence not only in his anthropological assumptions but also in his analysis of socialization, the assumption of roles, alienation, and anomie. As he blithely puts its, "ambivalences are removed for the alienated." Parsons says much the same for those who conform. In the manner of Parsons, Berger repeatedly alludes to the absence of conflicts once social roles are accepted, irrespective of what those roles are and who is forced to fill them. This is either tautological or myopic. Society as a human product gets short shrift. Almost without exception, these difficulties derive from a one-sided, one-dimensional view of being human.

If ambivalence is human, the attempt to ignore, deny, finesse, or flee must be human as well. One salient expression of this escapism is the difficulty of theorists in taking the perspectives and emphases of Marx and Durkheim equally seriously. Unquestionably this difficulty reflects emotional as well as logical obstacles in confronting ambivalence, but then gratuitous cultural and social support for the failure to do so is always close at hand. Marx and Durkheim, especially Marx, effectively segregate the poles. Yet if their respective contributions cannot be "seen together," our efforts will be one-dimensional misfortunes.

With this caution in mind, I will rely upon Durkheim and Marx to further develop and deepen the opposition of alienation and anomie, the better to eventually grasp their ultimate kinship. To proceed in this way, separating our fundamental discontents, may seem antithetical to our announced purpose of revealing their fundamental affinity. But not so. In fact, to do justice to significant differences, while combatting stark opposition, is essential. Dividing the two properly, we may come to understand their essential unity.

3

Marx on Alienation

If the product of labor is alien to me, if it confronts me as an alien power, to whom, then, does it belong?

Marx

Man first of all sees his nature as if out of himself, before he finds it in himself.

Feuerbach

You sought the heaviest burden, and you found yourself.

Nietzsche

Some commentators have argued that Marx's view of man has far more in common with the Enlightenment than the outlook of other nineteenth century figures like Tocqueville, Burckhardt, Simmel, Weber, or Durkheim. Somehow Marxist man seems to belong to the century or two *before* Marx invented him. Simmel has characterized the intellectual world to which Marxist man belongs with exceptional clarity:

> The inadequacy of the socially accepted forms of life of the eighteenth century, in contrast with its material and intellectual productions, struck the consciousness of the individual as an unbearable limitation of his energies .... [T]he oppressiveness of these and similar institutions which had lost their inner justifications, resulted in the ideal of the mere liberty of the individual. It was believed that the removal of these ties, which pressed the forces of the personality into unnatural grooves ... would lead society out of the epoch of historical unreason into that of natural reason .... [I]t was merely necessary to gain this freedom as purely and completely as possible to recapture the original basis of the existence of our species and of our personality, a basis which is as certain and fruitful as nature.[1]

The aversion to social institutions, social dependence and influences, is not only descriptive but constitutive of this outlook.

For this reason, man in general, man as such, is the central interest of the period; not historically given, particular, differentiated man. Concrete man is reduced to general man . . . . [T]herefore, all that is needed to make appear what is common to all men, or man's essence, or man as such, is to free the individual from all these historical influences and distortions which merely hide his deepest nature . . . . [T]he crucial point of this conception of individuality—which is one of the great conceptions of intellectual history—is this: if man is freed from all that he is not purely himself, if man has found himself, there emerges as the proper substance of his being, man-as-such or humanity.[2]

Simmel's eighteenth century individualism parallels Marx's idea of species man or being. For Marx species man was something of a substitute for a vision of man with explicit normative dimensions.

But is not the Marxist view of man thoroughly sociological? Marx is certainly *the* sociologist of conflict. He is likewise a sociologist of social control and coercion: the ways in which social classes were confined, coerced, influenced, rendered dependent and servile, subjected to forces beyond their control and consciousness. Yet on the positive side—the benign view of social influence and dependence on society; society as the source of nurture, the midwife of what is best and most progressive in us—Marx has very little to say. What he did say is found primarily in the *Economic and Philosophic Manuscripts of 1844*. Even there the message is perfunctory. Nonetheless it is the only extended example of the sociological apperception in Marx, as Dumont has pointed out.[3] In this respect the *Manuscripts* represent an aberration, even in light of *Grundrisse,* whose account of social man is timid and not well grounded in his earlier perspective. His view of communist utopia was "non-social" as well, in precisely the way the Enlightment view of man and individuality was: thoroughgoing opposition to any social influence or dependence, to anything that hints of social transcendence or the *sui generis* character of society. The emphasis throughout is placed on what Lane has aptly called sociological release. As with Enlightenment thinkers: the root, for Marx, is man. We must avoid positing society as an abstraction, as something transcending the subject. Marx was a sociologist to end all sociology.

Another aspect of this attempt to have it both ways is more obvious: his treatment of the division of labor. Marx's virtually lifelong rejection of the division of labor suggests a Faustian restlessness and megalomania, an unwillingness to be defined or shaped by one's roles, a feeling that the real sense of oneself must be found in one's uniqueness, one's differences from others. Simmel defines such attitudes in terms of nineteenth century individualism: the individualism of difference, incomparability, uniqueness. He argued that this provided the metaphysical basis for the division of labor. Durkheim thought along these lines as well. What Marx intuited and Durkheim did not is that the impulse behind this movement from the individualism of equality, or eighteenth-century individualism, to the individualism of difference was not about to stop with the acceptance of the division of labor, however meritocratic it might be made. Once man was freed from arbitrary social shackles and distinctions he set out to make distinctions of his "own." After all, the heirarchy of roles which constitutes the division of labor is not fashioned by the individual for his or her unique purposes.

Thus the next, more radical stage of the critique of society was a critique of the division of labor. Durkheim preferred to believe such attitudes were the sole property of a few vestigal dilettantes. Marx saw it otherwise, and this is one reason he continues to inspire the most advanced protest phenomena in contemporary Western societies. Marx regarded the division of labor as backward looking in the extreme, aside from its progressive role in developing and destroying capitalism. Durkheim, Weber, and Simmel saw the divison of labor as the very mark of modernity, despite their different evaluations of it. For Durkheim, the backward looking were precisely those who sought to destroy or reject the division of labor. The *most* backward were those who rejected the division of labor because they entertained futile, bloated, dated aspirations to become modern versions of Renaissance man.

In effect Marx advocated some sort of synthesis of the individualisms of equality and difference. Yet he does not succeed in making such a goal plausible, much less palpable. There is no such reconciliation in Marx, except by dialectical flourish and fiat. Both notions of individualism are present, to be sure; but they remain in a state of antagonistic mixture.

Freedom as Self-Realization, Freedom as Release

Marx's view of man did not undergo fundamental changes in the course of his career. To argue this in detail would be a lengthy distraction, but any discussion of Marx takes at least an implicit stand on this question. I will let the assumption be judged by its fruits.

Any sample of Marx's pronouncements on man and species man yields a number of adjectives which are overwhelmingly positive. Marxist man is productive, conscious, independent, creative, versatile, multitalented, dynamic, active. He is also free of psychic conflict.[4]

Merely listing qualities or attributes of man is crude and uninformative, of course. That most commentators resort to such lists reflects the fact that Marx had no integrated, coherent view of man. Instead we find a number of adjectives in search of a noun.

Some have attempted to express Marx's conception more succinctly and forcefully. Duncan makes the plausible argument that Marx adopted a philosophic commonplace of his time: the destiny of man is the completion or realization of all those abilities that are in him. This tends to overlook our ability to commit mass murder. Others correctly suggest that Marxist man desires freedom, and that this desire is rooted in the act of producing and gaining mastery over the material world. This seems to combine the impulse to escape the social yoke with the desire to realize oneself in productive activity and products, possibly in cooperation with others. But the cooperation Marx has in mind is of a peculiar and presumably rare sort: it must not reflect social influences nor hierarchic control. This effectively eliminates all imaginable social situations, interactions, and institutions, including the workplace.

In a similar vein, Schacht interprets Marx as claiming that productive activity is the medium through which individual personality expresses and realizes itself. Others stress the spontaneous and self-directed qualities of the activity, insisting that it must have no end other than the expression and development of one's personality. Kamenka suggests that, for Marx as for Hegel, freedom means self-determination in accordance with one's inner constitution, not being determined from without, by one's relation to other things. But we learn very little about this inner constitution, what sorts of political regimes we make of our self and its subordinate selves. Therefore, when we find Marxist man portrayed as being in perfect harmony with himself (in the absence of social contradictions which alone cause him psychic conflict), we can only assume that there is some marvelous Invisible Hand at work in the Marxist psyche, ensuring this harmony even in the absence of our insight into the process.

Such characterizations of Marxist man differ little in substance. Nor do they differ much in what they omit: an account of psychic conflict, what it involves and concerns; and a sense of man as a social being, not just a being coerced and frustrated by society. The latter contention holds true even in the face of the *Manuscripts of 1844,* the debatably sociological perspective of the *Grundrisse,* and the common interpretation of his species man as social in every sense. Instead of signaling the coming ascendancy of the sociological apperception in his mature thought, the *Manuscripts* appear to have inaugurated the inevitably individualistic perspective of political economy.[5] Yet Marx saw no inconsistency in adopting the economic method and perspective. The symbolic organization of capitalism was grounded in the market economy: capitalist economics was what capitalist society was all about. It had gained dominion over the ways and the means by which market society represented itself to itself.

It also seems to have captured Marx's own account. Marx tended to confuse the dominance of the economic, a specific and unique historical circumstance, with some kind of transhistorical truth about societies. This is deliciously ironic in light of his diatribes against the ahistorical. Sahlins has rightly observed that Marx was a pre-symbolic theorist, having been misled by the dominance of economic symbols and thoughtways in the nineteenth century.[6]

Horkheimer has suggested that philosophical anthropology represents a "desperate search for absolute meaning in a relativist world." What strikes the modern reader is that Marx's search was distinguished more by confidence (and brevity) than by desperation. He certainly had no fear of what might be found, of unleashing frightful antinomian as well as progressive forces. His unshakeable faith in species man encouraged him to proffer and promulgate conceptions of freedom that might otherwise appear unthinkably advanced. In denying the possibility that human nature itself was being degraded or destroyed, a certain recklessness concerning the fate of freedom became his prerogative. Without dismissing Marx's own inner struggle, it nevertheless seems that the real sociologists—Simmel, Durkheim, Weber—were decidedly more concerned, cautious, anxious, tormented.

Time and again Marx contrasts species man, self-realization, self-production, self-creation with any sort of dependence on society, or being influenced by it. The notion that communist men and women would collectively control their social destiny is fused with the notion that individual destinies are individually controlled. The concern with creativity is reminiscent of Nietzsche, yet Nietzsche saw this task as fraught with peril and not for everyone. Admittedly a few passages in Marx stress control, social influence, social determination, and cooperation. There is his much quoted remark about how much hard work is involved in creative activity. Another passage calls attention to the virtues of overcoming obstacles and resistance even in necessary tasks. But these stand out as the exceptions they are.

Marx's view of freedom went beyond mere absence of constraint: the question is where it went. His views on labour do not stress the joys and bracing, character-building discipline and duties of work. The emphasis is placed on productive activity as "spontaneous" and "self-directed," as the expression and development of one's own personality, free of coordination and control. When Marx suggested that freedom is the condition of man whose human powers are fulfilled, passing beyond absence of restraint to the active unfolding of all his potentialities, it is hard to think of this individuality as communal in nature or orientation. It is easier to imagine that others are supposed to keep their hands off. To see it this way involves reading between the lines. It may seem to confuse Marx with some of his more infantile modern epigones. But those who take for granted the social nature of Marxist man are reading neither the lines nor the spaces between with care.

For Marx, servility is an inhuman bugbear, and his belated assertions that man is *also* constituted by society convey neither enthusiasm nor conviction. The same pronounced emphasis on sociological release can be found in many other contexts. At one point Marx described the communist utopia in terms of the elimination of all intermediate loyalties, ties, groups, group influences, in language so blunt as to boil the blood of pluralists. His description of species man suggests a distinct distaste for social ties. Species man is a "man of all-round accomplishments whose full development is not hampered by prevailing social relations with their various forms of alienation."[7] The ambiguity in "prevailing" is significant. One possible interpretation is that species man is not held back because he is totally free of social entanglements. The other is that social relations under communism will be entered into because they are somehow free of the "various forms of alienation." The latter, no doubt the intended meaning, requires a defense it never received.

Or we can look at another way Marx spoke of alienation: as a result of attempting to assert one's independence in ways that make one dependent. On the one hand this implies that dependence and independence always work at cross purposes; on the other, that communist man would be exempt somehow from hard choices, resulting commitments, and dependency. It would have been simpler to express distaste for the bourgeois conception of independence, and the particular forms of dependence it establishes. Or he could have said that bourgeois man is independent in certain respects, which the bourgeoisie recognizes and overemphasizes; and dependent in others, which its ideologists and apologists tend to ignore. But this might imply that communism has to make the same kinds of trade-offs.

It is his critique of religion, however, which elicits and displays these positions most vividly. Someone has suggested that Marx exhibits an almost Nietzschean concern with human dignity, thought of in terms of independence and mastery over things. In fact he surpasses Nietzsche in his concern for mastery over *things*. The real focus in Nietzsche is the overcoming of contrarieties, individual as well as social and conceptual. Nietzschean notions of overcoming, of ambivalence not exclusively sociological, are foreign to Marx's outlook, especially after his brief flirtation with the idea of self-alienation in the *Manuscripts*. As Tucker points out, that flirtation ended abruptly with the notion that self-alienation can always be attributed to "another man."[8] All obstacles become external, alien. Man, and theorists of man, are free to concentrate on the mastery of external things, other men; to think of independence strictly in terms of the institutional and ideological obstacles.

So it is with the obstacle of religion, the critique of which is the "prerequisite of every critique." Aside from disentangling himself from Hegel's idealism and Feuerbach's abstractions, the critique of religion presents few intellectual or emotional difficulties for Marx. In terms of its social principles and impact, Christianity is a school for cowardice. It has stolen man's self-esteem, "which disappeared into the blue mists of heaven." The comparison with Nietzsche is again revealing. Nietzsche yielded to no one in despising the psychological counterfeiting of Christian asceticism, the brutality to the senses, the ressentiment against what is fine, noble, high-spirited, joyful, creative, sensuous. Yet he had a far keener sense of what the death of God might mean for man. He admitted that for many centuries Christian piety might have been the only path by which the Western spirit could have been refined and educated, and even expressed gratitude to such a perfect antipode. The death of God was not merely an embarrassment, or something to celebrate and hasten. It was a crisis of incalculable depth. It presented a profound challenge to articulate a code of ethics and a way of life which would take into account those human propensities and weaknesses on which religion had preyed, but do so in the service of autonomy, dignity, creativity, and self-overcoming. There was relatively little childish exultation over killing the Father, and profound concern with the difficulties of living in a world without fathers.

For all such matters Marx had little sensitivity. Christianity was an object of loathing, the same Christianity from which he and Hegel before him borrowed so heavily. Judaism fared no better. The dissolution of Christianity (or capitalism, or any feature of bourgeois society) is an altogether good thing. Total alienation will be followed by total freedom; slavery will be exchanged for the complete absence of social influence. From total subjection to total release, and on to total mastery of society. The total transcendence of transcendence. It is an intoxicating brew.

Self-Realization as Multidimensionality

Marx's view of the specifically human and his critique of the division of labor are associated with well-worn contentions concerning the all-round development of communist man.

Consider some statements on the subject, by Marx and sympathetic commentators:

> Communism is the time of full, personal appropriation. (Ollman)

> Universal man . . . is a man of all-round accomplishments. (Schaff)

> Freedom . . . is the condition of man whose human powers are thus fulfilled . . . [It] passes beyond absence of restraints to the active unfolding of all his potentialities. (Ollman)

> The detail worker of today, the limited individual, the mere bearer of a particular social function, will be replaced by the fully developed individual, for whom the different social functions he performs are but so many alternative modes of activity. (Marx)

> Freedom is the active striving of all faculties to attain their objects. (Fromm)

> Man is independent only . . . . if he affirms his individuality as a total man in each of his relations to the world . . . in short, if he affirms and expresses all organs of his individuality. (Fromm)

> The transcendence of private property . . . is the complete emancipation of all human senses and qualities. (Marx)

> Only at this stage does self-activity coincide with material life, which corresponds to the development of individuals into complete individuals and the casting-off of all natural limitations. (Marx)

To know what to make of these contentions we need some sense of what faculties will be unfolded, how malignant or benign, well-behaved or unruly. We need to know whether they prompt activity such that "the development of each contributes to the development of all." On these matters there is little. What little is said invariably concerns what "all round development" and "full personal appropriation" are not.

Nevertheless, on a few occasions Marx does reveal his conception of "human nature in general" (as opposed to human nature "as modified by each epoch"). "The whole character of a species . . . . . is contained in the character of its life activity; and free, conscious activity is man's species character."[9] Ollman has ferreted out a longer list of powers and needs regarded by Marx as species powers. These include "seeing, hearing, smelling, tasting, feeling, thinking, being aware (*Anschauen*), sensing (*Empfinden*), wanting, acting (*Tatigkeit*), loving."[10] Elsewhere in Marx, Ollman finds "creating, sex, knowing and judging" regarded as species powers.

In the absence of further information, particularly concerning attributes opposed to these, such ideas could well serve the causes of megalomania, madness, and mayhem. Slogans of this sort could be taken as prescriptions for anomie as easily as for utopian freedom—as prescriptions for infinite frustration, or for accomplishing even less than more reasonable expectations might achieve.[11]

Again the comparison with Nietzsche is instructive. Nietzsche is concerned equally with creativity and multidimensionality, sensitive to the conflict between individualism and the individuation required and bounded by specialized roles. But he sees this problem of expressing and accommodating all our faculties and propensities as far more demanding and problematic. He suggests it involves a kind of cruelty to oneself. In addition to neglecting such possibilities, in addition to offering us a narrow slice of "empirical" human nature, Marx fails to explain how all these qualities and potentials fit together. Even benign potentials compete for limited time and energy. And if we add back what Marx has subtracted and ignored—aggression, greed, envy, ignorance, passivity, dependence—the question of compatibility of desires can no longer be slighted or finessed. As for the question of social interaction, it suffices to note the virtual absence of tough-minded consideration of the possibility that the exercise of some of my powers is likely to diminish the possibilities for your exercise of yours.[12] This is another major respect in which Marx's utopia is sociologically naive. It resembles the liberal fantasy that there must be some institutional arrangements that will allow each and everyone to have his way.

So it is a spectacle both enlightening and disappointing: a powerful thinker with unimpeachable dialectical credentials, one whose stock in trade was the ceaseless clash and conflict of opposites, presenting such a harmonious picture of human desires and social interaction under communism. The neglect of individual contradictions and ambivalence is reflected in his neglect of anomie, and conversely. Indeed, Marx has little but scorn for the human needs and weaknesses that might make man vulnerable to anomie, prone to dependence, in need of belonging, and the like.

It might be argued that Marx's focus on alienation spoke adequately and appropriately to the empirical realities of individuals and society in his time. In this case his neglect of anomie would be merely ironic: an abstract and one-sided theory of society and history, overly influenced by particular, historically specific circumstances. But this ignores the fact that distinguished conservatives like Burke and de Maistre were deeply concerned with anomie in the generations preceding Marx. Tocqueville and Nietzsche placed anomie at the center of their theoretical outlooks. Nietzsche felt that the old world and "that which makes an institution an institution" were already in a state of advanced decay. Those who danced around the corpse to keep up their courage were both barbaric and misguided, and he was implacably opposed to these so-called "free spirits." The crucial difference is that Nietzsche's view of alienation is intimately bound up his account of anomie. Marx would have found this simultaneous concern with alienation and anomie conservative, promiscuous, or unintelligible. This is a measure of the one-sidedness of his dialectic, and a sign pointed straight at the heart of his difficulties.

Alienation According to Marx

The sociologists encountered earlier were accused of various subterranean psychological assumptions, despite (to some extent because of) their willingness to let the individual be the final judge of his state. Their dilemma is roughly as follows: either forego a theory of false consciousness, and thereby proceed with untenable naivete; or else risk being dragged into the abyss of depth psychology, possibly losing one's sociohistorical perspective on man. Marx generally opted for the first horn of the dilemma, which helps explain why his account of the specifically human lacks depth and density. Others attribute to Marx the depth psychology they themselves would have introduced had they been Marx. Many of these innovations are of such poor quality that not taking responsibility or credit for them is an excellent idea.

In Marx's early view all alienation is associated with the conditions and process of work. There is alienation from one's product, in that it belongs to someone else; from the process of production, in that it too is controlled by capital; from others, initially coworkers; and from our species nature (also regarded as self-alienation), since our free, conscious, creative activity is nil. Four years later, in *German Ideology* (1848), the division of labor assumes first importance as the symbol and vehicle of alienation.[13] Given his sweeping interpretation of the division of labor, given its applicability to the capital–labor split, the change was not a radical one, though the division of labor raises a somewhat different set of issues. Two additional aspects of alienation, whose continuity with the earlier conceptions is quibbled over but rarely doubted, are the alienation inherent in exchange and commodity fetishism. Both came to prominence in *Capital*.

Schacht suggests that there is nothing these various usages have in common except the idea of separation.[14] This is incorrect. What unites the usages is separation from self, thought of in terms of divergence from species nature. While the terminology was abandoned at about the same time it was introduced, the idea of self-alienation continued to provide a shadowy but indispensable normative standard for a theoretical system with a dearth of such standards. To be sure, topics such as the division of labor and commodity fetishism could have been treated after a fashion without the notion of self-alienation, without any notion of how individuals free of such impediments would develop, create, progress. But surely in the process these matters would have lost most of their meaning and interest. Self-alienation is central to his entire life's work.

With this in mind let us look at a series of attempts to distill Marx's conception, giving particular attention to the language employed and to embedded psychological assumptions. Ollman suggests that alienation can be regarded as a "splintering of human nature into a number of misbegotten parts." In addition to the specialization of task, this also conjures up the psychological phenomena of splitting, scattering, compartmentalization. The second interpretation suggests that we may be implicated in our plight. Schaff argues that alienation for Marx is submission to a reality which has "slipped out of one's control." This is also troublesome, as if reality were slippery. It is on a par with another ambiguous conception of alienation: we do not (or no longer) see ourselves in the world we have created. In most instances any one of us has actually created very little of it, and it is hard to imagine social institutions on any scale in which this would not be the case. To see oneself in all or most social relations and institutions may amount to a narcissistic delusion, facilitating identification with the oppressors or aggression toward imagined oppressors. Related to the problematic metaphor of reality slippage is the notion of alienation as a kind of forgetting.[15] This also suggests a partial psychologization of alienation. If forgetting were merely a matter of external censorship, if we were "forced" to forget, the word would convey little, and there would be little need for it. And why is it better to remember?

Schaff reminds us of another familiar formulation: "the life which he has given to the object sets itself against him as an alien and hostile force."[16] This eliminates a significant ambiguity, in that it refers directly to objects that the individual has actually been involved in producing. This view is not obviously compatible with alienation as forgetting, though it is possible that the object appears hostile *because* we have forgotten our authorship. More important is the unexamined question of whether the subject is reporting on the object, or instead some aspect of himself or others, attributing it to the object. The actual relationship to the object might inform this perception, of course: the actual experience of losing control over his product, of having wages and conditions of work dictated to him, and the like. There may be genuinely hostile and alien aspects to the object (process, form, institution). The point is that we often reveal as much about ourselves as the objects and situations we address. Any viable theory of alienation and anomie must not only take account of this most human tendency, it must begin here.

Other perceptions and conceptions of the object imply more or less cognizance of the alienated condition. One involves identification with one's oppressors, including those objects to which we have given life but which now rob us of it. This may involve self-alienation but does not involve the perception of the object as alien. On the other hand, it is not simply a matter of poor memory. This is the alienation of those who have learned to stop worrying and to love the Bomb, or other genuinely oppressive and menacing objects or institutions. Those who see such objects as alien and unfriendly are less alienated, or at least more perceptive, than those who have learned to love it. Of course this contention depends on an articulate account of self-alienation, on external standards of some sort. This is precisely what Marx attempted to set aside, and what modern researchers take such pride in jettisoning, along with Marx himself.

Another revealing definition is offered by Fromm: we are alienated from ourselves because we have become slaves to *parts* of ourselves. This is part Marx and more Fromm. The lack of any social referent is reminiscent of that loose humanistic blather about alienation from which Marx early on dissociated himself. Even so, Fromm's suggestion is based on the multidimensional, universal qualities ascribed by Marx to Marxist man. Marx himself often refers to the alienated as "crippled," "one-sided," and the like. The rub is that Marx's own conception of the qualities and faculties that would flower under communism is narrowed to exclude negative human traits and many neutral ones. By Fromm's standard, inspired by Marx, Marx's own neglect of the darker, weaker sides of human nature is clearly a form of intellectual or psychic alienation: domination of those forgotten or unmentioned human qualities by the relatively few which receive attention and recognition. On the other hand, Marx's list of species traits nevertheless manages to be altogether too open-ended, especially in light of the dynamic, expansive, world-building, aggressive behavior they imply. Marx offers a vision of society in which most individuals could be alienated, in the (self-alienated) sense which Fromm introduces; but simultaneously anomic, as a result of their one-sidedly dynamic, expansive, antinomian qualities. While the coexistence of anomie and alienation is central to the argument of this study, it is inexplicable in the context of Marxist theory.

Fromm suggests that this domination of the whole by the part is Marx's original conception of neurosis. This is twice wrong. It is not original, unless we take a narrow sample of exclusively Western literature. And even if Marx had offered these rudimentary ideas in more systematic form, they would by no means qualify as a theory of neurosis. To delve more deeply into why and how people come to be self-alienated leads Marxist theory toward the abyss of the unconscious, profoundly threatening a theory otherwise secure in its treatment of psychic phenomena as straightforwardly social, or nonexistent, or irrelevant. This is not at all what Marx had in mind.

To get to the bottom of Marx's view of alienation we can do no better than to approach Marx, as his son reputedly did, asking what he would consider to be the most despicable aspect of human behavior. With fervor and without hesitation he responded: "servility." Servility is the antithesis of human dignity, and dignity is surely Marx's overriding concern. But there is something odd about his answer. For servility is far more of a psychological matter than enslavement or oppression, words which Marx might have used if he wanted to emphasize helplessness in the face of objective and effective coercion. It implies that even the most wretched subordinacy can be aggravated and extended by psychological factors working to some extent independently of the enslaving circumstances. Yet to admit this outright might give Marxist theory an acute case of anomie.

We have seen that a number of modern theorists, academic as well as popular, claiming some allegiance to or descent from Marx, freely generalize the concept, imagining they are radicalizing rather than diluting it. While Marx would surely wish to dissociate himself from such promiscuous usage, he also must be held responsible for much of it. Alienation as unresponsiveness is not really that far removed from the indiscriminately antiauthoritarian spirit of so much of what Marx wrote. Marx proposed the "ruthless criticism of all existing conditions," argued that the proletariat will rid themselves of *everything* bourgeois, and spoke of total alienation and its eventual total absence in communism. The lack of concern with self-control, the thin and belated concern with communal control and self-denial, the failure to consider what individuals might have to contribute to the new society, the lack of appreciation for group sentiments, customs, rules, guidelines, authorities—all of this fuels the fire of those moderns who exult in the notion that nothing is or need be sacred, then embrace the most pitiful and tawdry objects in order to lavish and squander their deepest impulses and aspirations. How often our most advanced theorists proclaim that "nothing is necessary" and "nature is no guide" and then reveal in the course of their arguments a host of unexamined and virtually sacrosanct beliefs!

In truth, the diligent reader can find many belated qualifications to brave pronouncements of this sort. Marcuse, embarrassed and appalled by those who took certain of his unbuttoned pronouncements seriously, belatedly reminds his constituency that building the new society, as Marx himself belatedly said of creative activity, is "damn serious work." But if such qualifications and reminders have much to do with the appeal of Marx or his modern epigones, I have completely misread the temper of the times.

Marx the Alleged Psychologist

It will be instructive to lay bare some of the difficulties encountered in the attempt to make of Marx a psychologist. Recall two distinct ways of experiencing alienation which surfaced in the previous discussion. One of these is the idea of alien-and-hostile-forces, forces which the individual may have had some hand in creating. (Whether this is actually the case, whether alienation depends on its being so, is not always clear.) This characterization of alienation is prominent in Marx. It is akin to modern treatments which see alienation as a matter of being left out, marginal, alone, isolated, and so on. But this modern usage distorts Marx's meaning, as we argued before. The alienation he has in mind is visited upon those who are in the thick of things, the very heart of the society and its processes of production and consumption, the exploited rather than the excluded, or those who have in various ways opted out or excused themselves.

The situation he has in mind is one of being within society, playing a vital role, conforming more or less to the role requirements for the proletariat or the otherwise oppressed. Instead of having the perceptions or attitudes of alienation in the "alien hostile" or confrontational sense, it is likely that many of Marx's alienated experience the malady in ways that do not involve confrontation, the recognition of alien-ness, marginality, or an explicitly oppositional stance. Call it resignation, or being stuck in a routine, a job, a role, or a nook. Or call it servility. The point is that their condition and experience of alienation may not consist of open, conscious confrontation.

Being resigned or stuck calls to mind two of Merton's responses to anomie: conformity and ritualism. In Merton's view these are responses to anomie, but in the view being developed here they are forms of alienation. They are likely to be more common than responses to anomie like withdrawal and rebellion, which may or may not represent alienation. To be left out of the fold may involve isolation, doubt, loneliness, normative conflict and confusion: that is, anomie. Alienation is likely to be a condition of being stuck or trapped, rather than being marginal to the dominant society and culture. It may involve marginality, but marginality is in no way central to the malady. It may be conformist and ritualistic. On the other hand, anomie may also pertain to those who participate extensively in the society, if the society itself has anomic strata or sectors. Disorder may be institutionalized.

Similar considerations apply to the question of what causes alienation. At one point Marx seems to call his own sociologistic premises into question by means of his rather curious contention that alienation causes private property. One interpretation is that men are implicated in their support of alienating institutions over and beyond the threat of hunger or the dole; or the pressure, influence, coercion, terror employed in keeping them docile employees. But this gives ammunition to partisans of "human nature," particularly those who posit conservative personality needs. A variation on this is the straightforward dialectical point that institutions create the men who in turn sustain the institutions. The problem for Marx is that both arguments picture the alienated as "active," as contributors to their own continued subjection. Individuals are only actors for Marx when they exhibit his preferred qualities, not when they voluntarily conform, overconform, or identify with the oppressor, or continue the old ways when new conditions make new ways possible.[17] The idea of choosing conformity, security, passivity challenges the one-dimensional image of human beings, and those cherished propositions and utopian outcomes dependent upon it.

Three attempts to rescue Marx from this shadow side of human nature are worth a brief look. The first concerns false consciousness, the acceptance of ideological views counter to the interests of subordinate socioeconomic strata among those very strata. While these are powerful determinants, and while they act in myriad ways neither obvious nor easily combatted, Marx's analysis of ideology and false consciousness merely postpones the question of Marxist psychology, even as it makes it more pressing. At this late date, after the spirited efforts of many talented theorists, it remains unclear how Marxist species beings would be so consistently fooled as to confuse oppression, repressive desublimation, and the stifling sterility of their lives, with self-realization in Marx's sense. That is, unless there is a shadow side to Marxist man. The undoubted existence of false consciousness is not so much a refutation of human ambivalence and depth psychology, or a substitute for either, as a powerful argument on behalf of both.

The other two attempts are offered by Ollman, although neither is original with him. He suggests that in order to explain why men, especially the lower strata, do not behave and think as they "should" (according to their objective class position in society), we must rely on the existence of sexual repression and its contribution to the authoritarian mentality. This is a bit like asking Freud in to clean up the mess Marx made, then telling him to leave immediately afterwards. It is questionable whether human nature as Marx conceived it can survive the addition of Freud.

Ollman's other approach to this shortcoming in Marx is Fromm's idea of social character, which represents another attempt to explain the existence of views which are out of accord or poorly synchronized with the individual's social setting and historical position.[18] On closer look we find that what *does not* need explaining is inertia, much as conformity needs no explanation in Parsons's action theory. The doing and thinking of what was done and thought yesterday, the forgetting of what is possible today, these need no explanation. Human resistance, or fear, or passivity, or inertia do not qualify as actions or attributes of actors. Yet inertia and fear play prominent if unacknowledged roles in the analysis. How any of this can be reconciled with Marx's individual, who is nothing if not dynamic, is hard to fathom.

Alternatively, we can examine the argument suggesting that there is really no need to turn to psychology, since Marx himself was a master psychologist. Erich Fromm, departing significantly from his earlier analysis of social character, suggests that Marx was the author of a "new and original concept of neurosis," characterized by the domination of one part or passion over the rest.[19] We are alienated from ourselves because we are slaves to part of ourselves. Other symptoms of alienation, he maintains, include depression, dependence, idol worship, and failure to experience one's identity.[20]

Fromm contends that Marx was intimate with the idea of the unconscious (a conclusion apparently obtained by confusing the unconscious with false consciousness). As an example of unconscious motivation, Fromm offers us Adam Smith's Invisible Hand; individuals are conscious only of egoistic concerns, and not the altruistic effects of their behavior. On the other hand, Freud neglected the "social unconscious," the repressed awareness of social contradictions, shortcomings, inconsistencies. It is not our own dirty little secrets, our own contraries, which we repress. It is the dirty secrets of society, along with a multitude of related frustrations and aspirations. Why we repress, however, is never clear. Neither is it clear why or how we know those secrets in the first place. Fromm argues that repression for Marx was essentially the result of contradictions between the need for the full development of man and the given social structure. It follows that the society in which exploitation and class conflict have been eliminated will require neither ideologies nor repression, since the fully humanized society would have no social unconscious.

Fromm's central contention is that Marx made a monumental discovery: the distinction between love of life and love of death, *biophilia* and *necrophilia*. "Perhaps the most decisive question in Marx's psychology is whether a man, class, or society is motivated by the affinity to life or to death."[21] Fromm does not indicate what passages contain this discovery, nor even any passages which suggest the discovery was ever made. He ends with the gratuitous suggestion that Marx would have rejected Freud's psychology.

Fromm has gone far beyond what Marx said or meant. Yet this alleged psychology is not grossly inconsistent with Marx's occasional and fragmentary remarks bearing on human nature. Accordingly, the problems are familiar. Fromm stresses our multiple powers, emotions, faculties, potentials, yet neglects the fact that any particular path to self-realization involves an infinity of might-have-beens, a world of opportunity costs. Even if we neglect the fact that people bump together and impede one another's progress, being fully human in Fromm's sense would be the equivalent of a mad scramble among these powers, a mob of the senses and faculties. To establish priorities, to impose any kind of pecking or feeding order on potentials and possibilities is (for Fromm and Marx) an alienated state. And if we had instinctual guidance in sorting out these powers, such guidance could only be seen and experienced as alienation.

To fail to establish such an order is to flirt with what Fromm himself refers to as the failure to experience one's identity. Fromm sees this failure as one of the clinical aspects of alienation. In this he is half wrong. As Berger suggests, it is likely that the alienated have temporarily *solved* their identity problems by means of adopting an alienated state, whether or not this is what they had in mind. Identity is threatened by anomie as well as alienation. This is why anomie helps generate alienation, and identities strictly social. Marx and Fromm offer a virtual formula for anomie, and therefore alienation as well.

Fromm's equation of the unconscious with a form of false consciousness seems to assume that everyone unconsciously knows the truth about his objective self and class interests, as if everyone had read his Marx. This does not sit well with Fromm's other idea of the unconscious, as consisting of practically everything of which we are not aware. Here the unconscious becomes a kind of storehouse of our ignorance. The former view has possibilities, perhaps, if it could be explained why we ever knew these things in the first place and repressed them in the second. The latter drowns us in possibilities. The spaciousness of this unconscious is aptly illustrated by his notion that Adam Smith's idea of the Invisible Hand is an example of unconscious motivation. The implicit contention is that the unconscious motivation on everyone's part (the butcher, the baker, etc.) is to keep prices down, competition stiff and fair, and everybody happy. This is hokum. Smith's point is very nearly the opposite. This is why he turned from the study of moral sentiments to the study of economics, and why he grudgingly granted Mandeville's point that virtue is out of place in the market society. Fromm comes close to crediting this cavernous unconscious with containing *everything* of which we are consciously ignorant. One suspects that this social unconscious of Fromm's is a sly way of claiming that most folks really do see things as Fromm and Marx see them, even if they won't admit it.

An altogether more refreshing view of these matters has been offered by Adam Schaff, who bluntly suggests that the missing link in Marxist theory is man.[22] From a distinguished Marxist philosopher, admittedly partial to the humanist Marx of the *Manuscripts,* this is a significant admission. Most enthusiasts think these fragments are themselves the missing link. Undoubtedly Schaff is right, though we find ourselves tempted to argue that Marx brilliantly intuited one half of a valid view of man. But human beings do not come in halves. Human qualities make sense only in light of their opposites. The missing link is indeed man, ambivalent man. A satisfactory account of alienation and anomie awaits the forging of that link.

⋆   ⋆   ⋆   ⋆   ⋆

Every great philosophy, Nietzsche wrote, is a species of involuntary and unconscious autobiography. As a young man of seventeen Marx wrote an essay on choosing a career which is of great interest in connection with the themes we have put forward.

> But we cannot always choose the vocation to which we believe we are called. Our social relations, to some extent, have already begun to form before we are in a position to determine them. . . . [I]f we have chosen a position for which we do not possess the talents, we shall never be able . . . to fill it properly, we shall soon recognize with shame our own incapability and say to ourselves that we are a useless creature, a member of society who cannot fill his post. The most natural result, then, is self-contempt, and what feeling is more painful, what can less be displaced by anything the external world offers? Self-contempt is a serpent which eternally gnaws in one's breast, sucks out the heart's lifeblood and mixes it with the poison of misanthropy and despair.
>
> A deception about our aptitude for a position we have examined closely is a misdeed which revengefully falls back on ourselves, and even though it may not be censured by the external world, provokes in our breast a pain more terrible than the external world can cause.
>
> When we have weighed everything, and when our relations in life permit us to choose any given position, we may take that one which guarantees us the greatest dignity, which is based on ideas of whose truth we are completely convinced, which offers the largest field to work for mankind and approach the universal goal for which every position is only a means: perfection.
>
> Dignity elevates a man most, bestows a high nobleness to all his acts, all his endeavors, and permits him to stand irreproachable, admired by the crowd and above it.
>
> [T]he high opinion we have of the ideas on which our vocation is based bestow on us a higher standpoint in society, enlarges our own dignity, makes our actions unwavering.
>
> Whoever chooses a vocation which he esteems highly will carefully avoid making himself unworthy of it; therefore, he will act nobly because his position in society is noble.
>
> If a person works only for himself he can perhaps be a famous scholar, a great wise man, a distinguished poet, but never a complete, genuinely great man.[23]

No one should have their youthful writings held up for any sort of examination: all of us were so much older then. Yet one of the liabilities of the great is that we make exceptions in their cases.

What first strikes the eye here is that this essay was penned by an exceptionally ambitious young man, determined to be hard on himself above and beyond whatever negative judgments society might visit upon him. Part of this is the straightforward consequence of his goal of perfection, which he seems to treat as if it were some actual state of affairs that might actually be achieved—as if it were one of Hegel's "good infinities." Once this state is attained, perhaps he can take his rest. The more interesting aspect of this harsh self-censure and self-punishment, however, has no particular relation to the goal of perfection and the exacting demands of dignity. Or rather, it underlies those impossible goals. For there is an unmistakably self-punishing and self-denigrating quality to these dramatic swings he exhibits, both in his essay and his life.

Notice for example his reaction to the hypothetical discovery that he had chosen a position for which he lacks the talent. On learning this were the case, many would be frustrated and discouraged. Others might treat it as a learning experience, and move on to something different with little remorse. But Marx reacts with utter shame, and monumental pride in his shame. He seems hell bent on being more disgraced by any real or imagined failure than public or friendly opinion would ever demand, as if making himself miserable and insecure in this way were his primary source of satisfaction and security. Clearly, finitude itself is disgraceful. Under such conditions a job is never just a job, nor a career a career. Everything is charged with a significance almost cosmic; Marx is always on the verge of confusing and equating the particular with the universal. Living the life of universal man is confused with the pursuit of finite goals symbolic of the universal.

This extreme fear of being tied down to particulars, to choices that preclude choices, generates or possibly reflects the assumption that the choice of career is more or less irrevocable. He overlooks the possibility of a second chance—a second career, or a second post in which he serves with distinction—as if major choices were in all cases once and for all propositions. This is exceedingly interesting in light of the equally unrealistic assumptions he later makes concerning multiple careers and multiple talents of communist man. Communist man is pictured as the man who doesn't have to make choices. The fear of finitude generates the Faustian pursuit of the infinite. One famous portrait of this multi-valent, multi-talented man has him pursuing several careers at once, presumably with great satisfaction and success. Perhaps because he is so anxious and fearful over the possibility of being trapped and shamed, the idea of the abolition of specialized careers grows into his obsession.

Colossal ambition and pride in proportions almost divine also manifest themselves in many other assertions. We learn that self-contempt is the natural result of not being able to fill a post. This is anything but natural. To fail to meet the demands of one's specialized, appointed task is apparently some sort of sin. Then there is the shame of it all (most of it generated by Marx himself, no doubt to outdo all possible critics), the contemptible weakness it reveals. He was (self) deceived about his aptitude for a position. The self-contempt that inevitably accompanies failure sucks out his "heart's lifeblood," causing pain "more terrible than the external world can cause." The young Marx fancies himself better at everything, and can despise himself more than the entire external world put together.

Elsewhere the pride assumes a more positive form. He implies that he can do just about whatever he puts his mind to. He further assumes that his noble position will be recognized as such by society. Most significantly, he entertains the embarrassing fantasy of "standing above the crowd" while nonetheless receiving its plaudits and gratitude. Clearly, Marx had already conceived the idea of reaping the rewards of society without paying the price it usually exacts. From here he proceeds to wallow once again in his ignominious wavering, savoring the possible loss of all nobility and stature. It is as though he had been the center of some universe and then another universe had turned a cold eye on his childish desires and pretensions, and somehow he realized it was inevitable and just. Through it all we see the rapid and constant oscillation from the heights of self-glorification and pride to the depths of self-contempt and ignominy.

Another dimension of this marked ambivalence has to do with the conflict of social influence and individual self-determination. "Social relations," he complains, have begun to form "before we are in a position to determine them." This is odd. Some overeager interpreters have seen in this the anticipation of the materialist view of history. More likely it is a veiled protest against not having been able to choose the circumstances of his birth and upbringing, not getting to choose his parents, not getting to *be* his own parents. Perhaps it is a protest against not having the characteristics and the viewpoint of a universal man limited neither by space or time. Hence the dramatic transition from historical man to trans-historical man in Marxist theory, albeit conveniently relegated to the future. Perhaps the idea of having been dependent and helpless so long, during which time he was taking far more than giving and learning more than teaching—from his father, for example, who was stuck with the bills for his carousing and high jinks—is repugnant to him. Certainly there are elements of aggression and retaliation in his obsession with filling a high place in an incomparable manner. He intends to make such stupendous contributions to society that no one could ever retaliate in kind, nor pay him back completely. (What better way to deal with envy than to generate envy in others, with gifts that no one else can reciprocate?) The passages on the shock of finding oneself lacking, or incompetent, or merely imperfect have all the force of the bursting of the childhood balloon of omnipotence. Marx is out to prevent this from happening, whatever the cost. Perfection is all that is required. Another item significant in this connection is the sharp contrast he draws between those situations in which social relations do influence us and that marvelous time in which "we are in a position to determine them." This crude distinction has little basis in experience, unless it is the experience of an infant learning it is finite, individual and rather small; or the somewhat older child who learns of a sudden that he isn't the Mother's entire universe, after all. But out of just such crude distinctions, one suspects, came the idea of a future communist utopia, and the multi-faceted communist man-child who could do it all without ever being identified with or reduced to any one role or activity.

Marx will later draw the same kind of overdone distinction between life under capitalism and under socialism. Both images are projective in character. There is no hint in Marx of the Durkheimian formula of liberty by means of dependence, just as there are few such hints in all of Marxist theory. There also seems to be considerable ambivalence as to whether the achievement of nobility is a matter of occupying a noble position, or in some sense involves rejecting or transcending social roles, positions, norms. Marx clearly wants social approbation in the most desperate way, but he also wants to be his own man, in a most radical, no doubt impossible way. Thus he intends to be above the crowd, yet "still admired by it." There is the elaborate emphasis on filling a position properly, a treacherous enterprise in which the slightest failure is followed by infinite self-contempt, pain beyond all external pain, the serpent gnawing at his breast, and so on. This has the air of a ritual repetition of some long forgotten scenario, in which he did not get it quite right the first time. By the same token, he must also be telling us something of a virtual rage against having to be so grown-up, responsible and exacting, a rage against having to do one's duty under conditions of such misery and anxiety, against having to get it exactly right this time. And this is bound up, in turn, with the retaliatory aspect of his monumentally high ambitions. Given sufficient diligence and superhuman efforts, Marx will not only beat them at their social game but will propel himself beyond the game itself, and all its petty roles and rules.

From this adolescent outburst it is impossible to foresee the manner in which these Faustian inclinations and aspirations—by turns in savage combat and illicit alliance with an ascetic morality that would do many a Christian proud—would work themselves out. In part this is because of the indeterminate nature of close ambivalences, in part the indeterminacy of life events and the social channels into which ambivalence flows. The focus on choosing careers as society defines them, on nobility being connected to noble positions, on the extreme fear of failure certainly misleads us as to how unconventional a career this outwardly conventional humanist would take. At the same time, it helps us make sense of Marx's eventual path. The solution to this terrible bind of wanting to be recognized as noble, yet wanting to rise above any socially defined nobility, was to challenge the specialization that society forces on all but a privileged few, and to translate those humanitarian sentiments into the egalitarian belief that most men are capable of overcoming and shedding their dependence on socially defined slots. On the one hand we imagine that this great man defies the rules, sheds and scorns the roles of his society. On the other hand he does the greatest good imaginable for the society he transcends. In the end, "glowing tears of noble men will fall on his ashes," much like Mommy and Daddy would cry and mourn if something happened to their little boy. Marx was an inveterate utopian, and maybe this was the sort of utopia he always had in mind.

Marx did not invent these ambivalences. Neither is the struggle between social dependence and individual development unique to Marx. But few have been so audacious as to attempt to resolve this conflict by means of a theory which attempts to be both sociological and non-sociological, while offering no conception of human nature which would make this combination intelligible, much less plausible. Almost everyone daydreams of being the complete person, transcending social roles and valuations, but this need not produce an argument and program for the abolition of the division of labor, and a vision of a utopia populated by multi-talented individuals. All of us constantly engage in projection, but then few of us manage to project our conflicts onto the world-historical canvas, and have billions of others associate them with real conflicts between capital and labor. All of us have alternated on occasion between pride and self-contempt, but this rarely results in our splitting humanity itself into the praiseworthy and the contemptible, and building a formidable theoretical system on this basis. All of us desire the benefits of society without the constraints it imposes. But most of us wake up eventually.

A few years after writing this essay, Marx remarked (rather uncharacteristically) that all that was really necessary to achieve all needed political and social changes was for everyone to "awake, as from a dream." For waking us up, however, Marx needed a theory of dreaming and forgetting, repression and self-alienation, of ambivalence and the unconscious. Far easier to blame "society" or that "other man" for all these unpleasant obstacles. But if we construct an all-embracing theoretical system, as Marx did, on the basis of our unacknowledged and untamed ambivalences—if we thereby do not own up to our projections and repressed opposites—then how will we ever wake up? And how will we know, when we awaken with yet another vision, whether we have merely stepped into another dream?

4

Durkheim and Anomie

Irrespective of any external regulatory force, our capacity for feeling is in itself an insatiable and bottomless abyss.

Durkheim

The individual submits to society and this submission is the condition of his liberation.

Durkheim

The old gods are growing old or already dead; and others are not yet born. This is what rendered vain the attempt of Comte with the old historical souvenirs artificially revived; it is life itself and not the dead past which can produce a living cult. The only candidate for collective belief is precisely this religion of humanity whose rational expression is the individualist morality.

Durkheim

I always knew he would be an abstraction monger.

Henri Bergson

I stalk the thesis that Marx and Durkheim offer complementary one-sided perspectives on alienation and anomie, neither of which provides a view of human nature adequate to the task of putting the pieces together. However, Durkheim's view of individual and society is such that the maladies of excessive social control as well as insufficient social control both play a role. Anomie, control, constraint, and the maintenance of limits undeniably receive the bulk of his attention and concern. Yet his central contention is that dependence on one's society is the only real source of liberation. Marx never really faces this paradox. Durkheim tries to solve it by fiat, but it cannot be said that he fails to confront it.

A more orthodox account of Durkheim will serve as backdrop for my interpretation. In company with many others, Lewis Coser argues that Durkheim's overriding concern with social cohesion and order causes him to systematically neglect conflict and the fate of those who must conform to pathological or oppressive situations.[1] There is entirely too much rhetoric about society and too little consideration of subcollectivities and subgroups. This is surprising for a sociologist sometimes associated with the advocacy of social pluralism. The claims of the individual against society are consistently neglected. This is further aggravated by the virtual equation of society, morality, and received authority.

Durkheim slights class phenomena and treats the social question and the state as moral questions, not as questions of scarce power and wealth.[2] Similarly, he treats the various intermediate professional, occupational, religious, interest groups as complementary and productive of social cohesion, rarely taking cognizance of the fact that such groups clash, often with adverse consequences to other groups and to social order. In his treatment of both morals and religion, he seems to assume that their effect is always to restrain and to unite.[3] And whereas radical thinkers contrast a real state with an ideal state of some sort, it appears that normality is the best one can hope for in Durkheim's society.

By and large these generalizations are accurate. On the other hand they are misleading.

Overview of the Outlook

Miles apart in many regards, Durkheim and Marx were in agreement on a number of important matters. Both claimed to see the individual as a social being, and emphasized the social creation of needs. Both understood that society might develop capacities and instill desires which the society could not adequately fulfill. For Marx this meant eventual revolution; for Durkheim, the recurrent threat of anomie. For Marx this disparity represented injustice, but also opportunity; for Durkheim it was primarily a problem of social cohesion and control. Both situate their sociological propositions and philosophical anthropology in the context of history. "It is only by historical analysis," Durkheim wrote, "that we discover what makes up man, since it is only in the course of history that he is formed."[4] Similarly, the historicity of man and views of man is vigorously emphasized by Marx. Despite these claims, both held to an ahistorical conception of human nature as well.

Both sought the "laws of motion of industrial societies," and saw the division of labor as the crucial component. Durkheim's political outlook bears a resemblance to pluralism in American political science. Yet some commentators credit Marx with depicting the social and economic preconditions necessary to attaining and sustaining genuine pluralism. Both men were influenced greatly by the French utopian socialists, particularly St. Simon, and by Rousseau and Kant as well. Both considered utilitarianism their major ideological enemy. Durkheim condemned its failure to account for society, the egoism it sponsors, and the threat it poses to social order. Marx saw it as the false consciousness of bourgeois society, the ideology of ascendant capitalism and the professional and commercial middle classes. He pilloried its class based and biased account of human nature, its habit of using the English shopkeeper as the model for the species.

Spencer's attempt to deduce society from human nature and contracts among individuals and groups represented an assault on virtually every theoretical premise, moral conviction, and methodological postulate Durkheim held dear.[5] It challenged his patriotism, his conception of group attachments, the social bond, the very fabric of society. These assaults or insults were embodied in the attempt to model society as an aggregation of egoistic atoms: competing, colliding, establishing temporary liaisons, making contracts and bargains on the basis of self interest alone. Durkheim found this image of modern society inaccurate, unworkable, unhealthy, disgusting: a formula for disruption, disintegration, dereliction of duty, anomie. Spencer's fortunes might have been already fading, but utilitarian instrumentalism, in everything from personal relationships and the family to intermediate associations, politics, and the state, was anything but on the wane.

There was much else to dislike in Spencer. Particularly irksome was the attempt to portray freedom, not as a social product and the achievement of a particular kind of society, the product of a particular path of historical development, but as actually constitutive of the individual. Durkheim saw Spencer's doctrines as part of an attempt to deduce sociology from psychology, nonego from ego, and thus to deny Durkheim's defining characteristics of social facts: externality, objectivity, and constraint. This represented a challenge to the fledgling discipline of sociology. Underlying all such criticisms was the attempt to shape and moderate change in such a way that the new society would not tear itself apart in the mad scramble to realize the fruits of modernity. For this reason individualism and the false dualism of individual and society were central preoccupations throughout Durkheim's career. His attack on Spencer was merely the opening salvo in a lifelong battle with the unworkable and immoral egoism of utilitarians.

Durkheim agreed that there is at least some element of contract in all interactions. But also there is an element of the transcontractual in all contracts. This is dramatized by those exchanges which, despite the willingness of both parties, are not even allowed to take place. Each such contract or exchange is made possible by the context of laws, moral codes, customs, mores. These determine the character and conditions of the exchanges, what it means to violate these conditions, what penalties are assessed the violators, what corrective or punitive action is appropriate. Utilitarians must picture these exchanges as involving abstract men, without country, character, social location, sex, or any socially specific characteristics. What we manage to find out about these utility men can only be the result of snooping about, inferring a set of social and psychological characteristics that these phantoms without country or social location in fact do exhibit. There is nothing gratuitous or accidental in this practice of stripping men and women of their specificity, their sociological clothing, their historical setting. To admit that your analysis works best for Englishmen of the ascendent capitalist class in the mid-nineteenth century, with specific needs for noninterference or intervention by governmental authorities, on behalf of certain kinds of freedoms and rights but not others—all this moves us uncomfortably close to Durkheim's contention that human beings and human wants are essentially social and historical.

Durkheim's assault on egoism is lent impetus by the suspicion that the utilitarian model may well apply to increasing numbers. His persistent effort to distinguish blatant egoism from moral individualism, to initiate a cult of man, a social religion, sometimes strikes an anxious note, as if he were trying to convince both author and reader.

> The condemnation of individualism has been facilitated by its confusion with the narrow utilitarianism and utilitarian egoism of Spencer and the economists. But this is facile.[6]

It is not merely in Spencer or Bentham that he finds such a facile identification of the two. While he praises Toennies' characterization of *Gemeinschaft,* recognizing it as essentially his own view, he finds Toennies' account of social cohesion in *Gesellschaft* essentially atomistic and utilitarian.[7] The whole of his *Division of Labor* is devoted to turning the tables on the cult of community, by postulating a new "organic" solidarity based squarely on the division of labor. His belief or hope was that this would not only replace the mechanical solidarity of the old society, based on segmentation and similarity, but would simultaneously drive competing views of society, utilitarian as well as socialist, from the field.

Durkheim was uncertain whether a moral consensus or conscience collective would be rendered superfluous by the forms of solidarity entailed in the division of labor. He contends that the latter contribution to social cohesion would be rooted in the vivid daily impressions of larger purpose and interdependence that performing a specialized task supposedly produces. Moral individualism, this would-be cult of man, this secular religion of society, derives from the eighteenth century view of man, the "principles of 1789." Its twin pillars are freedom and equality. It received its consummate philosophical expression in Kant. "Far from making personal interest the objective of conduct," Durkheim asserts, "this individualism sees in all personal motives the very source of evil."[8] No doubt this had a quaint and dated sound even in his own day.

Writing in the midst of the Dreyfus affair, Durkheim apparently judged that this was no time for public confessions of doubt over the future of moral individualism. "Once we have stopped confusing individualism with its opposite—that is, with utilitarianism—all these supposed contradictions disappear like magic."[9] This is of a piece with the magic Marx believed in: Durkheim substituted utilitarianism for the capitalist villain. Moral individualism represents not the "glorification of the self but of the individual in general." It "springs not from egoism but from sympathy for all that is human, a broader pity for all sufferings, for all human miseries, a more ardent need to combat them and mitigate them, a greater thirst for justice."[10] The increasing differences among humans, as the division of labor progresses, will enhance the appreciation of the only thing they have left in common: their humanity, "the constitutive attributes of the human person in general." (How this squares with the proposition that our nature is solely social and historical is not clear.) There is no progressive alternative to this neo-Comtean cult of man: "everything converges in the belief that this religion of humanity, of which the individualistic ethic is the rational expression, is the only one possible."[11]

> Nothing remains which men can love and honor in common if not man himself. That is how man has become a god for man and why he can no longer create other gods without lying to himself.[12]

After all: "hereafter, to what can the collective sensitivity cling?"

These rather remarkable passages suggest the affinity between Durkheim's central perspectives and abiding passions and the Enlightenment faith of the "principles of 1789" (as well as the influence of Comte). They are reminiscent of Marx's own Enlightenment leanings. In these contexts Durkheim goes so far as to express concern over group attachments which infringe on the individual! There are numerous appeals to the idea of species man, and repeated hints of the Feuerbachian-Marxist theme of self-infinitization, man as god.

Durkheim's moral individualism, much like Marx's socialist individualism, actually contains or implies two varieties associated by Durkheim (and especially Simmel) with the eighteenth century and nineteenth century respectively.[13] Simmel called the former the individualism of equality, the latter the individualism of difference or uniqueness, associating it with the division of labor. Durkheim envisions the possibility of reaping the best of both. Marx, in his way, does much the same. Simmel sees them as fundamentally opposed, though he entertains the hope that they might be somehow synthesized. Yet to the extent that the individualism of differences or uniqueness is fostered by the division of labor, the place of any generalized conception of man is rendered vulnerable. Nor is the desire to be unique necessarily consistent with a given division of labor. Uniqueness, as Simmel and Marx understood it, implies idiosyncratic development, individuals for whom there may be no place in the given division of labor. Durkheim's consistent underestimation of this aspect of individualism, his confusion of uniqueness with the specialization of task, suggests that he never quite appreciated the nature nor full force of modernistic egoism.

As for the place of egoistic impulses in Durkheim's own theories, we may rely in part on his explicit account of human nature.[14] Man, Durkheim asserts, is *homo duplex*. He bases this contention on an appeal to everyone's sense of self. Something within us is more than us: sacred, moral, uplifting, altruistic. It is also constraining and authoritative. It had better be, for there is another voice within which encourages behavior that is asocial, anarchistic, impulsive, wayward, irrational, immoral. The first voice is that of society, and it speaks to us through our rational faculties. The second is that of our instinctual endowment and its derivatives, egoistic in nature. It is associated with the senses, with man as a biological creature. Thus he pictures a kind of ambivalence, though not the strictly sociological form encountered in Merton nor the instinctual ambivalences associated with Freudian theory.

The sore point is that the social side of the self could itself be egoistic. Durkheim shies away from this possibility in the same way that he avoids admitting that anomic goals and behavior can be socially promoted. Nor is the identity of these instinctual drives or derivatives revealed. All we know is that that they create a continual basis for antagonism between individual and society. Neither is it clear whether and how the two kinds of motives can be mixed. If they cannot, ambivalence threatens to degenerate into pathological splitting, with little or no communication between the social person and the egoistic individual. To offer such a psychopathology as a transhistorical view of human nature is odd. And if none of these instincts are encountered first hand, not until they are labeled and set within a nomenclature and social world, then it is not clear why they belong in his conception at all. If all instincts are socialized, why not blame society alone for egoism, irrationality, and the like?

The fateful conclusion Durkheim draws, or which draws him, is that we cannot be released from all constraint. While Berger argues that we are relatively lacking in instinctual guidance, Durkheim suggests that the guidance we have is worse than nothing. "It is not human nature which can assign the variable limits necessary to our needs," since "it is not within the resources of man's physiologically born character to set limits to desires."[15] In themselves these desires represent an "insatiable, bottomless abyss."

> How can we specify the quantity of well-being, comfort or luxury legitimately to be desired by a human being?[16]

This cannot be done by an individual, nor by any ethical system as such. It cannot be specified on strictly rationalistic grounds. "Society" must determine such matters by means of rational, rationally evaluated authorities. Again it is as though Durkheim had not fully appreciated the extent of the modernist revolt. That individuals or ethical codes or rationality cannot determine the fair distribution does not mean that society can readily do so, either on traditional grounds, by means of new constitutional conventions, or through national referenda. Recent work on the problem of "constitutional choice," for all its hyperactive technical sophistication, merely confirms the fact that the problem is neither technical nor institutional, nor is it a mathematical puzzle. The problem is disagreement. There exists no such moral authority, no society in general. Instead there are specific political and legal institutions, officials, interest groups, social institutions, religious factions, whose ability to specify what is "legitimately to be desired by a human being" is as questionable as that of the individual. Moral individualism is neither so simple nor so widespread as Durkheim thought.

Accordingly, the idea of constraint is built into his very conception of social facts, in hopes of making society safe for Durkheimian man and academia safe for sociology. Durkheimian society is not intended to be a bleak affair, although it is often sober to the point of somber. There is nothing more satisfying than doing one's duty. As Slater has suggested, Durkheim's society is in many respects a cross between Hobbes' coercive police state and the positive cultural model of society. We come to recognize that we owe to society most of what we are. It pleases us to pay it back, though doing so is not to be confused with fun. When stated so boldly, Durkheim's proposition is obviously vulnerable. Even so, the absence of this nurturing aspect of social relations in Marxist theory accounts for much that is implausible and unbalanced in Marx's treatment of alienation.

> Does not all constraint, by definition, do violence to the nature of things? It was just such reasoning that led Bentham to see in law an evil scarcely tolerable. . . . [And] doubtless the influence of the same viewpoint has led the major socialist theoreticians to deem a society without systematic regulation both possible and desirable.[17]

Durkheim's answer is an emphatic no:

> The totality of moral rules truly forms about each person an imaginary wall. . . . [For] the same reason that the desires are contained, it becomes possible to satisfy them.[18]

That individual selves are socially constituted does not mean that individuals do not affect what has affected them. But there are compelling reasons why this point is more asserted than examined and developed. One is his anxiety over the fragile state of French society. Durkheim worried about the French propensity for experimenting with exaggerated forms of individualism, thinking and writing for the world but falling short in their own political practice and stability. France (so proud of its Revolution that it continues to fight it to this day) had recently suffered a most humiliating and traumatic loss in the 1870–71 Franco–Prussian war. Durkheim's birthplace, Alsace, was lost to Prussia. In Durkheim's estimation, the Third Republic was basically on the right path of moderate reform at a moderate pace. He felt it needed all the help it could muster in order to survive and prosper. His keen sense of history and the patriotic mission he set for himself contributed to his preoccupation with cohesion and stability. His own geographical and ethnic origins contributed as well.

Similarly for his penchant for treating society, much like the deposed God, as something awesome and mysterious vis à vis the real, live, resourceful, active, creatures of blood and sweat who supposedly create it. Durkheim's society is not only *sui generis,* it sometimes appears *ex nihilo,* creating and propelling itself without human fuel. As Coser points out, he does not attend to the processes by which people fashion the rules to apply to their transactions. Nor does his limited view of politics and the state as the embodiment, interpreter and enforcer of the conscience collective and the guardian of social order help much. Society is typically presented as a given, constraining, objective datum. We learn little of how it got there, who built it, who benefits from allegiance to it, who really owns or runs it, or when compliance conceals coercion.

The upshot is that the dialectical and progressive aspects of his view of social man are buried under a pile of pronouncements which neglect or shortchange individuals. Often he appears to defend and rationalize alienation itself. But here again a closer look is in order.

Anomie, Division of Labor, Egoism

In his last major work Durkheim put forth an argument concerning religion that tells us a great deal about his personal hopes and fears for his society. There he contends that the distinction between what society considers sacred and what it considers profane is not only universal, it is of all distinctions the one most rigidly observed. Curiously, he offered this proposition precisely at a time when, from all appearances, it was rapidly becoming dated in European societies.

Contrary to Coser's contention, Durkheim did not take the decline of religion in his stride. For various reasons, he channeled his concern toward the consequences for social order and ethics rather than toward any specific religious doctrine, nostalgia for religious times, or blatantly religious solutions to social dilemmas. But his attitude is worlds removed from that of Marx. Feuerbach and Marx saw religion as the paradigmatic source of alienation: as ignominious, servile psychological counterfeiting, robbing man of his dignity, initiative, self-consciousness, and world-building will and capacities.

On one level Durkheim was sensitive to this view. On the other hand, he virtually equated the religious with the social. Oddly enough, this is not exclusively a conservative concern. For he associates religion with certain periods of "creative effloresence" in which society renews and forges or forges again its collective identity. In this context religion leads to the dissolution or disregard of structures, breaking down rigidities, forcing institutions to reform and be responsive: people come alive and experience their society as humanly constructed. (Weber's preoccupation with charisma inevitably comes to mind.) Durkheim was thinking of such climactic periods as the Dreyfus affair, the French Revolution, perhaps the Napoleonic wars. What Durkheim seems to appreciate about such periods is that they involve the overcoming of the alien unresponsivity of social institutions, and the realization that individual existence is thoroughly social. Given that he did not readily distinguish his cult of man from religion as conventionally and traditionally conceived, this is tantamount to associating religion with the overcoming of alienation. Marx would have been disgusted.

In Durkheim's judgment there is only one possible source of collective renewal and faith in modern societies: the cult or religion of humanity, in the specific form of moral individualism. He hoped that his criteria of normality and pathology would place reasonable limits on the otherwise boundless and impossible aspirations for change and for individual aggrandizement. The same was true for his functionalist criteria. Hence his persistent attempts to radically distinguish egoism from moral individualism. What would be the basis of the new order, absolutely essential in preventing a new and cataclysmic disorder? It is clear what we do not need. "In the modern period . . . needs and desires have become freed from moral constraint, so that they have lost any fixed point of reference . . . . [T]he malady of infiniteness torments our age."[19]

To be sure, Durkheim's first explicit view of the crisis of European culture had a rather complacent cast. He contended that the receding of the conscience collective represents a change in the nature of the social bond, not its destruction. As for anomie in the work place, his proviso is that the worker, however specialized, tedious, backbreaking, or monotonous his job may be, should have sufficient contact and communication with others in the enterprise to give him lively and regular impressions of the larger enterprise of which his job is a very small part. This appears to be a timid affirmation of the importance of finding or realizing the universal in the particular. It trivializes that problem, however. Durkheim did not even insist on the workman's task *symbolizing* for him the larger reality of which he is a part. Meanwhile, Marx projects the *literal* embodiment of the universal. To paraphrase Philip Rieff: these are positions that deserve one another.

Durkheim's other progressive proposals share some of the same timidity. The concept of anomie is also applied to collective bargaining in some industries, in which expectations and possibilities for meeting expectations have seriously diverged. He discussed another "abnormal form" of anomie, the "forced division of labor," in which workers cannot choose jobs, and alternatives are foreclosed. Durkheim suggested that Marx focused on this abnormal form of the division of labor to the exclusion of the normal, more benign forms. As to which is rule and which exception, the jury is still out. Durkheim's abnormal forms are supposed to disappear in time, but they continue to be most conspicuous.[20]

Durkheim saw these as aberrations, temporary and transitional. The solution was to perfect, not to reject, the division of labor: the problem contained its own solution. For Durkheim this meant making the division of labor spontaneous, whereby the choice and pursuit of specialized tasks and careers would not be coerced or circumscribed by artificial social barriers. Such equality of opportunity or meritocracy would eventually cause social and natural inequalities to coincide. Class conflict expresses "incomplete realization of organic solidarity," not intractable opposition to that solidarity or to the division of labor. He could not conceive of the division of labor as the fundamental locus or manifestation of class divisions, no more than he could countenance the constant focus on social conflict, or the class bias of social institutions from the educational system to the state. It would appear that the spontaneous division of labor is one of those Durkheimian abstractions of which Bergson rightly complained.

This confidence or complacency largely disappeared in subsequent work. In the preface to the second edition of *Division of Labor* (1903), he proposed the formation and encouragement of guild-like occupational groupings, resembling the professional associations to which Talcott Parsons (following Durkheim) ascribes such significance and benign qualities.[21] These would reduce industrial strife, reduce anomie and integrate the unattached and marginal. They would likewise serve as a counter-balance to centralized power, much as in Tocqueville, though this is not Durkheim's primary concern. While he still believed that anomic forms of the division of labor could be avoided, he also felt that it was no time for being smug about the automatically benign course of social evolution.

Accordingly, the mood of *Suicide,* his next major work, is considerably more sober and subdued, and not simply because it deals with suicide.[22] Durkheim viewed the apparent increase of suicide rates in the nineteenth century against a backdrop of the steady release from community, tradition, authority, group attachments. The results of this process, which Marxists and liberals alike regarded and applauded as progress, were widespread despair, insupportable loneliness, the free rein of anarchistic and irrational egoism, rampant hedonism, and the "maladies of the infinite." He pictured it as an age of Faustian ambition and megalomania, of philosophies of "hatred and disgust," combined with the pessimism that always accompanies unlimited aspirations.

The notion of the infinite appears only at those times when the moral system is shaken.... without any new system yet contrived to replace that which has disappeared.[23]

In connection with his effort to demonstrate that only a purely sociological approach could give an adequate account of the variation in suicide rates, Durkheim distinguishes four types of suicide: egoistic/altruistic and anomic/fatalistic.[24] Most interesting are the egoistic and the anomic/fatalistic, since altruistic suicide is presumably rare in modern societies. Egoistic suicide is committed by those who are cut off from group attachments, guidance, support. They are lost, lonely, lacking in purpose and meaning. The closely related anomic suicides are those whose aspirations have outrun their prospects. They suffer from having no intrinsic limit or ceiling to their desires, or because there is no realistic hope of having them satisfied. (The latter is the basis of Merton's treatment of anomie, though he narrows its scope considerably.) In either case the individual comes to demand what cannot be delivered. Finally there is fatalistic suicide. If anomic suicide is related to the deregulation of the passions, then fatalistic suicide is that resulting from excessive or oppressive regulation. Its victim is the person who is trapped, who sees no exit nor escape, whose future is blocked and passions choked. Significantly, Durkheim summarily dismissed its significance.

Yet it is of crucial importance. It conjures up the possibility that either Durkheim's vision of an anarchic and anomic society is mistaken—and instead, many are trapped and oppressed—or that the two maladies can co-exist in the same society. More disturbing still is the possibility that these two maladies could afflict the same person, or be so intimately related that they pass readily over into their opposite. They might even be the same malady, viewed in different or opposite ways that reflect our cognitive limitations, our language and logic, rather than their opposite nature. Durkheim missed an opportunity to offer a view of social maladies that comprehends both anomie (and egoism, its close companion) and alienation, as suggested by his category of fatalistic suicides. His own view of ambivalence as between the social and individual self might conceivably have provided the impetus and basis for this reorientation. There are other elements in Durkheim that might have assisted: his genuine appreciation of ambivalence toward authority and of the liberating aspect of dependence. By comparison, Marx maximized the conceptual distance between liberty and social dependence, generally opposing liberty and dependence in terms to which most liberals would subscribe.

A further problem concerns Durkheim's elusive distinction between egoism and anomie. Some have even argued that anomic suicide is actually a special case of egoistic suicide. Durkheim suggested that both types result from the insufficient presence of society in the individual. In the case of egoism, this is related to severed or attenuated ties to social groups. Egoism is the malignant, degenerate form of moral individualism, an index of the degree of social disintegration. Egoistic suicide results from the individual not having something larger, more solid and stable than himself to attach himself to. Anomie is defined and generally employed in connection with lack of control over the basic passions and desires: either because these are infinite, or in conflict, or because they thoroughly exceed what is possible in a given social setting.

While there are numerous life situations susceptible to anomie, Durkheim contended that the problem typically revolves about the economy, both in production and consumption. In *Division of Labor* he pointed to the plight of the worker under extreme specialization of task, to the unregulated scramble for advantage in collective bargaining and industrial strife, and to the repeated, increasingly severe economic crises. He saw the unrestrained pursuit of wealth as the paradigmatic case of the refusal of limits and the attempt at self-infinitization. Unlike those sociologists we encountered earlier on, Durkheim generally associated anomie with the successful, the better off, the upwardly mobile—with the culture of the middle classes, with society at its "best." Especially in good times, wealth creates the illusion of invulnerability, omniscience and omnipotence, and feeds the fever of more and more grandiose expectations. Measured against these expectations, the slightest setback or shortfall feels like a crushing defeat. Many of the poor are spared this particular disease by having their expectations routinely squashed to subhuman proportions. Poverty supplies its own discipline, Durkheim observed.

Living according to the rules and dictates of Durkheim's society might well be frustrating, and confining. Equally important, the moral consensus, society itself, could be productive of anomie. This possibility is slighted as well, if not to the same degree. Durkheim hedged on the question of whether egoism and anomie are in every respect social products, and did not consider that a society based on the division of labor and moral individualism might generate *both* alienation and anomie.

On those occasions when he discussed the spirit of the times in a general vein, he makes it clear that social order, moral individualism, normal forms of the division of labor are goals not yet achieved, and that ours is not only a transitional situation, but one marked by the maladies of egoism and anomie, the pursuit of "infiniteness." (Giddens comments that Durkheim "half understands" egoism and anomie are social phenomena.) "These dispositions are so inbred that society has grown to accept them and is accustomed to think them normal."[25] The sphere of trade and industry is "actually in a chronic state of crisis and anomie is constant, and, so to speak, normal."[26] Indeed: "the longing for infinity is daily represented as a mark of moral distinction."[27] By no means did Durkheim regard these pathologies as marginal phenomena affecting only marginal people, deviants, losers. His criterion of normality suggested the possibility that an entire society could be abnormal.

Durkheim implied that a person in an egoistic state, with few or tenuous social ties, will be unstable, lacking in a sense of purpose, alone and lonely. What is not at all clear is why this precludes his plunging ever more deeply into the pursuit of one of the inherently unattainable cultural goals of which Durkheim wrote. Perhaps there is no better way to lose one's way. Often we join and belong, as someone has said, in order to shun ourselves. Unless genuine "group attachment" is simply equated with contact or membership, the distinction between egoism and anomie seems all but superfluous. Similarly, the anomic person who pursues goals inherently unlimited and unattainable might well occupy a socially defined collection of roles with multiple contacts and ties to others and a measure of participation in social institutions. As Durkheim himself points out, the pursuit of the infinite is daily offered up as the mark of wisdom, good citizenship, patriotic consumerism. It is a key ingredient of business success, prestige, fame, and what passes for common sense.

Durkheim's Anomie, Durkheim's Alienation

We have touched on the idea of creative efflorescence which captured Durkheim's imagination; the forced division of labor, that he deplored; the enthusiasm he occasionally expresses in connection with the notion of realizing oneself in the process of creating society. We have also touched on some of the reasons he is not known for any of these positions.

With this in mind, look for a moment at the question of social justice. Horton alleges that Durkheim had no such concern. But social justice is integral to his concern with anomie. A society which develops a certain profile of talents and expectations among its population should see to it that those talents are employed and expectations fulfilled.[28] Durkheim felt that this criterion is rarely met in modern societies, especially in those strata infected with Faustian ambitions and diseases of the infinite.

The mass of men, he pointed out, must be content with their lot. In order for the division of labor to be a source of solidarity, the individual must be matched with the specialized task he chooses. Admittedly Durkheim's solution, the "spontaneous" division of labor, raises thorny questions which he neglected. Unquestionably his formulations are loaded (who is for "forced" division of labor? who is against "spontaneity?"), and his underlying principle ("to each according to his contribution") lacks majesty. Durkheim did not reveal how it is to be accomplished and whether it is compatible with "spontaneity" in the choice of jobs. Nor did he ever indicate the extent to which his principle necessitates intervention in the system of prices and markets, much less the extent of governmental ownership and control of economic enterprises.

Granting these qualifications, the essential point is that social justice is by no means swept under the rug by Durkheim's focus on anomie. Social justice, at least the widespread *feeling* that the society is fair in distributing its material rewards and that jobs are suited to individual's capabilities, is what anomie is all about. Durkheim's view of anomie and social justice does militate against overweaning ambition, infinite self-glorification and self-aggrandizement. But these are diseases of the affluent for the most part, whereas the aspirations of the lower strata are often surprisingly modest. The overall cast of his view of social justice does not deviate a great deal from modern liberal-egalitarian doctrines. The point is that he sees social order and normative guidelines as crucial to the achievement of meaningful social reform. This reflects his appreciation that anomie and anarchy can impair our ability to establish self-conscious, active, human control over social institutions. Any account of alienation, he implies, must include this anomic contribution. Durkheim's intuitive if limited understanding of this relationship is crucial to what really distinguishes him from Marx.

The notion that alienation has been built into the very marrow of sociology by Durkheim's rules of sociological method, by his very conception of the subject, is likewise misleading. To characterize social facts as exterior, objective, and constraining is not so much mistaken or pernicious as one-sided and undialectical. Durkheim was generally silent on the question of how these external facts come to confront us as objective facts, though his understanding of the social fact did not mean individuals had no effect on their society, its institutions, its direction. Any member of society "receives more than he gives," though he generally fails to note that what an individual receives may be grief. Nisbet is correct in asserting that Durkheim premises an active, dynamic person.

In Durkheim's last major work he was at least as concerned with reviving society as with ensuring adequate social control.[29] He looked forward to another of those periods of creative, collective renewals; intensely alive periods in which the intimate connection of the individual and the collective is realized, reestablished, symbolized with great force and vividness. In such periods, social facts and moral codes would presumably not be viewed so much as immutable, alien, external, but would be debated, changed, created afresh, lived. It is almost as if he had fully embraced the proposition that we can really understand only that which we have constructed. This could even be described as the overcoming of alienation: from social goals, moral codes, places of work, fellow workers, neighbors, and so on. The human character and origins of social rules, morals, and institutions—that truth so often made a dirty secret—would be re-affirmed and applauded. Durkheim by no means had revolution in mind. He thought primarily in terms of a creative, progressive reinterpretation of tradition and the establishment of a new order.[30] The point to emphasize, again, is that Durkheim was simultaneously expressing a concern with alienation as well as anomie.

The area in which Durkheim's concern with alienation seems least likely to surface is the division of labor. Other than stipulating that the good effects of the divison of labor on personality and social order are dependent on its being spontaneous, disagreement with Marx on this issue appears total. The other point concerns the way in which the division of labor is ultimately justified. Durkheim offers two arguments justifying the division of labor. The one stresses its joint contribution to moral development and social cohesion. The other defends its contribution to the individual's development, his uniqueness and "depth." But Durkheim saw scant difference in the two arguments and tended to equate contributions to social solidarity with contributions to personality:

> He who gives himself over to a definite task is, at every moment, struck
> by the sentiment of common solidarity . . . in the thousand duties of
> occupational morality.[31]

Durkheim explicitly linked the organic division of labor to his conception of self-realization. He viewed the attachment to something bigger, stronger, more stable than our egos—that is, social groups and institutions—in the same light. The ongoing division of labor in modern society implies the necessity and possibility of developing "profoundly" rather than "superficially."

To the extent that his arguments concerning job satisfaction, the profundity of specialized development, the contribution to the individual's personality (sense of well-being, competence, control), and his appreciation of the larger order in which his task is located are susceptible to empirical testing, they do not fare well. For example, it does not seem to matter much if there is continuous contact with workmates and supervisors: not if the worker must do a minute and mindless (or obnoxious) task over and over, one which would engage a tiny portion of the attention and faculties of an idiot. Durkheim's rosy view of the division of labor as a benevolent contributor to a richer, more individualized, more satisfying life, partakes of sociological romanticism.

The point to stress is that, aside from the alleged contribution of the division of labor to moral insight and social cohesion, Durkheim offered an argument that the division of labor, once perfected, would enhance the human personality. It is likely that the chosen means do not further the ends he prescribes, not to the degree he imagined. On the other hand the wholesale abolition of the division of labor has much to be said against it. Marx himself concluded that the divison of labor should be abolished only "as far as possible," an observation no more informative than the maxim that Caesar should be rendered what is his.

Here again, Durkheim's concerns are not quite so far removed from Marx's as popularly believed. Of course, there are the obvious and important differences, catalogued and scrutinized by Coser and legions of others. But the neglected, really significant difference is that in the last analysis, Durkheim could not bring himself to ignore human ambivalence, whereas Marx could not quite bring himself to face it.

Sociology and Socialization for a Time of Crisis

Durkheim's understated but unmistakable concern with both alienation and anomie is also reflected in his views on moral education.[32] Durkheim was anxious to combat what he believed to be false and pernicious doctrines of morality and its relation to society. His targets include the utilitarians, the socialists, and "moralists." Above all he wished to stress that there is no inherent opposition between liberty and authority, independence and dependence. He takes issue with the moralists because they abstract ethics from society, and argue as though each of us carries with us all the necessary elements of morality. Reason itself is subordinate to society; many fundamental questions of morals and world views cannot be adjudicated by reason. (At one point he suggests that even the law of non-contradiction may be a social product.) Morality can not be contained or expressed in a "very general, unique formula," as in Kant's categorical imperative or Bentham's greatest happiness principle. We must be taught the necessary facts and aspects of morality. So-called laws of morality can only be crude approximations to a complex reality. One does not appreciate nor appropriate this reality by applying simplistic rules which could not conceivably apply to the countless moral choices confronting everyone. To learn about morality is to learn about society, and society is complex and culturally idiosyncratic.

As for the utilitarians and the socialists, their glaring mistake is to neglect the role of discipline in creating a moral agent. Bentham considered both law and morality as pathological and pathogenic. Marx very nearly did. Durkheim believed that what socialism actually advocates and encourages is anarchy, anomie. The utilitarians had sought "to trace what is creative and free almost exclusively to processes of separation from institutions and traditions . . . in release rather than membership."[33] He saw the socialists, and no doubt Marx and Marxists, in much the same light.

"Theories that celebrate the beneficence of unrestricted liberties are apologies for a diseased state."[34] This is a not a blind dismissal of creativity, or innovation, or invention. Nor is it a mindless objection to any and all deviations from tradition. His point is that "creativeness and innovation cannot be separated from tradition . . . the great man of thought and action . . . works with materials he has inherited, through ways normatively given."[35] Creativity is the product of straining against tradition, probing and testing authoritative ideas of what is true, what techniques are effective and appropriate. When boundaries are in general disarray, when there is nothing authoritative to overcome, when authority is so fragmented or splintered that it is confusing and ineffective, the bowstring goes slack. Such are the insights that Bentham and Marx, in their horror of that which might prove constraining, frustrating, oppressive, confining, never really appreciated. It is for this reason that the fate of Marx's creative society resides under a cloud. Whatever liberates our spirit without giving us mastery over ourselves, Goethe said, is destructive.

Durkheim suggests three elements of morality: discipline, group attachments, and autonomy.[36] By discipline he means the spirit of discipline, not the mindless observance of all rules under any and all conditions. The spirit of discipline is as opposed to slavish adherence to rules as it is their mindless rejection. Human nature is becoming ever more "vigorous," he admits, and those who would limit us to what our forefathers did are no less than "arrogant." The spirit of discipline does not encourage "blind and slavish submission." (Or servility, to use

Marx's epithet.) Our very specialization of self implies and entails limitations and restrictions. The more unique we become, the more we depend on society to complement us. Individualism-as-specialization promises a deeper sense of accomplishment than a life of wayward, restless, self-contradicting whimsy and impulse, or that of a jack who masters no trade.

In words worthy of a schoolmarm, Durkheim points out that discipline promotes regularity and provides determinate, realistic goals. However, like most schoolmarms, when Durkheim refers to discipline and duty he means it. He does not promise that it will always be experienced as fun. On the contrary. The marked emphasis on duty derives from Kant, whereas his rather niggardly affirmation of satisfaction represents a concession to the utilitarians. By no means are they perfectly compatible: "one is inconvenienced in doing his duty."

His treatment of attachment to social groups as an element of morality devotes too little attention to the fact that groups can likewise be the source of irrationality and disruptive behavior. Recall that the absence of group attachments is the defining feature of egoism in his taxonomy of suicide. For Durkheim the individual's attachment to groups is typically an asymmetrical affair, with communication a one-way street and hierarchy the norm. The tendency for the group to loom larger than it is in life is powerful, and operative even in the smallest and most intimate of groups. As for why this is so, even when "unnecessary," psychoanalytic insight might be of considerable help here.

Finally there is autonomy, grounded in reason, strictly opposed to the heteronomous influence of the senses. Kant is again invoked. Reason is "geared to the general and the impersonal; our senses, on the contrary, have an affinity for the particular and the individual."[37] This traditional view is more asserted than scrutinized. He does break with Kant in arguing that reason is not a transcendent faculty, that it needs constraint and bounds which can only be provided by society. He suggests that society must provide the Kantian imperative with content. Through the practice of moral rules, guided by reason, discipline, and the benign influence of group attachments and practices, we gain the only kind of liberation Durkheim regards as meaningful. We achieve self-control and self-governance, the dignity of voluntarily restricting ourselves by accepting and following an impersonal code of behavior.[38]

The sense in which this submission to moral codes is voluntary is not clear. To the asocial being inside all of us, such submission can only be coerced. As for the social aspect of the self, it is not clear why any real decision is involved. Durkheim admits that "the part played by each generation in the evolution of morality is quite restricted." Nor can democrats take much comfort in these views of autonomy, morality, and discipline. For Durkheim, human dignity resides more in submitting to impersonal codes than in participating in their formulation, interpretation, or application. By contrast, Rousseau's General Will has no existence apart from the citizens who divine and apply it. Despite his frequent references to Rousseau, it is Kant who is the greater influence.[39] In Durkheim's view, Rousseau is primarily a Kantian moralist and incidentally a democrat.

For all this, we must not lose sight of his central proposition. Morality must be defined, not "through liberty," but rather in terms of a "state of dependence." Liberty itself is a product of dependence. Morality is liberating, as Durkheim understands morality and liberation. This is the organizing principle of his treatment of morals and education, and for that matter all his work. It is also his personal credo; here as elsewhere, Durkheimian theory bears the stamp and signature of a powerful personality. Despite this insight, with its implicit affirmation of ambivalence, Durkheim too often implies that this harmonious relationship of liberty and dependence automatically obtains. The belief that this is so is rooted deep in his conservative instincts, and the resulting conceptions of individual and society with which he both advanced and shackled the study of society.

Morality as Self-Realization

To find or insert dependence at the heart of moral behavior, to posit dependence as the basis of liberty, are acts of provocation deliberately aimed at those who, like Marx and Bentham, tend to see dependence as despicable whatever the context. Durkheim reverses the formulations of radical individualists, socialists, and utilitarians in dramatic fashion. Society, he tells us rather feverishly, "is the producer and repository of all the riches of civilization, without which man would fall to the level of animals."[40] Yet it might be argued that, compared to the heinous crimes against humanity committed by organized societies, the fall of humans to the level of animals would be a short fall. Were modern-day Lebanon to descend to a genuinely Hobbesian state of nature, without social and religious differences and factions, it might well be less dangerous and no more anarchic. Nietzsche observed that individuals are rarely insane, while groups are insane as a rule.

If Durkheim overstated his proposition, it was because he feared such truths were in danger of being inundated in the tide of utilitarianism, hedonism, egoism, anarchism, socialism. Thus the timely exaggeration: "it is from society that there comes whatever is best in us . . . . [H]e is not truly himself, does not realize his own nature, except on condition he is involved in society."[41] The problem is that "being involved in society" distinguishes no one from anyone else. All are involved in some way and to some degree. Probably he refers to the dangers of egoism and the loss of group attachments, or the general withdrawal of affect (if not contact) from society. Nevertheless, the evidence suggests that his carelessness on this crucial point served as a kind of model for subsequent theorists invoking his name and authority.

He goes even further: "morality is a preeminently human thing, for in prompting man to go beyond himself it only stimulates him to realize his own nature as a man."[42] This is one of many statements which call into question his oft-emphasized historical and social understanding of human beings. There is a minimal sense in which any moral code, however repressive, life-denying, laden with ressentiment, or anal, assists man in going beyond what he would do or be in the absence of all society and morality. Nietzsche subscribed to this proposition, attempting to rank moral codes and precepts in terms of degrees of "overcoming." The problem is that we learn so little from Durkheim about "overcoming," what realizing one's own nature as a *person* could mean. This is no accidental omission. In some descriptions of *homo duplex* Durkheim pictures us as little more than vessels into which society pours its contents. Ego exists only in the specific form of egoism inculcated and sponsored by society.

Where this leaves the self that is not exclusively social is unclear. Durkheim certainly flirts with the proposition that it is the nature of man to go beyond himself, to overcome himself, to overcome the dualism of individual and society rather than submerging and suffocating individuality. He chafed under the intellectual regime he himself established in connection with human nature and social control, and the stoic and severe personal regime he imposed upon himself. After a series of decidedly reckless claims for the good effects of embracing society and its morality, he offers numerous qualifications. To discipline ourselves in this way is "not the same as inculcating a spirit of resignation, nor curbing legitimate ambition."[43] While we must always work with inherited materials and pursue ends planted by culture, man rearranges, redirects, interprets, extrapolates, and so on. Durkheim hints of some notion of individuality independent of society, by means of which we can choose among moral directives. His ideal of moral individualism, the modern cult of humanity, itself implies a notion of self-realization.

While the alleged dualism of human nature appears to be the beginnings of an ahistorical account of the species, Durkheim has no qualms in asserting that the nature of human nature is primarily historical, however much he appears to renege elsewhere. This is because of the marked predominance of the social aspect of the self. Durkheim's dualism of human nature is decidedly asymmetrical. This is reflected in his frequent appeals to the historical juncture and to "present conditions." "Under present conditions it is above all the faith in a common ideal that we must seek to elicit."[44]
By contrast,

> when . . . morality has yet to be established, when it is still nebulous and unformulated, then to achieve this end we must have recourse to the active and imaginative forces of the conscience, rather than the purely conservative ones.[45]

Indeed, he occasionally betrays his suspicion that it is really the second situation which characterizes present conditions.

The attempt to develop rational substitutes for spiritual and religious phenomena may be inherently contradictory. Rationalism itself is one of those irresistible historical currents which has helped render religion emaciated, disoriented, and demoralized, with severely reduced claims to moral ascendency in society. To think of society as itself a religious phenomenon may well reflect and contribute to the erosion of any distinctively religious sphere, as fundamentalist preachers and various would be prophets have long warned. It is questionable whether religion can be completely socialized or rationalized and remain religious. Outlining a rational case for religion both reflects and promotes a certain distance from the unquestioning acceptance of rules which are "all commandment," from that unambivalent and unquestioned faith in a common ideal. The vehicle may be incompatible with the destination. The more ludicrous aspects of the Comtean cult of humanity serve to remind us of this.

Durkheim contends that "respect for authority is in no way incompatible with rationalism as long as the authority is rationally grounded."[46] The cure for rationalism is more rationalism. Thus he naively attributes to rationalism the appropriately respectful and reverential attitude toward authority. He attempts to drum out of rationality any instrumentalist–utilitarian attitudes, knowing full well that even rational-legal authority can be dissolved in the *aqua regia* of egoistic calculation, and that rationality and the pursuit of self-interest are increasingly identified.

Durkheim's hopes for moral individualism ("the only system of beliefs which can assure the moral unity of the country") rest on the assertion that as we become more particular, more specialized, more individuated, we become more aware of the other individuals who must complement us, of our resulting dependence on them to sustain and complement our independence. Paradoxically, we become increasingly sensitive to the category of "man." Our humanity is all we have left in common. In Marxist terms, Durkheim is suggesting that we become more aware of our species nature as specialization progressively alienates us from it. Appropriately enough, the problem surfaces in connection with the pluralism he intermittently advocates and the specialization of task which he generally affirms. Evidence of his own uneasiness can be seen in "Individualism and the Intellectuals,"[47] in which moral individualism and "man in general" receive all the praise, and pluralism and group attachments are trampled underfoot by patriotism and the concern for national unity. Even the division of labor, supposedly so important in the achievement of organic solidarity, is unceremoniously dropped. But never for long. Addressing educators and future educators, the abstract ideal characteristics of man as man succumb again to sociological relativism, the pluralistic and the particular:

> Let us make use of classical writings, not in order to allow the child to know that abstract and general man which is the ideal type of the 17th century, but to show him man as he is, with his almost endless variety.[48]

It is doubtful that this oscillation represents simple confusion. More likely, it represents an unsuccessful synthesis, a conflictful mixture, of the individualism of equality with the individualism of difference. On the one hand, the belief in moral individualism is necessary. On the other hand, as Whitehead suggests, any general idea is a potential danger to the existing order.

The same tension hounds his treatment of democracy. The Rousseau to whom he appeals argued that democracy was precisely the overcoming of specialized interests and perspectives. In a democracy, Durkheim argues, learning self-control is especially important: much more is demanded of the citizen. This is particularly the case in French society, "enfeebled" and plagued by excessive individualism and military adventurism. Our duties in modern democratic society are clear: to concentrate, specialize, set for ourselves definite tasks, immerse ourselves in our work and social obligations, and push our specialization of self as far as the social order requires. This is *our* human nature. These duties to society are simultaneously duties to oneself, contributions to one's mental and emotional development, stability, equilibrium.

It is an illusion that personality was more complete in times when the division of labor was less developed. The individual's activity "was not really his own," and his liberty was only apparent. His personality was borrowed. Moreover, to flit from job to job, to play the dilettante, is to develop "superficially," compared to the profundity of establishing a particular, unique self, a new and unique window onto the world: doing *something,* as Weber urged, better than anyone else. Everything basic in us partakes of the particular and the partial. Society specifies the general and universal, lending meaning to the otherwise meaningless, providing the whole of which we must be parts. We should quit "trying to make of ourselves a sort of creative masterpiece, quite complete, which contains its worth in itself and not in the services it renders."[49]

Utilitarianism, vanquished in direct assault, now creeps through the back door in functionalist guise: pleasures and pains, costs and benefits, are now cast in terms of collective goals. What again surfaces is the conflict between the individuation implicit in the division of labor and a deeper desire for uniqueness. The latter is a far cry from the acceptance of a specialized role some institution or someone else defined for you. Maybe Durkheim understood this more than he lets on or we realize. Maybe he just did not want to cry in front of the troops.

Together with the dilettante, who is doomed to superficial knowledge and achievements, the artist takes severe lumps, as both symbol and embodiment of what is pernicious and corrosive of social order and responsibility. Art and artists are associated .with self-indulgence and dilettantry. The free-spirited artist, as well as the escapist, boundary-violating qualities of art itself, come in for heavy-handed criticism. Durkheim stops just shy of questioning what a masterpiece does for the GNP; and why artists do not go out and get a real job as real men do. He enlists public sentiment, which "reproves the tendency of dilettantes to refuse to take part in occupational morality." He deplores their withdrawal from social responsibilities, their delight in all sorts of "boundary games," their propensity to mix the heretofore segregated, to regard the sacred as a kind of target for their slings and arrows. They are also dangerously detached from the "real world." "Exaggeratedly aesthetic culture turns us away from the real world and relaxes the springs of moral action."[50] Truth is a matter of action and accomplishment rather than "constructing beautiful images in the silence of the mind." Worst of all, artists weave tales that deceive and inflame us: a complaint straight out of Plato.

> How often the poets make us accept themes which are scientifically absurd and we know to be such! For the artist, there are no laws of nature or history that must always be respected.[51]

And he strikes an ominous note, warning that at some point "the implausible becomes intolerable."

We have art, Nietzsche suggested, so that we may not perish from the Truth. The notion that scientifically absurd themes can have no *other* justification than scientific is not only provincial, it neglects the contribution of fantasy to the wellsprings of scientific creativity and progress. But Durkheim has other objections:

> There is genuine opposition between art and ethics. Art . . . detaches us from reality, from the concrete beings—individual and collective—that compose it. People say, do they not, that the real service that art performs is to make us forget life as it is and men as they are?[52]

It is a peculiar man who cannot sympathize with short stints in imaginary environments, nor with occasional attempts to forget "men as they are." It precisely is the Philistine's world that does not permit flights from itself. This "detachment from reality" which Durkheim pillories can produce perceptions and conceptions more vivid, and plastic, less rigidly encased in mummified form. Durkheim so fears anomie that he fails to appreciate its potential connection with the creative process. To cling to given forms, whether in thought productions, personal habits, performance of tasks or organization of work—to establish no distance whatsoever from that which poses as eternal, natural, immutable—is to dry up the source of creation and innovation. It is a kind of death. Overcoming this excessive fear of the formless is essential in realizing his vision of moderate, progressive change, supporting the social bond even as we withdraw support from given, imperfect social forms. The further irony is that it is essential to Durkheim's own creativity, his demonstrated if uneven ability to stand apart from the received wisdom and conventional pieties. Visions such as his, and those of all the great social and political theorists, are unmistakably aesthetic as well as analytic. Our failure to remember this coincides with the production of theories neither analytically powerful nor aesthetically satisfying.

Durkheim's basic formula of "liberty through dependence" assumes that dependence and moral discipline inevitably enhance and promote liberty. The centrality of his insight, together with its central flaw, is brought home by the comparison he develops between the child and the tyrant. Both child and tyrant are at the mercy of any whim, impulse, drive, bright idea they might have. Both are bounced about, willy-nilly, one way then another, filled them with all sorts of contradictory inclinations which collide with one another and come to nothing. The despot, like the child, is not master of himself.

"Self-mastery is the first condition of all true power, of all liberty worthy of the name."[53] For this reason his "apparent omnipotence dissolves into genuine impotence." The same dynamic explains the apparent paradox that children are not only creatures of habit, but also creatures of inconstancy. The inconstancy reflects the enslavement to impulse. Once something suitable, secure, and familiar—though not necessarily free of trauma—has been found, the child is often observed to repeat the routine or ritual countless times, and to suffer genuine trauma at its cessation or interruption. Such observations led Freud to the death instinct. They lead Durkheim to the notion of inadequate instinctual guidance, and to an argument on behalf of steady and considerable discipline for the child.

> The absence of discipline... produces confusion, from which those suffer most who would seem to flourish on it. One no longer knows whether this is good or bad, whether this should or should not be done, whether this is permitted or is illegitimate. Hence a state of nervous agitation, of contagion, a feverishness unfortunate for the child.[54]

Clearly, the child resembles the anomic adult:

> If he is *not* subservient to custom, it is because his sequence of ideas and feelings have continuity and persistence.... [T]hus, excessive change, far from being incompatible with routines, paves the way for it and re-enforces its dominance.[55]

But Durkheim has considerable difficulty specifying the circumstances under which this coincidence of apparent opposites obtains. He lacked an explicit and systematic view of ambivalent human nature which would underpin, refine, generalize, and apply this crucial insight and intuition. As a result he cannot begin to distinguish among self-overcoming, self-control, and masochism: nor between dependence which is genuinely liberating or grossly oppressive. Durkheim needed a psychology which does not load the dice so consistently in favor of society and specialized social roles. Much of what is valuable in his work stems from an intuitive appreciation of the presence and significance of human ambivalence. Most of what is confusing, unacceptable, and seemingly contradictory stems from the failure to pursue and develop this intuition and to ground it theoretically.

The many matters on which Marx and Durkheim are fundamentally at odds are well known and much rehearsed. These differences are also overemphasized and misunderstood, to the detriment of social theory. Their respective strengths, their undeveloped notions of what is specifically human, are in fact fundamentally complementary. Ambivalence itself makes the recognition of ambivalence difficult, and with it the deep truth and fundamental affinity of these seemingly opposite outlooks on individual and society. In the absence of a view of human nature which posits a fundamental ambivalence and the ceaseless effort to overcome it, which understands social discontents of alienation and anomie as grounded in human ambivalence, their views will continue to appear irremediably opposed.

★   ★   ★   ★   ★

Consider the following passage, in which Durkheim contrasts two "extreme and opposed types in men's moral character":

> With some people, it is the sensitivity to the rule, a disposition for discipline which predominates. They do their duty as they see it, completely and without hesitation, simply because it is their duty and without any particular appeal to their hearts. These are the men of substantial intellect and strong will—Kant is an ideal example—but among whom the emotional faculties are much less developed than those of the intellect. As soon as reason speaks, they obey; but they hold their feelings at a distance. Thus, their bearing suggests firmness and resolution and at the same time conveys a sense of coldness, severity, rigidity. The power of self-control is characteristic of them. This is why they do not go beyond their rights, do not trample those of others. But they also have little capacity for those spontaneous impulses in which the individual gives or joyfully sacrifices himself.
>
> Other people are characterized not by self-control and a tendency to withdraw but by a love of spending themselves, by an outward expansiveness. They love to attach, and devote themselves to others. These are the loving hearts, the ardent and generous souls. But their behavior, by contrast, is regulated only with difficulty. If they are capable of great deeds, they find it hard to tie themselves down to the performance of mundane obligations. Their moral conduct lacks, then, that consistent logic, that beautiful moral bearing of the former. One is less sure of these passionate men. For passions, even the most noble, blow successively hot and cold under the influence of chance circumstances and in the most erratic ways.[56]

The first of these types is a thinly disguised self-portrait. Yet the very brilliance of the second portrait is suspicious. It is as if here, too, he had personal knowledge whereof he speaks. The two types, Durkheim's masterful versions of the Apollonian and the Dionysian, cry out for synthesis. Something tells us they are equally vital aspects of a human reality whose unity we cannot express directly but must nevertheless try to convey and achieve. Something prompts the continual attempt to envision that unity, beyond, prior to, in spite of language and logic and their irreducible oppositions. Similarly for Durkheim's own conflicts, and his poignant, barely submerged lament that the separation is so sharp and seemingly irremediable. In truth, the two types are two sets of human qualities which everyone must accommodate in some manner and proportion. We are fortunate that Durkheim was not really so adept at separating these opposed aspects of his own character, despite an emotional make-up which constantly endeavored to confine him to the Apollonian, and to given forms. By comparison, Marx seems to have settled such issues to his satisfaction. But maybe his exaggerations betray him, together with the brilliant blindness of his own vision.

In his outstanding biography of Durkheim, Steven Lukes relates the following revealing anecdote.[57] The story has it that Durkheim's nephew and student, Marcel Mauss, was sipping coffee one day with friends at a sidewalk cafe. Presently he saw Durkheim striding purposefully across the square. Terrified that he would be publically reprimanded for engaging in such frivolous unproductive activity (why wasn't he at the library?), Mauss sprang up and climbed out a rear window of the cafe. In light of what we know of Durkheim's stern character and stoic habits, the delight he took in reminding us that duty is not always fun, his nephew's strategic retreat appears quite rational and prudent.

There is another Durkheim, however, equally unforgettable and appealing, if rarely seen or heard from. When his son was killed in the war, Durkheim was so devastated he could not bear to discuss his grief. According to a friend, "an almost feminine sensitivity" struggled against his usual contained, controlled, distant, forbidding manner. While he desperately fought for his peace by means of even heavier contributions to the war effort, he slowly lost interest in life, and died one year later.

★   ★   ★   ★   ★

Karl Kraus wrote that there are people who are followed all through their lives by a beggar to whom they have given nothing. If Durkheim did not starve his beggared self, then he was certainly niggardly in sharing the wealth. The irony we must ponder and pursue is that the emaciation of his life and social theory was such a damnably principled affair, seducing us even as it saddens.

5

Freud on Ambivalence

Now the separate propositions of psychoanalysis are nevertheless so intimately related that conviction on a single point easily leads to the acceptance of the whole theory. It might be said of psychoanalysis that if you give it your little finger it will soon have your whole hand.

I like to avoid concessions to faint-heartedness. One can never tell where that road may lead one; one gives way first in words, and then little by little in substance too.

It really seems as though it is necessary for us to destroy some other thing or person in order to guard against the impulsion to self-destruction. A sad disclosure indeed for the moralist! . . . [B]ut the moralist will console himself for a long time to come with the improbability of our speculations.

Freud

We seek an approach to human nature which will connect and underpin the apparently opposed maladies of alienation and anomie. This calls for a look at certain seminal thinkers who have dealt directly with the clash, the play, the overcoming of opposite human dispositions and needs. Freud is an obvious point of departure.

Freud was one of those conservative souls whose basic fear is that one thing will lead to another: "one can never tell where that road may lead." Yet he had the courage, mixed with dogged determination, to follow most disturbing matters he encountered to the bitter end, much like the Oedipus he honored as the nucleus of all neuroses. Next to Nietzsche, no one has done more to locate ambivalence in the depths of the psyche. Thus it is most appropriate that the foremost student of paradox and ambivalence himself appears ambivalent. Ambivalence is central to his personality and his intellectual outlook. Accordingly, while Freud's life and work represent a magnificent monument to the life of critical reason, it is his merciless exposure of the fanaticism of reason, the human costs of civilization, for which he is remembered and revered.

That same sense of responsibility is reflected in his warning against possible seductions by psychoanalysis itself. Poking about tentatively and innocently, one could lose a hand. The abyss he conjures up is the slimy, murky world of ambivalence, wherein any love may prove hateful and all negation masks assent. From another point of view, it is the dark underworld of the unconscious, haven of the childish, spiteful, rebellious, the downright disgusting; rising up against Aristotelian logic, Kantian categories, cognitive and social forms with Satanic cheek. Or it could be the notorious death instinct, which the lucky individual manages to direct outward, while the unlucky turn it on themselves, refusing the loan of life and dying needlessly day by day. Little wonder that he recommends the world of ambivalence with considerable ambivalence.

His warnings also reflect a certain pride in the allegedly tightly interlocking propositions of psychoanalysis. Were we to judge the matter on the basis of whether his doctrines and the movement he founded have come down to us intact, his belief in their essential unity might appear the height of hubris. Scandalously, many of his most brilliant disciples defected in his own lifetime. Most were original, able thinkers in their own right. Some departed because they chafed under Freud's authoritarian leadership, but many left because of long-standing, significant intellectual differences. Succeeding generations of renegade psychoanalysts have often attacked the Freudian corpus like so many beginning butchery students. This, too, has its basis in Freudian theory.

Three Freudian doctrines are particularly relevant to our enterprise: ambivalence, the unconscious, and the death instinct. The unconscious, in its most familiar Freudian formulation, is the home of sides of our ambivalences that we repress: the unacceptable, unthinkable, unofficial, disreputable thoughts and feelings which therein prosper, plot, fester. The death instinct, along with Eros, the other great protagonist of late Freudian cosmology, constitutes the primary example of instinctual ambivalence. Other ambivalences and instincts are usually seen as belonging to one of these two classes.

The relationship of the three hypothesis is close in another respect: they are often viewed as the most critical elements of psychoanalytic theory, critical in the sense of indicting the social order, seemingly any possible social order, on behalf of the forever recalcitrant and frustrated individual, chained to his desires. The connection with a philosophy of the collective or with "critical theory" is less obvious. Nevertheless, the curious feature of recent cultural and intellectual history is that those who seek a radical reinterpretation of Freud's message have gravitated to precisely these aspects of psychoanalysis, despite the obstacles each seems to pose to collective ideals and the reconciliation of the social with the individual.

How the death instinct might contribute to such a project is unclear, nor is it obvious how the postulate of instinctual ambivalence can issue in a message more hopeful than the message of pessimistic resignation or modest liberation Freud himself gleaned from it. Psychoanalytic therapy as he conceived of it was less of a cure than guidance in learning to live with our maladies, in transforming hysterical misery into everyday misery. With every self-assertive and aggressive act dogged by guilt, every love comingled with hate, the best Freud looked forward to was a little less anxiety, the exchange of manageable, everyday misery for the futile pursuit of illusory dreams, for fantasies altogether too real, for violent fluctuations from self-infinitization to self-degradation. Such were the lessons of ambivalence. We are thereby condemned not only to a war with civilization which we are fated to lose, but also to an internal war which part of us always loses. Meanwhile, the death wish stalks through our lives and loves, painfully separating what was painstakingly united, destroying and rendering formless what was carefully constructed and carefully formed, decaying the once vital and vibrant.

Yet the affinity of these dark doctrines to a wide range of social criticism is a matter of record. The impossibility of achieving something, Nietzsche reminds us, is among the attractions of trying to do it. And maybe these post-Freudian social critics see or sense something passed over in the naive common sensical view. One thinks of Max Horkheimer's observation: "the death instinct is deeply right." Perhaps only something so terrible as a death instinct is equal to the task of explaining barbarism so widespread, systematic, heinous that it beggars the imagination of history itself. If the hypothesis is wrong as a matter of fact, it may nevertheless be profoundly true as a symbol, warning, reminder: "deeply right." In hard times like these, even positive thinking liberal critics can be drawn to the death postulate. Somehow it seems to defend the individual, his integrity and basic needs in ways liberal environmentalism and social engineering cannot. It represents a fundamental facet of being human which a sick, slick, manipulative culture cannot permanently coerce, finesse, buy off, or ignore.

Similar arguments apply to the idea of the unconscious. Similar ambiguities obtain. And to instinctual ambivalence, an idea toward which would-be reformers, socialists, and believers in progress are understandably ambivalent when not downright hostile. From Freud's point of view all these attempts to deny or overcome ambivalence, proffered solutions secular or religious, are so many failures of nerve and manhood, failures to face the psychic facts. All such interpretations are likely to be regressive, reverting to arguments Freud had demonstrated the reasons for forever discarding, simplifying that which he had proved complicated or necessarily ambiguous, resurrecting solutions and nostrums religious and political he had proved (as in the case of dreams) are illusory by function and design.

Freud contends that the "separate propositions of psychoanalysis are so intimately related that conviction on a single point easily leads to the acceptance of the whole theory." On the other hand, the propositions themselves underwent continuous reformulation, were often discarded only to reappear and live on beside new theories, and were sometimes left in an unfinished or confused state such that Freud himself openly expressed dissatisfaction.

Freud on Ambivalence

In psychoanalysis, Adorno has remarked, only the exaggerations are true. His remark is an exaggeration, so perhaps it is true. Psychoanalysis is an embrionic science of exaggeration, and the opposed emotional truths thereby revealed. It sets for itself the task of determining when we can safely take what is being said and done as good approximations of what is meant and felt.

In early formulations of instinct theory Freud often hedged on whether all instincts came in opposed pairs. It is arguable that he never settled on the nature or source of ambivalence. What is indisputable is the constant and over-riding emphasis on ambivalence: "there is no neurosis without conflict between contradictory and opposed wishes," whereby "one side of the personality stands for certain wishes, and the other stands for opposed wishes."[1] Our character traits always represent certain combinations or fusions of opposite tendencies. Ambivalence is at the bottom of the otherwise perplexing phenomenon of the *taboo,* strong prohibitions, unquestionable moral injunctions. Taboo is itself a word which expresses ambivalence. Its basis is a "prohibited action, for performing which a strong inclination exists in the unconscious."[2] In like manner ambivalence underlies the Oedipal crisis and its resolution, the development of conscience, morality, and "many important cultural institutions." It is the basis of all compulsiveness, and the rigidity characteristic of neurosis. It can be seen most vividly in behavior which simultaneously reflects opposite emotions and motivations: in manic-depression, in which manic and depressive states not only alternate but often seem to coincide; the behavior of the passive aggressive, the helpless ones who use helplessness to control the situation; the all-too-familiar figures of the ascetic libertine and the filthy minded pure. It is likewise reflected in the readiness with which emotions and behavior pass over to their opposites.

There is another piece of telltale evidence: most of us stoutly deny our ambivalence, protesting our innocence of it, even as we go about revealing it in our behavior. Such evidence cannot be ignored. A depth psychology which timidly disallows vigorous denials and exaggerations as evidence of opposite motivations deprives itself of a basic tool. Denying ambivalence in our lives and theories, we go on to formulate or legitimate crude and false opposites, choosing one and banishing the other. Thus, Nietzsche said, we send life crashing into life.

Freud was far more certain of the omnipresence of ambivalence than of its origin or its exact nature. This is reflected in the inconsistency of his terminology. Freud acquired the concept from Breuer. In Breuer's usage, ambivalence refers to a coupling of opposite tendencies such that the opposite which is in the "minority" is passive, is refused a direct voice, yet speaks powerfully if indirectly to the trained or sensitized observer. It does not refer to mere succession in time of opposite attitudes. But Freud sometimes uses the term to refer to "ordinary ambivalence" as opposed to instinctual defusion or the ambivalent mixture involved in perversions like sadism. Elsewhere it is all labeled ambivalence. He sometimes implies a distinction between ambivalence and antithesis which is not clear. A number of other terms are employed: mixture, fusion, alloy, blend. These have significantly different connotations. Fusion suggests the dissolution and destruction of the original elements. A mixture might involve elements more readily distinguishable and detachable, in which the opposition continues more or less unabated.

Freud neither makes these distinctions explicit nor uses them with consistency. His failure to do so is certainly crucial and probably revealing. What is at stake is nothing less than the question of overcoming ambivalence, and the possibility of a coherent self.

But let us approach these matters indirectly, by way of his discussion of the origins of ambivalence:

> We know nothing of the origin of this ambivalence. One possible assumption is that it is a fundamental phenomenon of our emotional life.

But it seems to me quite worth considering another possibility, namely that originally it formed no part of our emotional life but was acquired by the human race in connection with their father-complex, precisely where the psychoanalytic examination of modern individuals still finds it revealed at its strongest.[3]

Several years later he uses similar phraseology in rejecting the hypothesis that ordinary ambivalence might be a product of defusion, as in the defusion of instincts which is the "essence of a regression of libido": "ambivalence, however, is such a fundamental phenomenon that it more probably represents an instinctual fusion that has not been completed."[4] Here ambivalence is on its way to fusion, not on its way back.

In a similar oedipal vein he suggests that

Love and hate did not originate in a cleavage of any common primal element, but sprang from different sources and underwent separate developments before the influence of the pleasure-pain relation constituted them as antitheses.[5]

Only when the genital organization is established does love become "the antithesis of hate." Elsewhere he admits that the "sadistic" subphase of the oral stage, which involves both the attempt to assimilate and the attempt to devour and destroy—biting the breast—"may be designated ambivalent."[6] By contrast, "there is no ambivalence at all in the relation to the object—the mother's breast" in the first oral subphase.[7] In virtually his last word on the subject he contends, in reference to sadism and masochism, that

We have before us two excellent examples of the fusion of two classes of instinct, of Eros and aggressiveness, and we proceed to the hypothesis that this relation is a model one—that every instinctual impulse that we can examine consists of similar fusions or alloys of the two classes of instinct.[8]

Here he sees ambivalence (or fusions, alloys) almost everywhere he looks, and again it seems that this is by no means an invention of the oedipal crisis. Accordingly, he describes ambivalence at the breast in a manner rivaling Melanie Klein:

These early object-cathexes are regularly ambivalent to a high degree. A powerful tendency to aggressiveness is always present beside a powerful love, and the more sensitive does it become to disappointments and frustrations from that object; and in the end the love must succumb to the accumulated hostility. Or the idea that there is an original ambivalence such as this in erotic cathexes may be rejected, and it may be pointed out that it is the special nature of the mother-child relation that leads, with equal inevitability, to the destruction of the child's love; for even the mildest upbringing cannot avoid using compulsion and introducing restrictions, and any such intervention in the child's liberty must provoke as a reaction an inclination to rebelliousness and aggressiveness.[9]

Ambivalence has been pushed back past the oedipal crisis, but the question of whether it is activated or actually created in the pre-oedipal period is left open. If ambivalence is produced, then for some reason it is *always* produced to some degree, even under the best of circumstances. In this sense it resists socialization, changes in the care of the child.

There are indeed inconsistencies in his treatment of this central psychoanalytic doctrine. On the other hand, what catches the eye and retains our attention in Freud is the psyche in perpetual conflict with itself, and not merely the battle of recalcitrant unregenerate instincts with overbearing culture. It is hard to resist the conclusion that the the Freudian doctrine of instinctual ambivalence is decidedly dreary and defeatist, permitting a modest liberation at best. Rieff summarizes the apparent implications of ambivalence as follows:

> Every new permissiveness leads to self-reproaches, leads to renunciation of a possession of liberty, experienced psychologically as repression and publically objectified as law or taboo.[10]

He goes on to suggest that psychoanalysis exposes

> the wrongheaded and futile drift of psychological science of today, with its not only utopian but impossible aim of freeing the individual from the burden of opposition.[11]

Strong language and bitter medicine, but surely closer to the Freudian word and spirit than Marcuse's flirtation with psychoanalysis, whereby ambivalence is eventually abandoned; or Norman O. Brown's brilliant Dionsysian obfuscations; or the pleasant homilies of Erich Fromm, wherein evil and illness alike are by-products of a life unlived in a sick society, and ambivalence is drowned in a sea of pablum. At best they do Freud the dubious honor of putting their arguments in his mouth.

The Unconscious: Adjective or Noun?

The repressed unconscious has been hailed by many as Freud's most critical assumption, both in the sense of being crucial and of guaranteeing a permanent conflict with culture and society. Yet there is another unconscious, or another way of viewing the unconscious, which Freud never really rejected despite its ambiguous relationship to his mature theories. It was timidly introduced and virtually neglected.

Yet Freud regarded it as his most significant discovery: This unconscious consists of contents unconscious by virtue of their structure and logic, not necessarily their unacceptability to consciousness. Freud referred to it as "the true psychic reality," a contention he never repudiated. Its most systematic treatment is in his 1915 article on the unconscious, to which much attention has turned in recent years.[12]

After making the case for unconscious mentation ("the mental, like the physical, is not necessarily in reality just what it appears to be"), he divides the unconscious into the unconscious proper (*system Ucs.*) and the preconscious (*system Pcs.*), which is merely latent and thus capable of becoming conscious. The decisive censorship occurs between Ucs. and Pcs. Already, however, the animistic image of the censor blurs a crucial distinction: between material in such a form that it is *inherently* incapable of attaining consciousness and material whose form does not preclude its becoming consciousness.

This distinction would be of little interest if the unrepressed unconscious, material prevented by the very form it takes from becoming conscious, were empty. But this is by no means the case. This retrospective assessment of the issue was published in 1940:

> We have found that processes in the unconscious or the id obey different laws from those in the preconscious ego. We name these laws in their totality the primary process, in contrast to the secondary process which governs the course of events in the preconscious, in the ego.[13]

He adds that he has thus far found merely "indications of the difference (between Ucs. and Pcs.) and not the essence of it."

This is excessively modest. Freud did grasp the difference, logically speaking, in the two modes of mentation. The following is taken from his justly celebrated summary of these structural differences:

> There is in this system no negation, no subtlety, no varying degree of certainty....*Negation* is, at a higher level, a substitute for repression.... [I]ntensity of cathexis is mobile in a far greater degree in this plan in the other systems. By the process of *displacement* one idea may surrender to another the whole volume of the cathexis; by that of *condensation* it may appropriate the whole cathexis of several other ideas....[T]he processes of the system Ucs. are *timeless*; i.e., they are not ordered temporarily, are not altered by the passage of time, in fact bear no relation to time at all....[T]he processes of the Ucs. are just as little related to reality. They are subject to the pleasure principle; their fate depends only upon the degree of their strength and upon their conformity to regulation by pleasure and pain....[L]et us sum up: *exemption from mutual contradiction, primary process (motility of cathexis),*

timelessness and substitution of psychic for external reality.[14] [Emphasis added.]

These features of unconscious mentation, obtained from dream analysis and observation of neurotics, suggest that the criterion of *consciousness* is ill suited to the task of making the significant distinctions among the various aspects of Ucs., Pcs., and Cs. "Consciousness stands in no simple relation either to the different systems or to the process of repression."[16] The more basic distinction is structural, between systems—secondary and primary processes—whose modes of logic and mentation differ radically. "In proportion as we try to win our way to a metapsychological view of mental life, we must learn to emancipate ourselves from our sense of the importance of that symptom which consists in 'being conscious.'"[16]

Freud's modest evaluation of his accomplishments in this murky area ("the profound obscurity of the background of our ignorance is scarcely illuminated by a few glimmers of insight") is inconsistent with judgments he expressed elsewhere ("discoveries like this are vouchsafed only once in a lifetime"). Even so, the discovery was essentially left to the proverbial gnawing mice. Worse still, the undifferentiated unconscious was subjected to the ravages of Freud's own subsequent formulations.

Freud's Death Instinct

Freud vacillates between maximizing the shock value of his alleged death instinct and minimizing its distinctiveness. He dramatically declares that "the aim of all life is death," but then points out that death is but one of two basic goals of life. Elsewhere he takes great pains to point out the consistency of the death instinct postulate with his previous preoccupations and with the overall trajectory of his thought. At one point he endeavors to show the strong affinity of his formulation to common sense notions of life and death, love and hate, and the bland forces of attraction and repulsion operative throughout the physical universe.[17] To contend that the death instinct is neither exceptional nor controversial is decidedly ingenuous. Yet he is justified in emphasizing the continuity of the death postulate with previous preferences and preoccupations: for example, the perception of ubiquitous intrapsychic conflict; the preference for irremediable dualisms; the belief in the conservative nature of the instincts, whereby they seek to restore an earlier state of rest.

Prior to 1920 he saw these conflicts in terms of ego-instincts, concerned with self-preservation, and sex instincts, concerned with the preservation of the species: hunger and love. At this point the phenomenon of narcissism intruded, hinting broadly of the ultimate unity of the two, or at least suggesting the transformability of one into the other. This prompted Freud to undertake a revision of instinct theory. The ego instincts had always been a kind of residual category, whereas sexual instincts had carried the burden of his actual accounts of behavior. Perhaps his interest in avoiding monism was as strong as his interest in determining which of the contending alternatives fits the data.

As Freud describes his "discovery," a clinical phenomenon of which there is indisputable evidence provided the first clue. This is the propensity or compulsion to repeat, even when what is being repeated could only be a source of renewed pain and trauma:

> We come now to a new and remarkable fact, namely that the compulsion to repeat also recalls from the past experiences which include no possibility of pleasure, and which can never, even long ago, have brought satisfaction, even to instinctual impulses which have since been repressed.[18]

Why remarkable? From the start he dealt with neurotics who regularly raked themselves over the coals by dredging up and reliving past trauma. The notion that this is done entirely for pleasure is at least as unbalanced as the notion that there is no pleasure in it whatsoever. Freud was no stranger to masochism, neither as human being nor therapist, but the softer dualism of ego and sexual instincts seemed to handle masochism at least as well as his new formulation. As he himself quipped: it is not fair to saddle ourselves with the hypothesis of the death instinct just because a few poor souls get their kicks from bizarre sex. Hence the importance ascribed to the compulsion to repeat.

Recall that Durkheim singled out the same phenomenon to make virtually the opposite point about instincts. To him the repetitions of children's play suggest an alternation of habit and impulsivity which supports his assumption that children (including many adult children) have inadequate instinctual guidance for their behavior and have not yet acquired cultural controls. Habit and impulsivity are by no means incompatible: they cooperate in generating one another.[19] For Freud, however, the phenomenon of repetition yields something quite different. Children's activities exhibit "to a high degree an instinctual character and, when they act in opposition to the pleasure principle, give the appearance of some 'daemonic' force at work."[20] Irrespective of how traumatic the experience originally was, it is meticulously duplicated. In Freud's (new) view the repetition, as such, cannot be pleasurable. "Novelty is always the condition of enjoyment." This neglects the novelty of repeating something that is past. It also neglects other, opposite kinds of pleasure. Indeed, if Freud had taken proper account of other sources of "enjoyment"—security, familiarity, comfort, peace, passivity, inertia—would the death instinct have been necessary? Or so terrible?

Experiences which contained nothing of the old and familiar would be both unintelligible and horrific. Stimulus redundance provides the backdrop with respect to which the new is tolerable, enjoyable, even distinguishable as new. Durkheim suggests that the constraint and inertia involved in habit and repetition may well be preferable to the confusion and anomia which would obtain in the absence of such repetitions. But Freud is not content to find at the bottom of this behavior a mere refuge or defense, nor inclination, nor learned propensity. The last thing he is prepared to do is to view it as Durkheim did, as a result of *inadequate* instinctual guidance. Nothing but a new instinct, or class of instincts, implacably opposed to pleasure and Eros, will do.

> But how is the predicate of being instinctual related to the compulsion to repeat? At this point we cannot escape a suspicion that we may have come upon the track of a universal attribute of instincts and perhaps of organic life in general which has not hitherto been clearly recognized or at least not explicitly stressed. It seems, then, that an instinct is an urge inherent in organic life to restore an earlier state of things which the living entity has been obliged to abandon under the pressure of external disturbing forces; that is, it is a kind of organic elasticity, or, to put in another way, the expression of the inertia inherent in organic life.[21]

This line of reasoning leads to the death hypothesis proper: "the aim of all life is death."[22] Everything dies or attempts to die for internal reasons. The sexual instincts differ from the others only in that they disturb the equilibrium of life and propel it forward, so that every organism may die in its own time as well as in its own way. The death instinct, deflected outward by the muscular apparatus, manifests itself in aggression, conflict, strife, hate. Eros, whose task is to build up, join together, make ever greater unities—creator of culture, of civilization—must embezzle instinctual energy from the death instincts, curbing and sublimating aggression. It thereby burdens mankind with an ever increasing sense of guilt, based on destructive impulses and fantasies which are proscribed and prohibited at every turn. "Holding back aggressiveness is in general unhealthy and leads to illness."

The activities and vicissitudes of these instincts transcend the topographical categories of the psyche:

> There can be no question of restricting one or the other of the basic instincts to one of the provinces of the mind. They must necessarily be met with everywhere. [23]

Rieff calls our attention to the fact that in a theory awash with name-giving and neologisms, Freud fails to name the destructive energy which is the counterpart to libido. Moreover, he admitted that so long as that instinct is not externalized as aggression—so long as it operates internally, as a death instinct—it remains silent.

So much for an initial look. Lest we deal exclusively in terms of our idea of Freud's idea, here is his account of the ultimate goals of life and death instincts:

> After long hesitancies and vacillations we have decided to assume the existence of only two basic instincts, *Eros* and *the destructive instinct* . . . .[T]he aim of the first of these basic instincts is to establish ever greater unities and to preserve them thus—in short, to bind together; the aim of the second is, on the contrary, to undo connections and so to destroy things. In the case of the destructive instinct we may suppose that its final aim is to lead what is living into an inorganic state, For this reason we call it the *death instinct*. If we assume that living things came later than inanimate and arose from them, then the death instinct fits into the formula we have proposed to the effect that instincts tend towards a return to an earlier state. [24]

One has the sense that the death instinct is Freud's bad idea of a good idea, and that nimble critiques and dismissals score many good points in missing a very big one. Much the same could be said of those who would dispose of ambivalence and the unconscious simply because Freud's formulations are flawed and inconsistent. Still, even at the risk of staring so long in the abyss that it stares into us, the central Freudian doctrines require further scrutiny.

In this connection I am reminded of a certain country preacher who one Sunday received a resounding Amen! from a prominent member of his congregation each and every time he itemized and condemned yet another mortal sin from his long and all-inclusive list. He could not help but notice, however, the strained silence which greeted his passionate condemnation of corn whiskey. After church the prominent parishioner explained it to him: precisely at that point, it seems, the preacher had "stopped preaching and gone to meddling."

Given that we all have our sacred cows, the preacher had probably been meddling with someone or another all along. In any case, with respect to ambivalence, the unconscious, and the death instinct—and their place in social theory—let us proceed to meddle openly and earnestly.

6

Life as a Matter of Life and Death

We must sound the inside and see what springs set us in motion. But since this is a high and hazardous undertaking, I wish fewer people would meddle with it.

Montaigne

That which removes itself from our consciousness and for that reason becomes obscure can on that account be perfectly clear in itself. Becoming obscure is a matter of perspective of consciousness.

Nietzsche

We appear as insects here, Each with a little stinger, That we may fittingly revere Satan, our sire and singer.

Goethe

We have suggested human ambivalence as the appropriate focus of a view of human nature; now we require an account of the nature of ambivalence. Freud associated the fundamental ambivalence with life and death instincts. In later formulations the unconscious itself became a kind of reservoir of instincts. The obvious difficulty is that we can know little of the instinctual as such, aside from its social and symbolic expressions. But this in no way diminishes the significance of those basic attitudes, emotions and fantasies surrounding matters of life and death, nor their relevance to the question of a fundamental ambivalence. It simply calls for shifting the focus from instinct to psychology, and the symbolic life of the species. Thus in the following two chapters we substitute the "death" (or "life and death") problem for the question of life and death instincts, psychological ambivalence for instinctual, and pursue the issue in connection with the psychology and symbolism of life and death. This in turn will lead us to a different model of the unconscious, in which instinct as such plays a minor role.

This exploration involves a number of diverse sources. What they have in common is the effort to delineate and defend basic human polarities which are neither instinctual nor social, at least in the sense of being determined by social structures. As we shall see, resurrecting the "death problem" entails rescuing the idea from subversive supporters as well as defending it against outright detractors. The outcome of this exploration and disputation is the hypothesis that there are two fundamental modes of thought and being, the differentiated and the undifferentiated. Alienation and anomie can then be seen as pathological relationships between the two modes. This primal distinction is treated as the expression or locus of a basic human ambivalence. I subsequently argue that it is likewise the basis of a division of the mind into the conscious (differentiated) and unconscious (dedifferentiated, or less differentiated) faculties and modes.

Why the Death Problem Continues to Show Some Life

Freud's death instinct has been resurrected so many times that it hardly deserves its title any more. Having been given its final rites about as many times, it has some claim to it. R. E. Money-Kyrle offers "an inconclusive contribution to the theory of the death instinct"[1] which delineates the difficulties both in subscribing to and rejecting the idea. What is innate, he suggests, "should be thought of as a range of possibilities, and what is acquired as an actuality selected from them under the influence of a particular environment." In a manner reminiscent of sociologists and anthropologists, he argues that the instincts of higher animals are more plastic as to their destination and expression than those of the lower. Psychoanalysis is concerned with the fantasy responses which may precede and motivate behavior, and the study of such fantasy patterns is actually the study of instinct in man. This view breaks down old conceptions and classifications of instincts by suggesting that the same primary fantasies can be associated or expressed in connection with a number of different instincts.

How could we have developed a death instinct?

> Since instincts, in the Darwinian sense, are developed by the selection of such mutation as favor the survival of offspring, and so of parents to produce them, how can we imagine the development by selection of an instinct of destruction?[2]

One possible evolutionary explanation is that the individual's ability to recognize the danger from potential enemies is based in some way on the aggression felt within itself: the advantage would go to those who are thus sensitized. However, this is not the death instinct. It is the "fear of a projected aggression originally evolved in the interests of self-preservation. " This fear might well explain the aggression that is turned back on oneself in love. Or instead, the felt threat to oneself which has no connection with genuine threats in one's environment may date from the time in which the self-object distinctions drawn by the baby were rudimentary or absent altogether. The baby's aggression against others might be experienced as aggression toward itself. But this hypothesis also appears to dispense with the death instinct.

Money-Kyrle nevertheless maintains that in analytic practice "we can also detect a primary threat to the self which is not derived from anything."[3] Freud derived the destructiveness he found in man from a conservatism reacting against the life forces that brought them into being. Can this not be linked to the concept of catabolism in biology and entropy in physics? Moreover, "are we to attribute psychic equivalents only to system maintaining processes, and not to the disruptive processes they counteract?" There are good biological and analytical reasons for regarding the *fear* of death as one of the basic motive of life. In analysis "we meet this fear in its more primitive forms, and it seems to be linked with the awareness of a self-destructive force."[4] Maybe this is some kind of psychic correlate or representative of entropy, of the catabolic process in our brains and bodies. But if it is an instinct it is a most peculiar instinct, one which could not possibly have evolved on the basis of self and species preservation.

Liam Hudson, another English psychologist, encourages us to bypass the sterile dispute between the biologists and those who stress the role of norms and mores, and instead to concentrate on separating three aspects of instincts: the *origin* of the need or drive, the *psychological function* that it performs, and the *biographical consequences* its existence or activity entails.[5] To know that a difference in disposition is hereditarily determined says nothing in itself about either the psychological function of the disposition or its effect on the individual's life.

Attempts to specify basic human needs have generally failed, he points out. Such lists are either "too simple to be credible or so diffuse as to lose their explanatory power." The alternative scheme he offers turns on the contrast between two levels of need: the levels of *primitive energy* and *symbolic preoccupation*.

> At the primitive level, this scheme acknowledges the existence of a variety of needs—sex, jealousy, aggression, competitiveness, the need to belong—but is concerned with the distinction between two categories of impulse: the pleasure-seeking and the destructive.[6]

Both categories can be transformed or sublimated. Once transformed, pleasure seeking becomes the desire for exploration and discovery, the need to probe the nonrational, forbidden, or exotic. Destructive impulses are transformed into the need for order and control, to avoid the ambiguous and the confusing, the new and the strange.

Another way of putting his distinction is of special interest: the transformation of pleasure seeking energies leads to the transgression or dissolution of boundaries and distinctions, while the transformation of the destructive impulses leads to a preoccupation with boundary maintenance and fortification. Later he refers to the forces of self-expression and those of control, the desire for spontaneous utterance and the necessities of discipline and restraint. He goes on to associate this pair with Eros and Thanatos: "the need to express, relate and explore on the one hand, and on the other, to control and restrain."[7] The ideal relationship between the two is that of an unending "dialogue" in which neither force ever wins out entirely over the other. Hudson's name for that dialogue is freedom.

In effect he has dispensed with the death instinct, as such. This is welcome. His contention that pleasure-seeking and Eros can be equated with boundary transgression or dissolution is most troublesome, however. Eros, as Freud put it repeatedly, labors to bind together ever larger unities. No doubt it crosses boundaries of various kinds in the process. Presumedly it does so on the basis of affection, "sympathy," and the like, not as a reflection of sheer acquisitiveness or aggression. Boundaries are relativized, conserved, overcome, but not destroyed. Yet there is no obvious reason why the act of violating boundaries could not include motivations and results of either sort.

Freud's own account was not free of this difficulty; witness his ready acceptance of Hering's classification of the basic instincts, assimilatory-constructive or dissimulatory-destructive, as confirmation of his death and life instinct hypothesis.[8] He does not consider the different ways in which this assimilation can take place, nor whether what is being assimilated has given its consent. Unless this distinction is made clear, one could equate love with Hitler's creation of *Lebensraum* for the German people. Hitler transgressed and dissolved Polish boundaries with vicious abandon. Why boundary maintenance is inherently aggressive and destructive is as mysterious as why pleasure seeking and boundary dissolution are always loving. Curiously, such difficulties derive from the violation of a maxim in which Hudson himself places great stock: life miscarries when either life or death forces seek to suppress the other. But theories, like Hudson's own, can miscarry for the same reason.

Elsewhere Hudson offers numerous examples of the benign consequences of the simultaneous affirmation of apparent opposites, the acceptance and overcoming of ambivalence. For example, he follows Durkheim in suggesting that

> the very reluctance of the permissive parent to exercise an arbitrary authority—to say, "this is right and that is wrong"—may cut the child off from vital advantages that the acceptance of a given framework can provide.[9]

The same insight is applied in many other areas of experience. The impact of a landscape painting suggests how the fixing of boundaries has the paradoxical effect of enhancing "life's sensuous possibilities." Similarly in the case of snapshots, and all those perceptual and conceptual snapshots by means of which we spot and chart movement. By freezing what is fluid we see more than could ever be seen without such distortions. To be completely immersed in the flow might produce no sense of movement at all.

In the same vein Hudson points out that in art "it is a lifetime's struggle with technical constraint that is formative of a vision beyond the merely facile."[10] This echoes Nietzche's contention that convention, far from being an obstacle to great art, is in fact the condition of it. In like manner, any successful academic training both focuses and restricts the meanings its students are free to perceive. Bounds must exist in order to be transcended, Simmel emphasizes. All such examples suggest that

> the pursuit of freedom is self-stultifying the moment it detaches itself from the processes of order. It seems that Eros and Thanatos are locked together in such a way that we cannot enjoy the first without submitting to the second.[11]

The problem here, which also plagues Durkheim's surprisingly similar conclusions, is that we can easily imagine all manner of dialogues, differing significantly as to the kind and degree of freedom promoted. At some point we must also ask whether it is freedom that is enhanced when these opposites are brought together in various ways.

We likewise need a better characterization of the polar forces at work. The connection of boundary transgressions to the "binding together" that Freud sees as the essence of Eros is not obvious. Boundary transgression can be most aggressive; boundary maintenance is not necessarily destructive or aggressive. Binding together is an important aspect of what we understand by love, but all bonds are not of the loving kind. To characterize love in this manner it would be necessary to add elements of respect for individual boundaries as well as their violation. Freud's use of Eros certainly hints of such elements. But to the extent that it does, the idea of Eros in dialogue with something else begins to seem superfluous or ambiguous. Nor does Hudson escape this difficulty.

One way out of this quandary might be to forget Eros and death, and to speak simply of boundary dissolution versus boundary maintenance. The *synthesis* of these opposites might then approximate our understanding of Eros. Eros would then be the kind of union in which the respective parts and boundaries are maintained and respected yet somehow overcome. Indeed, this conceptual innovation will prove most valuable.

Deadly Dualisms, Fearsome Fusions

The question of boundaries crops up repeatedly in discussions of the two classes of instincts. These boundaries are mental and physical, internal and external, cognitive as well as affective. But attitudes toward boundaries seem to issue from two opposing camps, and yield opposite conclusions. Two diametrically opposed views of boundaries and the death problem will amplify the point.

Norman O. Brown suggests that salvation lies in the fusion of life and death instincts, the obliteration of various dualisms—subject and object, life and death—which plague us and make us the sick animal. By contrast, Erich Fromm finds such fusion (of life and death "affinities") to be virtually the root of all evil. He advocates strict separation or extirpation of death-loving impulses, washing one's hands of the love affair with death, and various purification ploys and prescriptions. Fromm proposes to deliver the death instinct the *coup de grace*. What his spongy, sanitized brand of psychoanalysis actually accomplishes is to make us nostalgic for the death instinct, or at least for certain prophylactic qualities the idea seems to possess.

Ostensibly with the help of Marx, Fromm has arrived at the most fundamental distinction applicable to human beings:

> There is no more fundamental distinction between men, psychologically and morally, than the one between those who love life and those who love death, between the *necrophilous* and the *biophilous*.[12] [Emphasis added.]

As Hegel suggested, there is a certain kind of theoretical discourse, purged and purified of such contradictions, which manages to be inferior even to common sense. The confusion it generates stems from the very attempt to purify, to eliminate contradiction and confusion. Rigid distinctions such as Fromm's not only run up against the reader's disposition to complement difference with equality, form with formlessness, but the author's disposition as well. Faced with fundamental differences, or the contention that differences are fundamental, we crave fundamental similarities. We proceed to discover them. Faced with distinctions and rigid form, we perversely will the indistinct and formless. Faced with allegedly absolute distinctions, we rebel, we engage in boundary games. Accordingly, Fromm—after separating life and death affinities as with a cleaver—is eventually inundated by no longer suppressible connections and similarities between love of life and love of death. The ultimate effect on his prose and message is much like that of a swamp as dusk falls. Nothing is well defined; everything might well be something else. These are precisely the results which he sought to stave off with his sharp, absolute opposition of biophilia and necrophilia!

Fromm's necrophiliac resembles Freud's anal-sadistic character, though Fromm rejects Freud's account of the genesis of such syndromes, their source in erotogenic zones. Necrophilia is his substitute explanation for the psychic phenomena and social behavior that led Freud to the death instinct. Necrophiliacs are "attracted to and fascinated by all that is not alive, all that is dead: corpses, decay, feces, dirt . . . . They come to life precisely when they talk about death."[13] (Nietzsche wrote that "heavy, heavy-spirited people become lighter precisely through what makes others heavier, through hatred and love, and for a time they surface."[14]) According to Fromm, they also live in the past, love all that does not grow, all that is mechanical. They crave control, and are deeply afraid of life because it is inherently disorderly and uncontrollable. They want to return to the darkness of the womb. They have an insatiable craving for certainty. This underlies their efforts to make life controllable and themselves invulnerable by transforming life into death, the "only certainty in life." Only death is dependable, certain, eternal. Rejecting the death instinct, he replaces it with a thoroughly ambiguous Darwinian contention: "it is an inherent quality of all living things to live, and preserve their existence." But Fromm, like Freud, has another drive to offer. Biophilia must contend with necrophilia, "the one answer to life which is in complete opposition to life."

Whether Fromm has actually described a meaningful constellation of attitudes and attributes is uncertain. The component parts are connected by a certain psychologic, and are undoubtedly significant, but it is possible that his necrophiliac is nothing more than an interesting composite sketched in support of his theory. We must ask, for example, why love of the past is necrophilous. Neither the present nor the future has meaning or holds promise without our coming to terms with our past: we back into the future with our eyes on the past.

Nietzsche repeatedly pointed to the necessity of actually living through the intellectual positions, the conflicts and contradictions of the past. For him this was little more than coming to understand ourselves: we *are* all these things. To overcome them is not to ignore them, or flee in fright from them. We must earn these dangerous "modern ideas," our radical liberation from the past, by means of the past. Fromm's persistent inability to deal with such elementary paradoxes marks him as a true son of Enlightenment rationalism, as does his overdetermined conversion from Freud to Marx.

Necrophiliacs also love all that is mechanical, Fromm contends. Are we to believe that past eras were more mechanical than our own? And is not the "mechanical" the wave of the future?[15] Some of the most future-oriented sectors of the population are those who deal with machines, impersonal data, automated systems, computers. Computer personnel, systems engineers, management consultants, technocrats of all stripes are presumably among the representatives of Fromm's "mechanical." They tend to believe, with some justification, that they are the progressive new wave, in business, politics, and academia. Marx located the universalistic tendencies of capitalism in just such activities and strata. His faith has not been totally vindicated. The agility and flexibility demanded by their work is often more than matched by the rigidity with which they arm themselves elsewhere. Their politics may prove repugnant and reactionary; the jury is out on the political orientation and significance of the "new class." But are these lovers of the mechanical backward looking? Backward, possibly; backward looking, hardly.

The difficulty with his argument cannot be eliminated by simply tinkering with the sub-categories of love of life and love of death. To see this, focus on Fromm's account of the one fundamental perversion, "the blending between life and death." "Many rituals which deal with the separation of the clean (life) from the unclean (death) emphasize the importance of avoiding this perversion."[16] He does not attempt to document his point. He neglects those rituals which, far from making absolute the distinctions in the category system of the people involved, allow them to temporarily upset and reverse the usual evaluations and categories. Such rituals, at least at certain "liminal stages," reflect and promote the understanding that on a human level these social distinctions, and social structure itself, are arbitrary and even pernicious. They suggest a general human perspective underlying and transcending given, socially structured differences.[17] If he is not neglecting such rituals, then he is surely missing one of their central features.

The irony is that his naive association of the clean with the life-affirming partakes of the very qualities—the anal concern with the orderly, the niggardly, the clean—which define for him the love of death. The real message of many of those rituals Fromm ignores or misinterprets is that life runs in currents clean and dirty. If dirt symbolizes death (certainly it is an attractive candidate) then death must be part of life. We arbitrarily delimit life with a rigid anal prejudice for the pure and the clean. The contradictions we do see are ones we have created, the result of imposing categorical systems—socially structured, cognitive differences—on a life which defies them. We complain of our inability to capture life with our concepts and forms. Still, some of the time, most of us are delighted and relieved to see life escape. Often we tag along, happily mocking our previous fetters and jailors.

In this way Fromm misreads the alleged fascination of dirt, feces, and the corpse over which Hitler reputedly stood. These and most of the other matters which fascinate the necrophile are marginal, borderline, boundary phenomena: dirt, symbolizing disorder, incipient formlessness, disintegration; feces, neither fully organic nor inorganic; the corpse, alive only hours before, neither alive nor fully dead. No doubt the most important margin is between life and death, but a larger conception of life suggests there is no more important boundary to challenge and cross. The rigidity with which the distinction is held is the important thing, because it is the rigidity itself which is life-denying, and which eventually causes the eventual destruction of the distinction. This point by no means gets Hitler off the hook, but it does give him many more relatives and far more company than Fromm's rather select group of necrophiles. Fromm's own sharp distinction between the biophiles and the necrophiles is of a piece with the anality that the rest of his theory describes and deplores. He draws his distinction in a deathlike way, supposedly on behalf of life.

Primitives seem to understand this better than Fromm: many rituals are precisely those limited times and carefully delineated circumstances during which otherwise sharply distinguished categories (adolescence and manhood, men and women, human and social, kings and commoners) can touch boundaries, or be reversed, or even obliterated. They deal with the mysteries of transitions, equality in the presence of difference, continuity amidst change, the pulse of life flowing through but never fully captured or exhausted by social masks and forms. Fromm's cleanliness rituals would be welcomed by precisely those anal characters and peoples he takes such pains to denounce. Those obsessed with cleanliness or purity, like Lady Macbeth repeatedly washing her hands, must have particularly dirty sins to wash away. As Nietzsche would say: *they* are the ones who really *do* need to clean themselves.

A final point concerns Fromm's conception of the true relationship between Eros and death. It is admittedly the most fundamental contradiction which exists in man,

> but this duality is not one of two biologically inherent instincts . . . but one between . . . the most fundamental tendency of life—to persevere in life—and its contradiction, which comes into being *when man fails in this goal.*[18]

Thus "the death instinct represents psychopathology and not normal biology." We are thereby encouraged to concentrate exclusively on the repressive, death-dealing society and its cultural contradictions. Destructiveness is the outcome of an unlived life. Having begun his treatment of life and death with such a sharp, immutable distinction between biophiles and necrophiles, Fromm inexorably moves toward a static, sterile, monistic view of life, and the wholesale confounding of categories. Such oscillation from rigidity to formlessness, untenable dualism to toothless monism, exaggerated distinctions to formless mush, is more of an unintended advertisement for the relevance of psychoanalysis and ambivalence than an alternative to either.

Turn now to Norman O. Brown, who writes with equal passion and conviction on what appears to be the opposite side of these issues.[19] Fromm finds the fusion of his basic dualism pernicious, while Brown finds in instinctual fusion "our only hope." He is intent on no less than the "resurrection of the body," a project which resembles the burial of the mind. Accordingly he assaults those Freudian doctrines which constitute the heaviest stones blocking the tomb: instinctual ambivalence and the death instinct. Resurrection awaits their removal.

Brown is particularly prone to attribute his own innovations to Freud: a procedure which is a revealing mixture of the modest and the immodest. Generally his method is to ascertain whether Freud said it, or something like it, somewhere in his forty-plus years of publications. When Freud did say it, Brown rarely questions whether it happens to be the case, what data might help settle the question, what competing hypotheses have been or could be offered. He generally trounces alternative arguments and findings with a mere reference to Freud, the same Freud that Brown's interpretation, despite its virtues, often distorts.

Brown bases his "hopes for mankind" on the postulated existence of a golden, unconflicted, unrepressed age to which we are always trying to return. The age is early childhood, though he nowhere indicates how early is early. He contends that Freud himself anticipated this emphasis:

"in his later writings, dependence on the mother is increasingly emphasized." One would think that Brown would proceed to consult and rely on such figures as Klein, Spitz, Winnicott, and Mahler, in addition to Freud. Klein, one of the dominant influences in British psychoanalysis, has strongly emphasized the pre-oedipal origins of neurosis and manic-depression in the early relationship of the baby to the mother's breast; yet her noteworthy theoretical departure is not even mentioned in this erudite book. Such omissions are convenient, for he entertains a rather un-Kleinian (and not particularly Freudian) view of matters at the breast. For Brown, things are not only fine there, they are exquisite. "At the mother's breast, subject-object dualism is overcome."

> There are, of course, other dualisms which affect adult life, also missing at the breast. . . . [T]hus psychoanalysis suggests the "eschatological" proposition that mankind will not put aside its sickness and its discontent until it is able to abolish every dualism.[20]

To contend that the subject-object dualism is *overcome* at the breast is rather odd, as if the dualism is alive and well at an earlier point, and that our sojourn at the breast is our only time of "overcoming." Perhaps, instead, that first object relation represents the birth of distinctions. Under favorable circumstances it may eventually entail, as Klein emphasizes, the birth of the capacity to make reparations for aggression toward the loved object, and with it the capacity for integration with the object on a new basis. In all events, if our utopian dreams and transcendent yearnings have to do with our experience at the breast, it is doubtful that the mindless fusion that Brown advocates is the essence of those yearnings. For those who have experienced psychological birth at all, it is likely that some synthesis of individuation and fusion, difference and equality, constitutes the true core of utopian thought. Brown may have unveiled the breastly origins of our utopian project, but he seems to have misunderstood its nature. In Kleinian terms, Brown misses the point of the breast.

Brown wants to abolish dualisms. This entails the destruction of love and dialogue as surely as the destruction of individuality. Brown is free to offer fusion as an alternative ideal, but to attribute it to Freud is underhanded. "When not theorizing," Brown rather cagily contends, Freud "admits" that "in the earliest phase there is no ambivalence in the relation to the object, that is, the breast." This is of little help in sorting through the numerous contradictory speculations Freud offered on the subject. When Brown offers his basic "Freudian theorem," we are tempted to ask him to speak for himself.

> The instinctual life of man starts from a primitive undifferentiated fusion

of the two instincts—a fusion in which they are not mutually antagonistic—and, in so far as it is fixated to childhood, seeks to restore instinctual fusion. The relation of child to mother's breast remains our ideal because it represents such an instinctual fusion.[21]

For those who traffic in eschatological propositions, irreducible ambivalences must be disposed of somehow. In the end, much in the manner of Marcuse as well as Fromm, Brown concludes that "the ambivalence of love and hate is not an innate datum of human nature." Neither is it a necessary result of separation and individuation. The contradiction of life and death instincts is now seen as a product of the family, that favorite whipping boy, and of course "society." The idea of instinctual ambivalence, so helpful to him in exposing the naivete, superficiality and unconscious wellsprings of other views of human maladies, is quietly dropped, without ceremony. Meanwhile he continues to speak as though there were a single truly psychoanalytic view of these matters, and that his is it.

"The only grounds for hope for humanity," he dramatically declares,

> are in the facts of human childhood.... [F]ixation to that first pre-ambivalent experience commits mankind to the unconscious project of overcoming the instinctual ambivalence which is his actual condition and of restoring the unity of opposites that existed in childhood.[22]

Here ambivalence is to be overcome, not abolished, nor fused. He proceeds to make it clear that this crucial distinction is not at all clear to him. Whereas Eros "seeks to preserve and enrich life," Thanatos endeavors "to return life to the peace of death." (Elsewhere he characterizes Eros as unification, and Thanatos as separation, much like Freud.) Under the auspices and tutelage of Dionysus he rejects repression, sublimation and negation. Instead of negating, Dionysus "affirms the dialectical unity of the great instinctual opposites." (He also contends that to see Nietzsche's mature understanding of Dionysus a synthesis of Apollo and Dionysus is "to sacrifice insight for peace of mind.") In effect he proposes to lead us back to the breast and on to the womb. This is regressive fusion, not dialectical union. Dualisms are abolished, not overcome, just as surely as he abolishes *that* crucial distinction, and would have us abolish all the rest.

Shortly after we are told to avoid all repression and sublimation, we learn that the "work" of constructing a Dionysian ego is immense. This is much like Marx, belatedly reminding us that to construct and to create are hard work, something different and more difficult than simply throwing off social shackles and destroying the old society. Brown calls repeatedly for the abolition of repression, for a "consciousness which does not negate any more, which does not observe the limit, but overflows." How an ego is to be "constructed," under these conditions, he neither says nor conveys. He stops just short of calling for the abolition of logic, since logic forces the mind to work under "general conditions of repression." Eventually, his dialectical instinctualism degenerates into an orgy of eschatological exhortations, vividly illustrating his argument at the expense of his argument.

Books must be brought to a close somehow, and American readers prefer upbeat endings. But Brown's inspiring conclusion is unusually bereft of support from his argument. In the end his book, exhilarating as it is, amounts to a counsel of despair. The "instinctual dialectic" which replaces "instinctual dualism" is achieved on the basis of "abolishing" dualisms, ambivalences, repression, sublimation. Rejecting the idea of a dialogue or synthesis between the Dionysian and Apollonian, making the questionable association of the Apollonian and death, Brown opts finally for one-dimensional, Dionysian fusion and chaos. He desperately attempts to associate Eros with fusion and fusion with life. But what is this undifferentiated fusion of his, if not death? What is this all embracing union, created at the expense of that which is bound together? How can it be all-embracing, if it does not embrace and nurture differences and distinctions?

Death and Dedifferentiation

We have seen that speculation on the death problem employs and invokes three different notions of life. In one interpretation life is seen as boundary dissolution, violation, fusion, a species of the Dionysian. Death is then associated with rigid forms, with sharp differentiation and impenetrable boundaries. In another version, it is death, not life, which is associated with fusion and related concepts; life is associated with forms and differentiation. In the third, life or love is seen as the force "binds together," creating higher unities which do not destroy past differences and boundaries so much as overcome and transcend them. Death is seen as differentiation or separation, much as in the second version.

As for the first interpretation: many authors do associate death with separations and defense of boundaries, either as Thanatos or Apollo, god of form, distinctions, individuation. Yet death is also associated with dissolution or destruction of boundaries, distinction, and form, sometimes by the very same authors. A case could be made for differentiation and form as the stuff of life, our distinctively human means of staving off death (formlessness, entropy) by establishing little islands of relative stability and permanence. Death would then be represented as dissolution or dedifferentiation, as Dionysus, as the entropic decline to formlessness. But often it is *life* which is associated with formlessness and dedifferentiation, paired with death as rigid form, boundary defense, separation. This second, opposed interpretation has much to recommend it as well. The very attempt to distinguish life from death tends to collapse into a formless mess.

David Bakan's treatment of death and life illustrates the difficulty which plagues the third interpretation, which associates Eros or life with building ever greater, more complex unities. His view is offered in the course of a psycho-theological study of "isolation and communion in Western man." The "villain" of his book is "unmitigated agency." The "moral imperative" is to try always to "mitigate agency with communion": Bakan adopts

> the terms agency and communion to characterize to fundamental modalities in the existence of living forms, agency for the existence of an organism as an individual, and communion for the participation of the individual as a part of the larger whole.[23]

Here is his summary of their manifestations:

Agency	Communion
self-protection, self-assertion, self-expansion	sense of being at one with other organisms
formation of separations	lack of separations
isolation, alienation, aloneness	contact, openness, union
urge to master	noncontractual cooperation
repression of thought, feeling, impulse	lack and removal of repression[24]

He observes that "the very split of agency from communion, which is a separation, arises from the agency feature itself." It thereby "represses the communion from which it has separated itself."[25]

Much like Hudson and Brown, he associates separations and boundaries with Apollo and Thanatos. He acknowledges that what he says about separations must also apply to the separation of the agentic and the communal. This proviso, and his contention that the villain is *unmitigated* agency, not agency as such, contrasts favorably with Brown. But slowly we realize that this agentic villain has no partner: for Bakan there is no such thing as unmitigated *communion*. Returning to his characterization of the communal, we see why. He attributes most good things, including what is worthwhile about the agentic, to his preferred alternative, "communion." Freud does much the same with Eros. We are so dishonest with our gods, Nietzsche complained: we do not even let them sin!

Given the resulting one-sided characterization of the respective "modalities," it is indeed hard to see why agency could represent anything but trouble for communion, nor why anyone would find it attractive or desirable. Communion has appropriated the more benign or desirable manifestations of agency. Communion has been purged of the less desirable features which, for good historical and sociological reasons, community has often been associated. Why, for example, is communion associated with lack and removal of repression? Bakan's is a special kind of community, with distinctly liberal qualities and practices. Since it has somehow incorporated certain agentic concerns at the very outset, it need not bother with a dialogue.

What we have is an interesting if one-sided critique of the agentic, and no critique at all of the communal. Bakan is correct in claiming that his conception of death and life is essentially an interpretation of Freud's view. The death instinct has become "agency" and its egoistic derivatives, and Eros or life has become communion. The very split between the two, he recognizes, is itself agentic. But he can't decide whether the effect of the communal is to destroy the split, through fusion, or to overcome it through a higher union. In this he follows Freud all too well. This is reflected in his inability or unwillingness to abstract and isolate a purely "communal" pole which does not already contain strong elements of the agentic. The result is that he loses sight of his original insight: it is the *relation* and *interaction* of the poles which is critical. This is what determines whether life or death, in the larger sense, are served.

There is one formulation of the life and death problem that addresses the difficulties in each of these three approaches, and which manages to synthesize much of what is valuable in each. It is contributed by Otto Rank.[26] While he makes an important case for representing life as division and individuation, his more important contribution is to concentrate on the dialectical relationship of life and death. Rank poses the death problem in terms of fear, not instinct. He points out, much as Hudson does, that even if there were death instincts we could only know them through their psychic representations. If we look simply at the emotional side of the question of death and life, what strikes the eye is fear. Irrespective of the existence of the death instinct, the indubitable *psychological* fact of death, as it manifests itself in human consciousness, is fear.

But death is not all we fear. "The child experiences his first feeling of fear in the act of birth—not fear of death, but fear of life." This inner fear, experienced in the birth process or brought along with it, already contains within it two aspects, the fear of life and the fear of death, "since birth on the one hand means the end of life (former, womb-life) and on the other carries also the fear of the new life."[27]

> The fear in birth, seems to me actually the fear of having to live as an isolated individual, and not the reverse, the fear of loss of individuality (death fear). This means that the primary fear corresponds to a fear of separation from the whole, i.e., a fear of individuation. On account of this I call it the fear of life, although it may appear later as fear of the loss of this dearly bought individuality, as fear of death, of being dissolved in the whole. Between these two fear possibilities, these poles of fear, the individual is thrown back and forth all his life.[28]

Rank's dialectical twosome is illustrated by the behavior of neurotics, who suffer simultaneously from the fear of going forward and the fear of going backward. The neurotic does not repeat his rituals nor does he suffer for the sheer fun of it, as an early version of Freudian instinct theory would have it. Nor does he thereby reveal the existence of the death instinct, as Freud concluded. He behaves this way

> because he must bribe life itself; for which, according to Schopenhauer's deep insight, we all pay with death . . . . [H]e does this through a constant restriction of life . . . . [H]e refuses the loan (life) in order to escape payment of the debt (death) . . . . [H]is self-punishment tendency has not so much the intention of granting him life as of escaping death, from which he seeks to buy himself free by daily partial self-destruction . . . . [I]t seems certain that the neurotic is that type which aims primarily not at pleasure gain but at the reduction of fear.[29]

The neurotic is therefore a failure at life, though Rank points out that this may be more of an indictment of life than of the neurotic. For life "demands partialization, without wanting to preserve or give out one's whole ego undivided in every experience." It is the familiar, profound problem of the part and whole.

One obstacle to partialization, in addition to the close ambivalence itself, is the de-stabilizing effect of human emotions. Emotions are total or totalizing by their very nature. They threaten to plunge the ego into a non-reflective and dedifferentiated state which conjures up death, even as it also symbolizes life at its fullest. The total is ultimately felt as the final, at least from the point of view of the differentiated conscious, the observing ego. Finality means death. For neurotics, life is a continuous crisis in which every situation, every decision, every attempt to move, is invested, polluted, infested with cosmic significance. The part is equated with the whole, rather than standing in symbolically for it. In this "symbolic" poverty, the neurotic resembles the schizophrenic, though the latter has such carried literal-mindedness to an ultimate disastrous extreme.

Symbolism is the coin of the unconscious realm, so that this amounts to saying that the neurotic and the schizophrenic suffer from an impaired relationship between the unconscious and the conscious faculties. This impaired capacity for partialization—this peculiar disease of the infinite, to borrow and stretch Durkheim's notion—means that the neurotic cannot give himself because he cannot parcel himself out.

> The neurotic type . . . makes the reality surrounding him a part of his ego, which explains his painful relation to it . . . . [T]he act of putting out, which the artist perceives rightly, not only as a birth but also as a dying, the neurotic can bring to pass in no way.[30]

As for the therapeutic implications: what will *not* work is Freudian psychoanalysis, since the morality underlying this therapy is "the Jewish-Christian morality which seeks to conserve." By contrast, the aim of Rank's will therapy is self-realization, "becoming that which we are." Its endeavors to help the patient realize and accept all his ambivalences. In this, as in much else, he echoes Nietzsche.

Where does all this leave Freud's life and death instincts? "The theme of fear," he asserts

> is so intimately connected with death . . . that all [other] fear theories seem to be scientifically rationalized attempts to deny the fear of death . . . [I]f the death instinct . . . is to be understood only as the expression of the physical principle of entropy . . . then this is too far-fetched as an explanation of psychic phenomena to mean anything for individual psychology. But even with the assumption that there is in nature such a striving after a condition of rest, and even if it is manifested biologically as death impulse, still psychologically only the attitude of the individual toward this fact would be of interest.[31]

Freud sought to give the death instinct a new meaning, Rank contends, in harmony with wish. Accordingly we stress instinct, rather than fear: "as if man is purely instinctual, and fear were brought in from the outside."

What distinguishes Rank's view of the "death problem" is his treatment of the dialectical relatingship between differentiation and dedifferentiation. Rank associates individuation and differentiation with life. The fear of life tends to arrest this process, rigidly fortifying our boundaries and differences, producing the pathologies Hudson associates with the death wish and Freud with the death instinct. These are among the human, psychological ingredients of alienation, I shall argue. The fear of death, the reaction of the conscious faculties to the prospect of dissolution and fusion, may result in boundary dissolutions, fragmentation, and chaos: these are among the psychological dimensions of anomie. The part-whole problem of individuation offers a fresh outlook on the division of labor, those anomic maladies Durkheim referred to as "diseases of the infinite," and their counterpart, diseases of the finite, or alienation.

From this kaleidoscopic array of views of life and death we have extracted two most primitive and promising modes of thought and being. Not only is it possible to characterize life in terms of either differentiation or dedifferentiation (individuation or fusion, and so on) it seems almost equally appropriate to do so. Of course we are tempted to settle on one or the other, or destroy the dualism, quell the disorder, and dispel such a basic confusion. We have seen that many authors yield. Or we could follow the advice of William James: when faced with a contradiction, make a distinction.[32] But one of the central features of the creative process is the temporary freedom from the compulsion to choose, to escape the contradiction and the ambivalence which is inseparable from it. For the moment, then, let us choose to not choose.

7

Life and Death, Differentiated and Dedifferentiated

What locks itself in endurance
grows rigid; sheltered
in unassuming grayness, does it
feel safe?
Wait, from the distance hardness is
menaced by something still
harder
Alas — : a remote hammer is poised
to strike.

Rilke

This chapter explores the psychology and symbolism of life and death, paving the way for the subsequent consideration of the unrepressed unconscious as the dedifferentiating mode of thought and being, and the conscious as the differentiating mode. We eventually rendezvous with the contention that human ambivalence can be expressed in terms of these modes, and that alienation and anomie, on the individual level, amount to two fundamental ways of attempting to escape this primal ambivalence.

Dirt, Spiders, Slime

Oscar Wilde once remarked that man was made for something better than disturbing dirt. The context of the quip was a discussion of socialism, but he was trying to convey something more than the fact that janitorial jobs are incompatible with human dignity. Dirt was created by the ordering, differentiating faculties of the mind. It symbolizes disorder, the inevitable by-product of the excessive concern with order.

Mary Douglas has written an entire book about dirt.[1] She argues that a meditation on dirt may tell us a great deal about disorder and order, formlessness and form, the boundless and the bounded. Our difficulty in focusing on dirt, or similar symbols such as slime or snakes or spiders, is itself instructive. We tend to react to the "distorting apparatus" as though our personal equilibrium, our own boundaries were being assaulted. Certain kinds of abstract art melt or challenge boundaries in the same way.[2] The viewer may well be absorbed. Psychoanalysis is dedicated to challenging outmoded defences and false boundaries, and is often treated as though it will take your arm if you give it your hand. One man's disorder may well be another's order, but no one need be smug. The other man is vulnerable to other kinds of disorder, other symbols of the difficult-to-categorize, the assault on distinctions and categories. Of course it would be a mistake to take our exaggerated disgust with dirt entirely at face value, especially when it is so great that it prevents us from cleaning ourselves.

Dirt is simply matter out of place: a "by-product of a systematic ordering and classification of matter." Dirt symbolizes that which refuses to fit neatly and securely into the categories that count for us. Its less differentiated quality suggests the entropic decline and possible collapse of the structure and shape of our experience, the reduction of everything previously distinct and individuated to a homogeneous pile. To dirt thou returneth. Nothing matches the disgust and fright such symbols inspire, unless it is our affinity for dirt and disorder. Pigs wallowing in the mud are fastidious amateurs by comparison with many of us. Nothing equals our effort to differentiate ourselves and flee from others and the natural world unless it is our impulse to fuse with both. Life runs in currents clean and dirty, as our minds do.

Dirt triggers "pollution behavior," the sometimes desperate defense of the purity, integrity, and chastity of our categories. This can take various forms. One defense against the ambiguous and the anomalous is to ignore them. Another is to remove or destroy the offending phenomenon. Douglas cites the infamous case of the night-crowing cocks who, if their necks are promptly wrung, do not live to contradict the Neuer tribe's definition of a cock: a bird that crows at dawn. Our forefathers gave suspected witches the choice between dying as a self-confessed witch or dying in such a way as to confirm everyone's suspicions. Until recently the disturbing anomaly of talented, intelligent blacks was dealt with by denying them the education and opportunities whereby they could make their abilities obvious and incontestable. If this failed, more drastic measures awaited uppity niggers. Unmistakably superior blacks were credited with having "white blood," that very special juice.

Other methods are more humane and sophisticated. Behavior may be modified in various noncoercive ways. Durable conceptual systems have room for certain acceptable exceptions, which in turn lend support to the total system composed of both rules and exceptions. The alternation of controls and releases from controls often serves the controls. Workers who claim they are satisfied with their lot are seen as victims and purveyors of false consciousness: exceptions and objections to Marxism are part and parcel of the theory itself. There are Catholic, liberal, sociological, born-again Christian, and psychoanalytic analogues of this system-saving, order-preserving device. Or an army of psychiatrists, parole officers, welfare workers, counselors, and group therapists may be enlisted in the effort to convince you that no sane person would think and behave as you do. The good citizen, the good soldier, must be fully armed not only against the enemy but against the ultimate enemy: doubt concerning who the real enemy is. As a last resort, or in cases in which the talking cure is impractical, more muscle and less sophistication may be required, as the case of night-crowing cocks reminds us. Or take the spider, that ancient innocent victim of the poverty-stricken categorical system of Leviticus. Douglas argues there was no conceptual niche for crawling insects, much less eight-legged crawlers. To this day we blame them for every untraceable bite and skin eruption. Witches and individualists, two categories traditionally associated with one another, are the social equivalents of animal anomalies like beetles and spiders.

In the final analysis the quest for purity is stalked by failure. The threat comes from within as well as without. "When purity is not a symbol but something lived it must be poor and barren."[3] Success in this enterprise resembles failure. It is peculiarly empty, since little internal dissension and difference can be tolerated once the personality becomes an armed camp. Rigid ideas (self-concepts and the like) disallow life's traffic across conceptual boundaries. Nor can we afford to differentiate our enemies with much care. "Unquestionably, the yearning for rigidity is in us all," Douglas contends. "It is part of our human condition to long for hard lines and clear concepts."[4] On the other hand, it is also impossible to discuss these matters of dirt and differentiation "except in the light of men's common urge to make a unity of all their experience and to overcome distinctions and separations in acts of at-one-ment."[5]

These themes can be further refined in connection with Sartre's celebrated "psychoanalysis of things," particularly his account of the "great ontological region of sliminess."[6] Sartre contends that things and qualities can be taken as "objective symbols" of being. What mode of being does slime symbolize?

> [the slimy] represents in itself a dawning triumph of the solid over the liquid—that is, a tendency of the indifferent in-itself, which is represented by the pure solid, to fix the liquidity, to absorb the for-itself which ought to dissolve it.[7]

Sartre's slime is Douglas's dirt, rendered even more sinister and treacherous. The problem is that Sartre's metaphysical commitments and personal preferences produce a decidedly one-sided view of slime. Granted, the slimy may suggest the dawning triumph of the solid over the liquid. Granted, this makes it frightening and disgusting. Does it not also suggest the dawning triumph of the liquid over the solid? At the end of *that* road is a formless swamp, dark and murky, constantly changing, alive with life and death, in which things scarcely distinguish themselves before being sucked under, dissolved, merged. It is dangerous: that knotty log may prove to be an alligator.

"Slime is the agony of water," Sartre asserts. But slime is also the agony of solids. It reminds us that the world cannot be trusted to keep the well-defined shape our categories and cognitive maps attempt to impose. Sartre admits that slime has an ambiguous character as a "substance in between two states," but he does not acknowledge that it can be on its way to either. More importantly, his existential psychoanalysis inhibits us from recognizing that *we* pull it in these opposite directions, attribute to it opposite qualities and modes of being. The psychoanalytic bugbears banned by Sartrean (or Cartesian) lucidity might well have helped him produce an account of the ambiguous object which does more justice to the ambivalence of the subject.

Next he attempts to appropriate the slime (he does not explain why). By a "curious reversal," it comes to possess him. Presumably this means that something we *are* allows or welcomes it; who is seizing whom is unclear, or it should be. Maybe the desire to appropriate coexists with the desire to be appropriated. "Its softness is leech-like," he observes, not observing that it was he who grabbed first.

> In one sense it is like the supreme docility of the possessed, the fidelity of a dog who gives himself even when one does not want him any longer, and in another sense there is underneath this docility a surreptitious appropriation of the possessor by the possessed.[8]

This leech-like view of slime suggests a common masculine fantasy of feminine treachery: the cunning, dastardly exercise of strength by means of weakness, getting one's way by being agreeable, pliable, seductive. (The dog also catches it from both directions for similar reasons. It is man's best friend, but it is also a dirty dog, an animal no human should be treated like.) This view of slime also suggests that "symbiotic omnipotence" some psychoanalysts have experienced at the hands of some of their patients: the use of extreme dependence and passivity to gain control of the analytic situation. Sartre is equally fearful he will lose control of his analysis, perhaps by losing it to psychoanalysis. He thinks of slime as a treacherous Tar-baby. Like Brer Rabbit, we grab at it and find ourselves stuck. The more we grab, the more we're stuck. This should be contrasted with a view of slime which conjures up dissolution, chaos, deindividuation, confusion, getting lost: without firm footing or reliable guides.

"There is a possibility that the in-itself might absorb the for-itself. . . . Slime is the revenge of the in-itself."[8] Sartre may be confusing observation with creation, as if slime were taking revenge on his own analysis, by obliterating this important distinction. Slime might also suggest the revenge of the for-itself, something solid on the way to liquidity, leaving fusion and confusion in its wake. Indeed, without adequately acknowledging it is so, he also fears this sort of revenge.

> If I sink into the slimy, I feel that I am going to be lost in it; that is, that I may dissolve in the slime precisely because the slimy is in the process of solidification.[9]

Images of sinking and getting lost suggest a fear of formlessness rather than of rigid form. To be lost is not to be trapped or stuck, even though the consequences for life may ultimately be the same. But then he abruptly returns to the notion of slime on its way to solidification. Why we may dissolve "precisely because" slime is in the process of solidifying is anyone's guess: we may be trapped and stuck but left intact, like mastodons in tar pits or mummies in tombs. The mummy's problem is not that it is lost.

Sartre also admits that slime suggests a "certain permanent possibility" which solid and well-defined substances possess, that of transforming themselves into a "homogeneous, undifferentiated fluidity." But again, when he does inject this opposite view he does not notice or note the fact. The significant difference between these two views of this "ontological region" is obscured: fears of arrested differentiation and rigidity on the one hand and excessive dedifferentiation and chaos on the other: being trapped, immobilized, frozen, mummified, petrified, stuck versus being engulfed, dissolved, confused, lost. The two conceptions of death appear to be diametrically opposed.

In *Nausea,* however, the analysis is entirely reversed. His protagonist Roquentin experiences a whole world gone slimy. Slime is form on its way to formlessness. "Things are divorced from their names," he complains:

> They are there, grotesque, headstrong, gigantic, and it seems ridiculous to call them seats or say anything at all about them. I am in the midst of things, nameless things.[10]

Roquentin has lost his control over his categories. A radical democracy of disorder has been restored:

> The diversity of things, their individuality, were only an appearance, a veneer. This veneer had melted, leaving soft, monstrous masses, all in disorder—naked, in a frightful, obscene nakedness.... [A]ll these objects... how can I explain? They inconvenienced me; I would have liked them to exist less strongly, more dryly, in a more abstract way.... [I]n the way: it was the only relationship I could establish between these trees, these gates, these stones. I tried in vain to count the chestnut trees, to locate them... to compare their height with the height of the plane tree; each of them escaped the relationship in which I tried to enclose it, isolated itself, and overflowed. Of these relations (which I insisted on maintaining in order to delay the crumbling of the human world, measures, quantities, and directions)—I felt myself to be the arbitrator: but they no longer had their teeth in things. And I—soft, weak, obscene, digesting, jiggling with dismal thoughts—I, too, was in the way.[11]

His every distinction is in the way of this surging, oozing tide of formlessness. Behind the labels, it seems, there were no things-in-themselves. His desperate attempts to contain the flow are increasingly arbitrary, ineffective, and counterproductive: further desperate attempts to establish differences merely hasten the decline of difference itself. In pace with his mind, his body becomes increasingly feminine, weak, mortal, dependent, vulnerable: "jiggling and digesting." The abdomen, Nietzsche pointed out, is why we do not readily mistake ourselves for gods.

What is obscene to Roquentin is the degeneration into formlessness. What is disturbing to Sartre in his philosophical treatment of slime is the movement toward solidification and rigidity. Far from being stuck with his person, habits, conceptions, identity, Roquentin finds himself and his distinctions increasingly incapable of containing and restraining the world, holding the oceanic flux at bay. Whereas Douglas asks us to reflect on dirt as a symbol of disorder, Roquentin experiences the real thing, a world gone dirty, slimy. And while Sartre the philosopher may romanticize such states, Sartre the man, Roquentin, is terrified and disgusted.

It might be hoped that this massive insecurity would be quelled in the last resort by the senses, and the common sensical world view they support. But even the senses are no longer reliable: "this black root . . . this black, amorphous, presence, far surpassed sight, smell and taste."[12] Finally, "this richness was lost in confusion and was no more because it was too much." So ends the manic exhilaration in losing one's conceptual blinders: the intoxicating realization that nothing we have created, formed, or distinguished, neither in politics, religion, society nor art is really necessary or fixed. Henceforth everything is possible, movable, fluid. Anything could be anything else, but none of it comes to anything.

Roquentin's crisis ends on a note of great interest:

> Had I dreamed of this enormous presence? It was there, in the garden, toppled down into the trees, all soft, sticky, soiling everything, all thick, a jelly . . . . [I] was frightened, furious, I thought it was so stupid, so out of place, I hated this ignoble mess. Mounting up, mounting up as high as the sky, spilling over, filling everything with its gelatinous slither . . . . [I] shouted "filth! what rotten filth," but it held fast and there was so much, tons and tons of existence.[13]

Filth is also matter out of place. *Nausea* gives us a moving account of the emotional and cognitive experience of a world gone filthy and formless, and the ambivalence of our responses. Once all matter is out of place, our attempt to hold our ground, to maintain our boundaries and differences, seems arbitrary and futile. Like the spider, or the night-crowing cock, we too are in the way.

But then we also complain about being stuck, and worry lest life will dry up and trap and make living mummies of us. The Sartre of *Being and Nothingness* certainly does. (The novel hints that this horrific experience helps restore Roquentin's ability to write.) Why should we not revel in being swept away by the tide? Sartre's opposed accounts of slime need to be introduced to one another, just as Durkheim's anomie and Marx's alienation must be juxtaposed and simultaneously confronted. We must begin by attending more carefully to the fact that we are not just talking about slime.

Double Death, Double Life

We have seen that those who entertain the notion of death as rigidity, control, boundary defense—as being trapped or stuck—often err by associating the qualities of rigidity and the like with differentiation as such. As Rank reminds us, differentiation is crucial to life, movement, growth. *Arresting* the process of differentiation produces rigidity and the obsession with control and boundaries. This cuts the ties, disrupts the flow of traffic and nourishment from other people, concepts, aspects of the self. That unreal separation represents the "awesome power of the negative," Hegel said. It is Death, Death proper, utterly opposed to Life. It might be labeled Masculine Death. But to equate Death with differentiation (form, difference, individuation) is to confuse the phenomenon with its extreme, the process with the perversion. Differentiation as such can certainly be regarded as life.

If we do so, then dedifferentiation represents death, the death that is part of and essential to Life, or what Simmel calls Total Life. Total Life is that all inclusive conception which symbolizes the union of life and death, the synthesis of this basic opposition. It is Death proper which presents obstacles to the harmonious relation between life and death. Thus dedifferentiation, while seemingly in conflict with differentiation, nevertheless prevents differentiation from becoming Masculine Death: rigid form, impermeable boundaries, and the like. It sustains the life process of progressive differentiation and individuation by maintaining flexible boundaries and relations with neighboring things, persons, concepts.

To conceive of difference in the absence of making similar or equal is to imagine a kind of absolute zero of frozen, lifeless form. Differentiation as life thus appears both in opposition to dedifferentiation as death, and inconceivable or perversely arrested without it. Simmel's Total Life symbolizes the overcoming as well as preservation of the difference between life (as differentiation) and death (as dedifferentiation).[14]

But the labels can easily be reversed: that is, dedifferentiation can also be viewed as life. The undifferentiated not only symbolizes death, but also life and birth, as the comparative study of myth, ritual, rites, and symbols conclusively documents.[15] Life is not only a matter of differentiation and form; it can also be viewed as a Dionysian whirl or Heraclitean flux wherein everything is well on its way to being something else again, and self-identical things are fading illusions born of conscious faculties incapable of functioning except by means of perceptual and conceptual snapshots. In this light differentiation and form are seen as deathlike, though essential to and part of Life. To be captured or carried away by emotion, with the dedifferentiation this involves, is properly associated with living life to its fullest. And yet in the extreme this too is a kind of Death. Life as dedifferentiation miscarries without the support of death as differentiation. The conclusion is that Life (Total Life) is the synthesis of differentiation and dedifferentiation, dividing and making equal, irrespective of which is considered death and life.

There is a quicker route to the same proposition. When we differentiate anything from anything else, we suppress divisions within the boundaries we set down and within whatever is designated as external to these boundaries. What is newly differentiated must manage to be equal to itself, however rich the divisions we later see or posit. By the same token, to equate something to itself is to differentiate it from everything else: to establish equality is to establish difference. This makes obvious our inability to definitively associate life or death with differentiation or dedifferentiation, dividing or equalizing, since either of the poles clearly contains, implies, and relies upon its opposite.[16] Thus the futility and inadvisability of rigidly associated life or death with one or the other.

By analogy to Life, then, there is Death, Death proper. It has two forms, Masculine and Feminine. Neither should be confused with the benign version of death which is the necessary complement of life. Both life and death are partners in Life, even though they conflict. The conflict itself may be an illusion born of the dividing mode. Death proper stems from the exaggeration of one of the modes: dedifferentiation or differentiation, fusing or dividing, irrespective of which of the two we associate with life. This is equivalent to an imbalanced relation between the two modes.[17]

These distinctions are also helpful in sorting out the ambiguities involved in Freud's idea of Eros, and the use subsequent authors have made of it. Consider the association of Eros and the pleasure-seeking impulses with the violation and dissolution of boundaries, and the destructive drives with the defense of boundaries personal and conceptual (Hudson, Bakan, Brown). Boundary crossing can be aggressive, violating personality or property rights. To be sure, we often profess love and compassion for such victims; this probably helps explain why they are victims. Conversely, to automatically associate destruction with differentiation (the "agentic") is untenable, as we have said.

The underlying error here is the conflation of life with Total Life: hence we have (as in Bakan) the confusion of "binding together" (or union, synthesis) with fusion and dedifferentiation (i.e., boundary dissolution). Freud's Eros and Bakan's "communion" combine and confuse the idea of fusion with the idea of incorporation and transcending of opposites. "Communion" seems to have *already* absorbed much of the agentic, yet it is supposed to be its opposite. In this way Bakan's agentic becomes practically the root of all evil.

These and other formulations also confuse death and Death, and the failure to see that Death proper has two variants. Given that these maladies (rigidity and chaos, and so on) are indistinguishable in the limit, probably just different ways of viewing what is ultimately one malady, this confusion is both understandable and significant. But Freud contributes some confusion of his own, with his own ambivalence as to whether a genuine union or synthesis of life and death instincts is possible. His official position was a species of diehard dualism. Yet he repeatedly spoke of Eros in terms of binding together. This tempts us to interpret Eros as (Total) Life. But Freud claimed to believe in no such overcoming of opposites, accommodating ambivalence without harshly repressing either side of it. In his famous scenario, aggressive impulses would continue more or less unabated while Eros did its good work in preventing external aggression. Our sense of guilt would grow in proportion to the repression of aggression.

A final argument appears to tip the balance in favor of designating differentiation as life. It is offered by the distinguished physicist, Erwin Schrödinger.[18] Life, he argues, is differentiation, by which he understands the process of reproduction and development of differentiated organisms. Physical laws are actually dependent on atomic statistics, and therefore can only be approximate. If atoms were not so incredibly small and numerous, then these approximations would be correspondingly crude, so that the lawfulness and orderliness of the human *Umwelt* might collapse or be severely compromised.

There is a striking, life-saving, and life-extending exception to the rule that orderly behavior can only be based ultimately on statistical regularities involving billions of atoms. This is the gene, which has at most a few million. The gene is not only the carrier of part of the code or blueprint for the organism's development, it is an active participant in that development. And the gene, the ultimate carrier of differentiation, is for all practical purposes permanent, passed along unchanged for centuries.

The laws of physics depict the movement from low entropy to high, from relative orderliness to relative disorder. The concept of entropy was of course one of Freud's inspirations for the death instinct. The one basic exception to the seemingly universal law of increasing entropy is precisely life itself, which establishes an ever more complex order through a never-ceasing process of differentiation of functions followed by integration, on a higher level, of what has been differentiated. For a while, life does successful battle with the entropic processes of decay, disintegration, dissolution.

Life seems to be orderly and lawful behavior of matter, not based exclusively on its tendency to go over from order to disorder, but based partly on existing order that is kept up.[19]

Schrödinger's argument bolsters the case for symbolizing life as differentiation, and death as dedifferentiation, the entropic process. The very genetic mechanisms which differentiate us and put and guide us on a path of individuated development are those which generate order in the very teeth of disorder, in the face of the apparently universal tendency for entropic disorder to increase. Entropy, increasing disorganization, and formlessness powerfully suggest and symbolize death. At least for purposes of reference and exposition, it makes sense to see life and death in these terms.

There may not be a death instinct as such: in evolutionary terms it is hard to account for. Nor does the process of increasing entropy necessarily have psychic representatives. (Dedifferentiation certainly *symbolizes* entropy, but this is another matter.) But this by no means implies the absence of powerful symbolic representations of life and death, whose psychological salience is of first importance. The most potent of these cluster about the concepts of differentiation and dedifferentiation. This potency is entirely appropriate, since the argument we have begun to develop here is closely akin to what Nietzsche attempted to do with the idea of will to power.

Perhaps, to paraphrase Shakespeare, there is little about life and death that thinking it so doesn't make it so. To be sure, whatever an individual associates with life or death tells us something of life-and-death importance about himself, and possibly the whole human race. But we mustn't take his word at face value, no more than the words of various theorists of life and death we have encountered. For it does make a difference whether we fuse and confuse life and death, or rigidly segregate them, or affirm both as complementary expressions of that higher unity we can neither achieve nor abandon the attempt to do so. The difference is Life, and Life makes all the difference.

8

The Undifferentiated Unconscious

What man performs unconsciously costs him no effort, and no effort can provide a substitute for it.

Schopenhauer

> You are aware of only one unrest;
> Oh, never learn to know the other!
> Two souls, alas, are dwelling in my
> breast,
> And one is striving to forsake its
> brother.

Goethe

There is as much difference between us and ourselves as between us and others.

Montaigne

Freud's fundamental discovery is not that of the unconscious . . . but that of a world—which he unfortunately called the unconscious—ruled by entirely different laws from those governing conscious thinking . . . [H]e was the first to make the fundamental discovery of this strange "Realm of the Illogical," that it submitted, in spite of being illogical, to precise laws which he found, in an extraordinary stroke of genius.

Ignacio Matte Blanco

The Structure of Unconscious Cognition

The preceding argument could have been couched in terms of conscious and unconscious faculties and structures, but the unorthodox view of the unconscious which is involved deserves a more detailed view. Our inspiration is derived from Freud's own tentative development of the undifferentiated unconscious. The notion that there are two radically different kinds of mental processes, the primary process and the secondary, is among Freud's fundamental contributions.[1] Freud shared this high estimation of the discovery of the primary process. Yet he made little progress on the subject after his *Interpretation of Dreams* (1898) and his 1915 essay on the unconscious. As Silvano Arieti observes, Freud "did not explore the primary process as a mode of cognition." The defining feature Freud attributed to primary process thinking, its "free cathexis," ignores or obscures the cognitive side. If rules of unconscious mentation exist, they must be formulated in terms of systematic violations of ordinary logic, given the dedifferentiated quality of unconscious thought. Freud had no great confidence in this enterprise, judging by the surprise he expressed once he stumbled upon the elements of unconscious logic.

Nevertheless, a small but hardy band of psychologists have sought to build upon Freud's characterization of unconscious thought. Silvano Arieti calls his version of the rules of unconscious mentation *paleologic,* a mode of thought which supposedly precedes Aristotelian logic both ontogenetically and phylogenetically.[2] While ordinary logic accepts identity on the basis of identical subjects, paleologic accepts identity or equates things on the basis of identical predicates: that is, on the basis of some quality or characteristic which they share. This amounts to making equal (or identical, if paleologic is viewed from within) what is merely similar to conscious thought. Moreover, there is little that cannot be viewed as similar, especially by an agile mind driven by compelling needs. Arieti offers the memorable example of the schizophrenic patient who, noting that she is a virgin, and that the Virgin Mary was too, concluded that she is the Virgin Mary.

Everyone employs paleologic, and there are strong reasons for believing it is indispensable to our mental well-being as well as our capacity for creativity. The unconscious constantly creates new identities of those objects and concepts considered different by the conscious, differentiating mode, anchored in culturally derived categories, language, the logic of given social forms, and logic itself. The difference between the healthy and the disturbed mind in this respect is that those who are disturbed allow conscious thought to be flooded by these unconscious equations, illogical and bizarre to differentiated thought, under the pressure of great needs and anxieties. The healthy non-schizophrenic makes such unwarranted equations as well, although traces of their transgressions on a conscious level may be indirect, relatively trivial and short-lived. And there are many other ways for such needs to intrude. "Emotional" or "experiential" thinking, which seeks to evade or avoid the dictates and limitations of logic in order to provide more "space" and satisfaction, is by no means limited to the pathologically disordered mind, nor to obvious, frontal assaults on logic. In effect the disturbed patient tries to create a new concept and fails. "The paleological thinker wants to transcend the particular, but his attempts lead him not to platonic universals but to transmutability."[3] The paleological syllogism never results in a new concept. Each subject (I, Virgin Mary) of the terms of the syllogism ("I am a virgin"; "Virgin Mary was a virgin") remains within the original concept of virginity. The conclusion must as well.

Again, this does not mean that the healthy psyche avoids paleological reasoning altogether. *Simultaneous* employment of the differentiated and dedifferentiated faculties, logic and paleologic, is of the essence of creativity, as well as the proper functioning of conscious thought in general. If the inundation of the conscious faculties is one pathological extreme, and the doomed effort to segregate the two entirely is the other, then there must also be various degrees of mutual interaction in which both modes conflict with, complement, or enter into various kinds of liasons. Overcoming this fundamental distinction between the conscious and unconscious, differentiated and undifferentiated modes, is tantamount to Simmel's notion of Total Life. The two basic ways of failing, two kinds of imbalance between conscious and unconscious, are Masculine and Feminine forms of Death. These will emerge, in due course, as alienation and anomie.

Dedifferentiation and the Hidden Order

Anton Ehrenzweig puts forward a model of the unconscious which focuses squarely on its dedifferentiating aspect.[4] Much like Arieti, he contends that the unconscious can be characterized more economically and meaningfully in terms of its less differentiated *structure* than by whatever *contents,* repressed, archaic, instinctual, it may have. Speaking of images, he argues that they are withdrawn from consciousness not merely because of the superego's censorship of certain offensive contents; they may become inaccessible through their undifferentiated structure alone.[5]

Ehrenzweig relies heavily on the idea of unconscious scanning, a process which supposedly involves less differentiated and more economical modes of vision and cognition. He sees the undifferentiated unconscious as crucial to normal thought processes, problem–solving, and creativity in all fields.

In the solution of the complex tasks the undifferentiation of unconscious vision turns into an instrument of rigorous precision . . . [U]nconscious scanning makes use of undifferentiated modes of vision that to normal awareness would seem chaotic. . . . [T]he primary process is a precision instrument for creative scanning that is far superior to discursive reason and logic . . . [T]he broadening of focus in undifferentiation brings about enormous increase in the efficiency of scanning.[6]

His "hidden order" is the less differentiated (even Gestalt-free) vision and scanning and sorting processes of the unconscious. He resembles Arieti in disengaging the unconscious from its previous identification with the repressed. The less differentiated mode is not chaos, not even at its least differentiated levels. It is likely that we are constantly cycling from higher to lower levels and back, or in some sense exist at all levels at once. It is seen and experienced as chaotic when it impinges on "pathologically rigid, dissociated surface functions." Those who maintain rigid, impermeable boundaries about themselves, their picture of themselves, others, the world, experience the onslaught or upsurge of dedifferentiated thought or imagery as the threat of death, as Sartre's masterful portrait of *nausée* reminds us.

Ehrenzweig buttresses his otherwise skimpy model with numerous vivid examples involving dedifferentiated vision and scanning. Gifted painters are capable of suppressing the distinction between figure and ground, he points out, sometimes to the point of being able to paint "on both sides of the brush." This basic spatial distinction is one which the gifted or lucky artist is somehow able to diminish or avoid. There is also the "uncompromising democracy" of artistic vision, the refusal to be intimidated or seduced by conscious distinctions and choices among the elements constituting the work of art. This "belongs to the essence of artistic rigour." Discipline, and what appears to be the lack of discipline, come together. As Freud recognized, the analogy with the peculiar discipline of the analytic session is close, especially in the case of poetic creativity. As in free association, the usual evaluation of details and elements is reversed. Both processes seek the suspension of conscious control. Somehow this controlled suspension of control, this disciplined rejection of discipline, this choice to suspend choosing, favors greater control over the final product. Apparent opposites, control and the release from control, come together in a rigorous, disciplined spontaneity which can only be expressed in contradictory and paradoxical language. This radical democratization of images and thoughts is capable of producing new and unique equations, as well as nonsense. The suspension or diminution of differentiations may lead to a new and sometimes superior order of distinctions. We conquer our obsession with choosing in order to make better choices. We dissolve present distinctions and forms in order to produce better, more lively, more inclusive, more effective concepts. We employ means suggestive of death in the service of life. We affirm that both death and life are integral to Life.

The creative search poses a set of difficulties for which conscious faculties are ill-suited. We must achieve a comprehensive overview of the many possibilities, without so much detail and so many sharp distinctions (quick fixes, premature closures) as to entangle, arrest and bog us down. This must be done in a radically egalitarian fashion. Every possible avenue, including those that consciousness and the categories of the day and place find distasteful or inconsequential, must be taken seriously—indiscriminately, in a sense. We are denied access to many solutions to puzzles and problems not because we are incapable of thinking of the solution, but we are impaled upon rigid distinctions we cannot think our way past, preferred approaches that we cannot abandon. We cannot look aside. How this comprehensive overview or scanning process works Ehrenzweig cannot say. It is doubtful whether creativity could be creativity if we knew very much about it. But the pairing of the seemingly dissimilar, the differentiation of new similarities, the resultant creation of new concepts and new perspectives on things, cannot be random. An infinity of possibilities lead nowhere, or in the wrong direction. We could never account in this way for the inventiveness, ingenuity, and creativity we daily observe and exhibit, not to mention the extraordinary and repeated achievements of genius.

Wittgenstein was concerned with the same mystery in connection with the use of language, and stressed the necessity of the same sort of overview. With reference to language acquisition, its creative use, and the problem of anticipating future usage of concepts, he pondered the fact that the child must master words long before he has an inkling of the full range of their proper future applications. This extraordinary ability is a part of every normal child's developmental capabilities. Once latency sets in, the child gobbles up new words and exhibits a genuine passion for the abstract, for the genus, as Schopenhauer observed.

> We are capable of understanding a word "in a flash" though its precise meaning is not yet definable, but will emerge only through the whole subsequent use of the word.[7]

The key to explaining such abilities is that unconscious, dedifferenti-ated scanning can grasp numerous future usages of the word, numerous linguistic ties, more or less simultaneously.

Another striking example of this kind of faculty is provided by the architect. This is of special interest because Marx thought of the architect as the archetypical creative communist man. The architect must anticipate potential uses and problems that he or she has no way of visualizing at the design stage: the total function as distinguished from its more detailed uses. Appreciation for this ability can be gained by sitting down to try to design a minimally functional and aesthetic home. For most of us the result is a collection of conflicting features or rooms in search of a house. Ehrenzweig points out that makers of constitutions, lawgivers, and legislators are faced with analogous problems. The same kind of foresight is required in creating a complex work of art, reading several parts of a musical score at once, framing a complex analytic argument, creatively categorizing a situation or problem, and so on. Far from being an esoteric possession of a gifted few, in some measure this ability is essential even to normal mental functioning and mundane tasks. Anything requiring that we think more than one thought at a time must rely on a measure of dedifferentiation. And in a sense, everything does.

Further examples of less differentiated thought will be helpful in gaining familiarity with the idea and in assessing the degree or depth of unconscious dedifferentiation. One approach to the latter question relies on the presumed connection between the emotional impact of the situation or experience and the "depth" of it. The impact of a dream image is often inversely related to our ability to adequately visualize or conceptualize it in the conscious mode. Most of us have probably had the odd experience of futilely trying to recall and visualize a dream image which seemed particularly vivid, important, true at the time. Though we are prone to attribute our difficulty to a weak memory of the dream, often this is not the problem at all. Rather, the imagery was "too general" for consciousness to accommodate and assign specific meanings to.[8] The conscious faculties must break up and divide an image and idea which is holistic, indivisible. Once divided, it tends to be less meaningful, less powerful, but more precise. Its reach is reduced, and we are more informed than moved or enlightened. In addition to the emotional impact, then, another crude measure of depth is the degree of difficulty in conceptualizing and visualizing the material.

The psychological and anthropological literature on dreams, myths, rites, and symbols, yields a host of dedifferentiated thought–images. A particularly striking example is offered by Geza Roheim, in his arresting account of the dream process.[9] Roheim argues that the basic dream conflict between differentiated and undifferentiated space is at the basis of all creativity. He refers to a spatially undifferentiated "dream-womb" in which "the dreamer enters his own dream womb while at the same time he leaves this inner space through the 'gates' of the dream." Roheim's dreamer meets himself coming back through his own womb, whatever her sex. This would seem to be the ultimate in dedifferentiated images. Yet it retains some intelligibility because of the continued presence of differentiated elements, even though their very use is to try to deny difference. There is a certain logical (or psycho-logical) aspect to this illogical image, though its sense is difficult to fathom and articulate. Or rather: we may grasp or intuit its meaning, but to specify it is impossible.

Or consider the myth of the White Goddess, in which the divine child ultimately absorbs the creative powers of both parents. He incorporates the mother's womb. He bears, expels, and buries himself in one fell swoop: an oceanic image, Ehrenzweig dryly comments, "that can hardly be visualized in its extreme undifferentiation." In a similar category is the race of people conjured up by Balso Snell, the hero of Nathaniel West's first novel. They are the Phoenix Excrementi. Their practice was to eat themselves, digest themselves, and give birth to themselves by evacuating their bowels. Whenever Balso thought of them, West reports, he shuddered.

The crucial phase of Ehrenzweig's model of creativity has creative dedifferentiation tending towards a "manic" oceanic limit where all differentiation ceases. The deepest oceanic experiences dissolve space and time (and therefore motion and causality) the very categories which make conscious experience possible. At its deepest levels, dedifferentiation plays no favorites. This, too, is consistent with Freud's characterization of the primary process. The manic-oceanic experience of death and rebirth, Ehrenzweig argues, differs from pathological mania. The latter *denies* death by seeking control. It is the obsession with control which makes dedifferentiation chaotic. The essence of the uncreative, sterile mind is its attempt to control as a means of denying death and mortality. Clinging to differentiated faculties makes Feminine Death (chaos) of dedifferentiation. The ego clings to its embattled surface functions, is thereby impoverished and rendered vulnerable to eruptions beyond its control. It cannot use disorder in the service of order, formlessness in the service of form, death in the service of life. When death no longer serves life, or life no longer allows it to, it is Death.

The Unconscious and the Unbounded

Another renegade psychoanalyst offers a model of the unconscious which promises to reinstate the undifferentiated unconscious as the "true psychic reality." Ignacio Matte Blanco has labored long and lonely in the no man's land between psychoanalysis and logic. He has set for himself a unique and ambitious task: to employ the tools of symbolic logic in constructing a model of the unconscious and its relation to conscious systems.[10] He contends that psychoanalysis "has wandered away from itself." Freud's "greatest discovery," the basic characteristics and elements of logic of the system unconscious, has played "no role whatsoever" in the development of psychology, not even psychoanalysis.

Matte Blanco argues that Freud never really abandoned his original conception of the unconscious. Yet his subsequent tripartitioning of the psyche reduced the unconscious to a sad shadow of its former status. No longer was it a world, a way of being or thinking. It became a mere province of the mind, and spatial metaphors came to reign supreme.[11]

> Whereas the old unconscious was present everywhere as the true psychical reality, in Freud's three-fold conception the old unconscious ... came out rather damaged, compressed... and disinherited.[12]

All that province contained were instinctual forces pressing mindlessly for release. But Freud was gradually forced to make these sharp boundaries more flexible and permeable, edging back toward a conception of the unconscious as contending for the whole territory of the mind. He expressed regret over his tripartite conception, openly admitting his misgivings.

Matte Blanco argues that this structural or unrepressed unconscious is actually compatible with, but more general than, the threefold conception.[13] The problem is that the later formulation has severely inhibited the investigation of the unconscious as a mode of cognition and being. Psychoanalytic ego psychology, with its alleged conflict-free zones of the ego and its conflation of self and ego, presents another barrier to the adequate exploration of unconscious forces. The same is true of the chief rival to the threefold conception, the internal object relations approach of Melanie Klein and her students—a disguised version of the id–ego–superego model, Matte Blanco claims. With these emaciated models psychoanalysis has neglected its potentially most distinctive contribution to the understanding of man. It has "entered the field of psychology like a humble beggar, divested of what were its most precious treasures."[14]

Starting with the observed fact that the unconscious establishes an identity between the part and the whole, Matte Blanco was led to Dedekind's definition of an infinite set. An infinite set is the only case in mathematics and logic in which it is possible to show the equivalence of part and whole. That is, we can set up a univocal or one-to-one correspondence between the elements of a set and a proper subset of the set. (A proper subset does not include all the elements of the set, and is not the null set.) An example of the result that so stunned Dedekind is easily constructed. Take the set of all natural numbers, N equals 1, 2,..., and place them in one-to-one correspondence with 2 times N:

N   = 1, 2, 3, 4,   5,   6,   7,   8, ... and so on.
2N   = 2, 4, 6, 8, 10, 12, 14, 16, ... and so on.

The sequence generated by 2N is a proper subset of the sequence of natural numbers: every odd number is missing from it. On the other hand there exists a unique element in the sequence of natural numbers for every element in 2N, and conversely.[15]

In light of the part-whole equivalence the unconscious establishes, Matte Blanco was led to the idea that the unconscious acts *as though* it were dealing with infinite sets. His initial goal is to give an account of unconscious mentation in terms consistent with ordinary logic. If this requirement is imposed, we must assume the presence of infinite sets. Later on he shows that the observed characteristics of unconscious mentation can actually be generated by a single more powerful postulate, *symmetry*, which violates ordinary logic. Eventually even symmetry is jettisoned, once he attempts to describe the characteristics of unconscious "from within."

The first of the principles associated with the undifferentiated unconscious is the *Principle of Generalization*:

> The unconscious treats individual things or elements as if it were a member of a set or class with other members; it treats this class as a subclass of a more general class, and so on.[16]

In itself this does not imply violations of bi-valent logic. It merely indicates that unconscious mentation proceeds by embracing wider and wider sets, each one of which is infinite, and a proper subset of the next.

It is his second principle that overturns conscious logic. The *Principle of Symmetry* states that

> The unconscious treats the converse of any relation as true—i.e., treats *asymmetrical* relations as if they were *symmetrical*.[17]

A relation R defines, for all x and y, a relationship between x and y. An *asymmetrical* relation, call it B, is one in which the order of the variables x and y makes a difference in whether the relation is satisfied. Thus if B equals "x is the brother of y," and if a given pair (Paul, Mary) consists of siblings, then xBy satisfies B (Paul is the brother of Mary). But yBx does not (Mary is not the brother of Paul). However, if the relation S equals "x is the sibling of y," the relation is reversible, or *symmetrical*. The second principle therefore states that all relations, whether asymmetrical or symmetrical, are treated as though they were symmetrical. In the previous example, Mary would be treated as though she were a brother to Paul as well as a fellow sibling.

The Principle of Symmetry defies logic as we know it. The Principle of Generalization indicates an important aspect of how depth cognition appears to manipulate its material. If we observe the unconscious treating successively wider sets as though the preceding proper subset were equivalent, then we know that we are in the presence of infinite sets. The Principle of Symmetry goes on to treat members of a given set, however wide, as identical.

Symmetry generates Freud's list of primary process characteristics in short order. Symmetry implies that the proper subset is necessarily identical to the whole set. If xPy is the relation "x is a part of y," symmetry implies that y is also a part of x. This can only occur when y and x are identical. Symmetry likewise implies no succession in time. Time in the sense of succession requires ordering, and ordering implies an ordering relation such that a given time (t) is earlier than time (t + l). Applying the law of symmetry yields the contradiction that time (t + 1) is also earlier than time (t). Cartesian space can always be ordered in like fashion, and its ordering will also yield a contradiction when symmetry is applied. At deep levels, the unconscious knows neither time nor space, or not in the sense that conscious faculties do.

Symmetry implies that all members of a set or of a class are treated as identical to one another: symmetry knows no individuals.[18] In ordinary logic, members of a class are treated as similar or equal in this or that respect. The relation or propositional function which defines the set is only one of many which the various members of the set satisfy. Two men may be equally tall, but not equally dark or handsome. While they are identical in satisfying the given propositional function, they are typically unlike, and regarded as such, in other respects, with respect to other propositional functions. But symmetry renders identical all those elements encompassed by a given relation. For the unconscious, then, relations are everything and individual entities are non–entities.

The further implication is that the principle of noncontradiction is denied when the principle of symmetry is combined with the principle of generalization. Matte Blanco offers the following example: assume that the set or class mentioned in the principle of generalization is the class of all elements defined by the proposition (P); (P) is defined as being alive. (Not-P) is therefore equivalent to all those elements satisfying the condition of being dead. The principle of generalization, however, may produce a new super-class, composed, say, of all possibilities regarding life. (This is our Total Life.) The resultant class is (P, Not-P). Applying symmetry *within* the class, (P) and (not-P), life and death, are rendered identical.

In like fashion displacement and adualism (a form of displacement which renders external and internal reality identical) are easily derived from symmetry. Symmetry implies that the object or person onto which thoughts or emotions are displaced is actually identical to the original object. This in turn means that those phenomena based on displacement (projection, sublimation, transference) are easily derived corollaries. When it is displacing "the unconscious does not treat both elements only as possessors of something in common, but in fact treats them as identical."[19] Arieti's schizophrenic patient did not simply believe that she and the Virgin Mary are both virgins. From the point of view of her dedifferentiated unconscious she and the Virgin Mary are identical. The difference is that in her case these equations or identities invade and dominate conscious thought, even though elements of asymmetry remain. Matte Blanco admits that the unconstrained application of the principle of symmetry is a formula for eventual mental death. Under these circumstances it is no longer possible to formulate rules for the rulelessness, the patterned violations of everyday logic.

What prevents the destruction of logic and consciousness is the fact that there are almost always aspects of asymmetry present even in the deepest unconscious phenomena, just as in the dedifferentiated images we have considered. The manifestation of this is that asymmetry must prevail *between* a given set and the more inclusive sets of which it is a part (i.e., between successive relations). *Within* these ever-higher-wider sets, symmetry renders all elements identical, indistinguishable. Even this contention must be subject to the proviso that the width or inclusiveness does not grow so much as to embrace all of existence. One of the striking features of a thought process governed by generalization and symmetry is that any given mental manifestation can in principle be traced on and on, through ever larger infinite sets. A given mental act has a given mix of difference and equality, dividing and equalizing. Yet it also appears to contain or imply an entire spectrum composed of every "version" of that mental act from total dedifferentiation to total differentiation. This is still another way of relativizing the distinction between life and death, of combatting our tendency to spatially segregate the two modes of being. Spatial analogies no longer work. In effect, space and time are enfolded (by means of successive relations and the infinite sets they generate) into smaller and smaller areas of ever greater density.

The principle of symmetry can be seen as a generalizing principle, whereas asymmetry functions as a restraining condition.

> Psychological manifestations in man may be viewed as the interaction between the principle of symmetry and the asymmetrical way of being... as a material being and as a biological being, man is "asymmetrical".... In his mental manifestations, instead, he has both asymmetrical and symmetrical aspects.[20]

The symmetrical mode of being is the equalizing or generalizing unifying aspect of man, whereas the asymmetrical being is the dividing aspect. The foundation of man's nature is the synthesis of the two.

> Inasmuch as we are symmetrical beings we are not independent from others because we are a unity with others. For asymmetrical beings, in contrast, this absence of individual limits is inconceivable. Consequently, whenever such an absence becomes omnipresent and, therefore, imperative, this is felt by our asymmetrical aspect as a loss of our identity as individuals; it is also felt as a danger of annihilation. Such a contrast between both modes of being would constitute the deepest source of conflict.[21]

Models which appeal to symmetry and asymmetry, however, do not quite satisfy his criterion for an inside look. The distinction between symmetrical and asymmetrical modes already implies asymmetrical relations, much as the distinction between differentiated and dedifferentiated modes already reflects the differentiated mode. Implicit in the concept of relation itself is the concept of asymmetrical relation. For this reason he reformulates his principles in terms of a homogeneous indivisible totality and a dividing, heterogenic mode.

> I. There is a psychical mode of being in man which appears as if it were... a homogeneous indivisible totality.[22]

In this totality, feeling and being are one and the same thing. No distinction is made between self and not self. It is alien to time, space, and death, he claims, since the idea of death entails division into parts.

> The essential unity of a living being, seen integrally and not differentially, is something that remains... above the metabolic vicissitudes.... [T]he basic core of the individual is preserved in the midst of all life changes.[23]

His reformulated second principle reads as follows:

> II. There is a psychical mode of being in man which can be

described . . . by saying that it treats or conceives or "views" or "lives" all
reality (including its own reality) as though it were divisible or formed by
parts. . . . [W]e might call this mode the dividing, heterogenic mode of
being.[24]

This mode is characterized by discrete, separated elements. Space and
time are divided into portions which are next to each other or which
follow and precede each other; self and not self are sharply
differentiated.

III. All human psychical manifestations are the result of the interaction,
co-operation and/or any other type of relationship between both modes
of being.[25]

He proceeds to show that all the characteristics of the system
unconscious follow from this formulation. *Condensation,* for example,
is simply a "divisible" way of "describing a homogeneous indivisible
reality in which what we see, from the 'divisible' point of view, as parts,
are homogeneously impregnating the totality."[26] As such, it represents
an attempt to express indivisibility in divisible terms. *Displacement*
depends again on the fact that the indivisible reality is the whole class or
set in which individual and class are one and the same: "when . . . there
has been a displacement, say, from father to an authority, we are simply
describing this indivisible reality in terms of parts or elements (father,
the authority)."[27] From the indivisble point of view, displacement does
not involve displacement at all. The same consideration apply to
adualism: "such a 'replacement' is a way of seeing two different realities
(parts) at the point where there is, for the indivisible mode . . . only one,
homogeneous, indivisible reality."[28] Time and space as we ordinarily
conceive them belong only to the dividing mode. Lastly there is absence
of contradiction, since contradiction is dependent upon division into
two opposite aspects.

The new formulation seems to go beyond the principle of symmetry, to
get nearer to the reality of man as formed by two aspects: a
homogeneous, spaceless-timeless, partless reality, and a reality
conceived as formed by or divided into parts. It . . . seems . . . to point to
more primitive psychological *experiences* which *in themselves* would be
tautological, even though they may . . . be described in logical terms.
These experiences would be: *indivisible* and *divisible*.[29]

The asymmetrical view of the indivisible distorts its essential character
even as it attempts to approximate its structure: to offer a logical
account of what is prior to logic lends a misleading intellibility to what
is necessarily mysterious. The rights of this mode of our being have
been systematically shortchanged because of the cosmic happenstance

that the homogeneous, indivisible mode is unconscious to the dividing, heterogenic mode. History itself has been written by and on behalf of the noisier and more accessible of the two modes. Psychoanalysis, true to its perverse profession, must proceed in opposite fashion.

In this connection Matte Blanco probes the foundations of logic and the interplay of logic and psychologic:

> The two ways of viewing the world (as divisible and indivisible) seem to be at the very root of our nature. For it is from both branches of this dichotomy that all the basic structures of human nature start. Logic (thinking), feeling, being, the unity of the world and the division of the world, are all either the consequence or the expression of this dichotomy. In this sense, this dichotomy is anterior to logic. The formulation of the principle of symmetry, by contrast, already starts from the side of logic, that is, after the dichotomy.[30]

At the basis of Wittgenstein's view of logic, for example, and Sheffer's not-defined concept of the propositional calculus (p/q : p is incompatible with q), Matte Blanco finds an "abundance of symmetry," and "an [unsuccessful] tendency to return to the indivisible world."[31]

> At the level of bivalent logic . . . the nature of man in terms of the symmetrical or homogeneous indivisible mode of being is . . . "forgotten," blotted out, in order to cultivate its "vocation" of fidelity to the principle of contradiction. . . . [T]his "vocation" does not mean that there will not be in the "dividing" bivalent logic a tendency to unite the world again, a form of nostalgia for the homogeneous indivisible totality: the concept of relation, which deep down is at the base of all bivalent logic, is a witness to this tendency. But the means employed by bivalent logic to unite that which it has separated, are not appropriate.[32]

He summarizes his extensive examination of logical systems as follows:

> Whatever part we take of the world, the homogeneous indivisible reality makes itself present. In the course of the book we have seen this as a psychological reality. Here we seem to have discovered the same thing as a manifestation of the logical reality.[33]

In short,

> the undivided totality comes before the division into facts of this totality. I believe we can go further and say that the homogeneous indivisible totality is the basic thing. Perhaps this is saying the same thing as Freud said when he affirmed that the unconscious is the true psychic reality.[34]

Matte Blanco proceeds to apply his model to the analysis of emotions, as well as a host of case studies. He argues that emotions are all but synonomous with the symmetrical, dedifferentiated mode.

Echoing Rank, he points out that emotions are natural extremists. They seem incapable of assuming a value which is near zero, and instead tend to rush off to positive or negative infinity. As symmetrical phenomena, they tend to generalize and deindividualize their object. Applying the principle of generalization to your idea of your lover eventually produces the class of all former, future, potential, perhaps all imaginable lovers. Applying the principle of symmetry within each class makes her identical to all such lovers. This might then be generalized to the class of all loving or nurturing things, all of which are seen as identical. In a few blinks of the eye, the whole universe is sucked up and made identical.

In this way the whole class of lovers, perhaps the whole universe, is engulfed by your lover, and vice versa. There is a sense of oneness: the very operation of symmetry implies the nonexistence of individuals. Only the class of lovers exists, and it tends to expand in size and emotional salience to infinity. Eventually it expands to the point of comprehending hate itself as an element of a higher, more inclusive notion of love. At particularly exquisite moments, feelings approaching timelessness and spacelessness may be experienced, and the fusion or overcoming of oppositions of all sorts, up to and including the law of contradiction itself. The greater the degree of symmetry, the greater the magnitude and extent of the affect. Together with Arieti and Ehrenzweig, Matte Blanco emphasizes that a deep level of symmetry does not necessarily mean a regression to an early level of development.

One additional comment concerning Matte Blanco's relation to Freud will round out this brief account. It concerns the place and significance of instinct. By the time of Freud's tripartite divisioning of the psyche, instincts had regained their former superior position. They were virtually synonymous with the id. For his part, Matte Blanco relegates instincts to a minor position. He claims that there is a "lateral insertion of instinct on mind," meaning that instincts are quite asymmetrical. In his view, instincts are intent on their objects, have direction, and are generally well-defined. In entering the psyche they more or less by-pass the symmetrical mode.[35] As for the ego-id-superego model of the psyche, he suggests that this is a set of categories which simply does not correspond to what is generally observed nor commonly felt. Ordinarily, one does not feel that one's id asks one's ego to do such and such and that one's super-ego tells one's ego not to do it. All of me wants to do it, and all of me feels that I should not do it. Moreover, partitioning the psyche in this way makes the "all," the self, most mysterious. The tripartite model suggests a compartmentalization of the psyche either pathological or impossible.

An attempt to make ambivalence and mental conflict intelligible, it makes the unity of the personality inexplicable. If it is meaningful to divide the psyche at all, this must not be the way.[36]

In any event, Matte Blanco manages to generate all of Freud's characteristics of system unconscious with essentially one proposition: symmetry. Using the idea of symmetry in tandem with the principle of generalization and the concept of infinite sets, he is enabled to analyze dream material; emotion, and specific emotions; the relationship between psychology and logic; and a wealth of clinical material in a fresh, economical, insightful manner. His model of the undifferentiated unrepressed unconscious dovetails with our emphasis on the dividing and equalizing modes; the equalizing mode is in fact the unrepressed unconscious. He demonstrates that the two modes are not just matters relating to concepts or logic, but basic emotional and existential alternatives at all levels of existence. In all this he serves us well.

Unconscious Compensation

The idea of some sort of unification or reconciliation of the two modes of being has already been invoked from time to time. In the absence of such a possibility, it is not entirely clear why the pathological forms, anomie and alienation, are pathological.

The idea of balance is related to the notion of unconscious compensation. The unconscious, less differentiated mode "communicates" those missing opposites banned (or "repressed") by the law of contradiction, by differentiated consciousness. Just as differentiation implies, requires, and in a sense contains dedifferentiation, specific opposites on which consciousness is focused or fixated must be complemented by their opposite poles. "It is the opposite which is good for us," Heraclitus observed.

Unconscious compensation and the related idea of the *coincidentia oppositorum* are all but universal ideas. Mircea Eliade has collected a large number of traditional rites, myths, theories associated with the union of opposites.[37] He finds the pre-history of the coincidentia oppositorum in the idea of the Creation as a fragmentation of primordial unity. Thus we witness God's inability to complete the world without the aid of the Devil, and the almost cordial relationship between Goethe's God and Mephistopheles. Indian religions are obsessed with the idea of a Unitary Being hidden behind a veil of multiplicity and variety.

Another locus of these concerns is the theme of the ambivalence of the divinity, a "theme constant to the whole religious history of humanity." The idea of the *androgyne* as the perfect man reflects the same preoccupations, specifically the idea that "one cannot attain a particular and well–defined mode without first knowing the total mode of being." To know difference is to know equality, identity. The Urgrund of the Tantric yoga contains all dualities and contraries gathered into a state of absolute Unity. The celebrated "middle way" of Taoism is that of the union of opposites. Similar conceptions are found in the writings of Nicholas de Cusa, Meister Eckhardt, Pascal, Goethe, Hegel, Schopenhauer, Nietzsche, Bergson, Simmel, and Jung. Even Freud was not completely immune.

Two versions of the idea of the coincidentia oppositorum will serve to suggest its core meaning and connection with unconscious compensation. The first is derived from Taoism, which influenced Hegel, Schopenhauer, and especially Nietzsche. "The Tao that can be told is not the real Tao," we learn, "and the name that can be named is not the real name."[38] To name is to distinguish, while the Middle Way is beyond opposites, divisions, forms, distinctions. A name would imply the existence of that-which-is-not-what-we-have-named, and "the Tao has no opposite." (In this respect the Tao resembles Matte Blanco's indivisible, homogeneous totality.) Furthermore, to name is to oppose oneself, as subject, to the object: "if we speak of the One then the one becomes the object, with ourselves as the subject, and oneness exists no longer in its higher unity."[39] Hence the futility of ever approaching such truth solely by means of the dividing mode. Bergson taunted Mill and Dewey for their attempt to do so: they desire an intuition, he said, and they think that their analysis will produce one.

"Tao is able to be the Mother of the World, the grand interfusion."[40] In this realm, as in the deepest levels of the unconscious, there exists no space or time.

> The Gate of Heaven is non-being . . . a realm absolutely free from limitations and distinctions . . . . Non-being is the one-without-contrast; that is, the unity of all things . . . . In this unity everything breaks through the shell of itself and interfuses with every other thing . . . all selves dissolve into one, and all ourselves are selves only to the extent that they disappear into all other selves.[41]

It is called "Mother, because . . . it is the realm from which all birth issues forth and to which all death returns."[42]

A significant Western variation on the idea of the coincidentia oppositorum is provided by the fifteenth century Christian mystic Nicholas de Cusa.[43] The coincidentia oppositorum is the "least imperfect definition of God." Undoubtedly it is the symmetrical unconscious pervading the dividing, differentiated mode, which provides the human inspiration and approximation to this "vision of God." The unconscious may be, for better and worse, the God within. Cusa's vision is a lean and straightforward account of the union or overcoming of opposites, largely stripped of distracting anthropomorphic images. Rarely has the coincidentia oppositorum been offered so explicitly and economically.

Cusa makes it clear that the human vocation is to try to understand and then approximate that union of opposites attributed to God. One secularized version of this idea is undoubtedly the *Gattungswesen*, or species being of German philosophy, so charged with significance for Feuerbach and Marx. It is but a short step to Marx's multi-faceted multi-talented, communist man. The various directions this idea was taken, particularly by Marx, Nietzsche, Simmel, and Durkheim, dominate the intellectual and political history of the nineteenth (and twentieth) century and enter into the analysis of alienation and anomie in a most intimate way.

> I Marvel, Lord, seeing that Thou beholdest at once all men and each individual . . . how the universal coincideth with the particular in Thy faculty of sight. . . . [T]hy vision, Lord, is Thine essence.[44]

Cusa is not content to marvel. He beseeches his Lord to "teach me . . . how at one glance Thou discerneth both all together and each in particular."[45] This is reminiscent of Ehrenzweig's comprehensive dedifferentiated overview, except that God's vision of particulars is supposedly differentiated as well as comprehensive. It also can be read as a plea for unconscious compensation, the health and creativity associated with a balance of conscious and unconscious modes. It reflects the suspicion that both modes are us, and that the fundamental human project is both to affirm their difference and their identity.

Yet there is a formidable obstacle blocking the path to such knowledge, the more formidable because it is thought to be the very vehicle with which we negotiate the path.

> I have learnt the place wherein Thou art found unveiled is girt round with the coincidence of contradictories, and this is the wall of Paradise wherein Thou dost abide. The door whereof is guarded by the most proud spirit of Reason, and, unless he be vanquished, the way in will not lie open. Thus tis' beyond the coincidence of contradictories that Thou mayest be seen, and nowhere this side thereof.[46]

Reason, or what usually passes for it, is tantamount to the dividing mode, the defense of firm distinctions and oppositions, the observance of the law of contradiction. It bars the door to less differentiated material, thereby inhibiting unconscious compensation and any possible coincidence of contraries.

Since the overcoming of ambivalence is clearly what is at stake, we should not be surprised to find ambivalence at the heart of Cusa's enterprise. Whether he feels awe, or envy, is not always clear: "my yearning, bright with Thee, leadeth me unto Thee; it spurneth all that is finite and comprehensible, for in these it cannot rest, being led by Thee to Thee." The goal may well be a state of rest and repose, but what also strikes the eye is the restlessness, the infinite aspiration to transcend the finite and the merely comprehensible. (This fascinated Pascal, who commented on the desire for rest and peace underlying our restless frenzy.) In Cusa's world, man's yearning is divinely inspired, yet it is but a short distance to the realization that God (or Spirit, his quasi-secularized successor) realizes himself through the efforts and activities of man, or (as in Feuerbach and Marx) the projection of all of the best qualities of man. Cusa inadvertently charges God with fomenting the desire and disease of the infinite, much as if he were anticipating Weber's analysis of what made the Puritans run. Impossible goals and unbearable uncertainty have a great advantage in motivating us.

Rank's duality of life fear and death fear represents a secular characterization of essentially the same ambivalence. Recall that Rank thinks of life in terms of individuation, differentiation, and partialization. Life-fear underlies our tendency to get stuck or trapped, immobilized, unable to contemplate, recognize, or initiate significant changes. Each "giving out" of oneself is seen as total, final, and therefore smacks of death. Cusa spurns "all that is finite and comprehensible" ("for in these it cannot rest"). For Rank this suggests death fear, the fear of getting stuck, tied down, paralyzed, ossified, strangled by distinctions (roles, niches) which suffocate, clothes that constrict, houses that have no mercy. Death-fear causes life to resemble a Tar-baby, just waiting to get us stuck if we involve ourselves in it at all. Partialization, social roles, specialization of tasks are so many different ways of dying. The idea of having the partial stand in symbolically for the total (the best Rank hopes for) does not occur to Cusa, no more than to Marx. Why finite man, aspiring to infinity, can hope for much more he does not say. In this way *death fear* leads or amounts to *anomie*. For all those soul-squinters who cannot or will not keep pace, who get tired and defensive, there are always cheap comforts, secure nooks, frog-perspectives. Death fear passes over into life fear, which leads to and buttresses alienation. This is Rank's version of Berger's proposition: alienation as a protection against anomie. The difference is that Rank posits and demonstrates a dialectical relation: alienation aggravates death fear, which aggravates anomie, which aggravates life fear, which aggravates alienation, and so on.

The idea of unconscious compensation plays an important role in Schopenhauer, Schiller, and Nietzsche: godlike creativity and the workings of the unconscious are all but equated. Sometimes the process is thinly disguised, to author and to audience, as projections onto the cosmos or social cosmos, as in Hegel, Feuerbach, and Marx. More recently, various forms of the idea appear in Adler, Horney, Rank, and Jung. Freud himself offered a gloomy version of it, whereby the repressive demands of culture and civilization have their implacable foe in the unconscious, with its mindless Utopian program of satisfying every impulse and desire.

The figure in modern psychology most closely associated with the idea of unconscious compensation and the coincidentia oppositorum is Jung.[47] Rieff has suggested that for Freud the unconscious is all that is not conscious; whereas for Jung the unconscious is all that consciousness can become. Freud suspected Jung of trying to solve the "God problem" by making a God of the self. Yet Jung's analyses are filled with warnings of the dangers of unconscious "flooding," psychic "inflation," the perils of calling projections home too fast, too soon. Jung's unconscious, even in its capacity as compensating agent, is not necessarily positive, pleasant nor productive of desirable syntheses: various modes of responding to unconscious symbols result in various modes of being. These include explosive possibilities as well as the achievement of a better balance and less fragmentation. What he did suggest is that to ignore the necessity of unconscious compensation is the most dangerous of paths. Unconscious compensation is something to be achieved, created; unconscious pollution or intrusion requires no effort, and will take place in any event. Even now, millions strut about as if they had no unconscious, no shadow dogging their steps. Millions imagine that they are only what they care to know about themselves.

True to Rieff's characterization, the main endeavor of Jung's analytic psychology is the realization of the shadow. The means, the coin of the realm of unconscious mentation, is the symbol. Symbols suggest and comprehend oppositions which discursive reason would of necessity have to separate and oppose. On the other hand, in order to unpack their meaning, symbols must be translated into a differentiated terms. An infinity of possible meanings and motives can be among the freight carried by one symbolic vehicle. This is why psychoanalysis is known for its colorful interpretations more than its trustworthy predictions. The solution that Matte Blanco offers is the "translating function," which selects from an infinitude of possible levels and meanings the one appropriate to the subject at hand. This is more description than solution. But to suggest that psychoanalysis does not qualify as science *because* of these translating difficulties may amount to blaming it for having the subject matter it does.

Much like Freud and Matte Blanco, Jung argues that in neurosis there always exist two tendencies standing in strict opposition, one of which is unconscious. The spotting of imbalance and the marked ambivalence which accompanies it is a matter of searching "extravagant and exaggerated" behavior. Without opposition there is no balance, no system of self-regulation. The fundamental cause of rigidity is therefore the "fear of the problem of opposites." We might add that this is likewise the cause of chaos.

As for unifying and overcoming, there is much that conspires against it. The reconciliation of opposites is inseparable from the activity of the dedifferentiating unconscious; and Jung echoes Ehrenzweig in suggesting how much strength must be summoned in "exposing oneself to the dangers of being devoured by the maternal abyss." What is involved, he contends, is admitting and accepting what has been projected previously: a process that flirts with the possibility of positive or negative inflation. In the first variety of inflation I fancy that I become all these things. In the second the ego is overrun by "unconscious contamination" and I am next to nothing.

What exactly does the coincidentia oppositorum mean on the level of individual personality? Jung argues that this is the work and essence of the self, as opposed to the conscious differentiated ego or the unconscious dedifferentiated shadow. The self is the "uniting symbol" which epitomizes the "total union of opposites." As such it is nonrational, like Cusa's God, and can be expressed only in terms of symbols. It does not abide in Cartesian space or successive time. Human wholeness can only be expressed in terms of oppositions, antinomies and antitheses. Jung's self, then, *is* the coincidentia oppositorum, or the coincidence of particularly salient oppositions. Jung takes Cusa's idea of God and makes of it a universal human project.

Even if godlike aspirations were totally pernicious, it would be unfair to shoot anyone who brings the news that more and more of us entertain such aspirations. This may simply be the point at which Western culture, at least its most advanced sectors, has arrived. Besides, Jung can rightly argue that the really dangerous deifiers and infinitizers of man are those who do *not* seek to realize the shadow. The coincidentia oppositorum, understood in this finite-humanistic way, may imply moderation as well as balance. It suggests the standard by reference to which alienation and anomie are pathological, and promises to help rescue these concepts from the sociological relativism that has made a mess of their study and measurement. On the other hand, as Nietzsche tirelessly stressed, it is a perilous and conflictful balance. Opposites must be experienced, lived through, tamed and accommodated, not ignored nor destroyed.

By now it should be obvious that the discussion of differentiated and dedifferentiated modes, conscious and unconscious, could have been couched in terms of the themes of alienation and anomie. In the interest of highlighting the underlying view of the specifically human, the social manifestations of these discontents have been temporarily relegated to the background. Now they press forward and clamor for attention.

9

Thou Shalt Overcome

And life itself confided this secret to me: Behold, I am that which must overcome itself again and again.

An unspeakable amount of painfulness, arrogance, harshness, estrangement, frigidity has entered into human feelings because we think we see opposites instead of transitions.

Today the individual still has to be made possible by being pruned: possible here means *whole*. The reverse is what happens: the claim for independence, for free development, for *laisser aller* is pressed most hotly by the very people for whom no reins would be too strict.

Nietzsche

Overcoming What Oppositions?

Overcoming a given opposition passeth human understanding. A galaxy of oppositions are candidates for overcoming. But all involve and invoke the dualism of differentiated and undifferentiated, and our perennially fascinating, profoundly troubling dualisms and oppositions seem to be closely related to this most primitive pair. Here I argue that alienation (self-alienation) and anomie can be characterized in terms of two basic pathological relationships between these two basic modes of thought and being.

When a given opposition or ambivalence does not directly suggest these two modes, they nevertheless underlie it. Every distinction (difference, form) we establish or recognize can be viewed as either a dividing—establishing difference from that which it is not—or as an equalizing—setting or making something equal to itself. In fact it is both, but we cannot think both, simultaneously. Therefore the dedifferentiated material which accompanies any distinction is relegated to the undifferentiated unconscious; this is the insight at the heart of our model. If we go on to focus on what the material "inside" this distinction or form, or what is "outside," then we differentiate those areas initially rendered equal or identical. This is equivalent to bringing them to consciousness. This in turn is accompanied by and dependent on further unconscious dedifferentiation, and so on.

Ambivalence in this sense is in the nature of a universal relation or form, into which specific ambivalences find their way. The conscious half of specific ambivalences appears as the differentiated or preferred pole. Since differentiation is always accompanied by (unconscious) dedifferentiation, the conscious pole is in effect always accompanied by its opposite; given that on some level of dedifferentiation, opposites are seen as identical to one another. This applies to any distinction drawn or difference asserted, to any linguistic, cognitive, or social form.

Ambivalence in this sense is clearly universal and human. It is not exclusively social. It counts, in ways we have suggested and sketched. To assert its omnipresence and paramount significance does not tie us to those oppositions salient to particular cultures, specific social strata, or given individuals. It does not limit us to the study of psycho-pathologies, not in the conventional sense. On the other hand, it does link social theory to social discontents which all individuals and cultures are humanly prone. The posing of opposites, that fundamental faith of metaphysicians and common folk alike; the underlying primal opposition this invariably reflects and promotes; the ambivalent emotional freight this always carries—these are the constituents of this view of the inescapably human.

At the same time it is thoroughly social, albeit in a sense which must be carefully specified. Social, cultural and linguistic forms are always involved. We do not express ourselves or act except in ways that are intrinsically social. We do not experience ambivalence as abstract individuals, but as social beings in specific contexts. The conscious mind always focuses, always differentiates something, finds something specific to compare and contrast. Particular oppositions trouble and excite us. In this sense ambivalence is never pure. The conscious mode exists in historical time and social space. Putting the matter another way: in addition to being the form for any particular ambivalence or opposition, this fundamental ambivalence can be considered the content or raw material of any form, since any form may be expressed as a combination of differentiation or dividing and equalizing. This is true of the self, that form symbolically uniting conscious and unconscious modes, or striving to do so. This means that any form we differentiate/equalize (conceive, perceive, imagine) has the same basic structure as the self. In this sense, all objects are subjective. (This is a version of Nietzsche's proposition that it is according to the model of the subject or ego that we have invented and fashioned things.) Moreover, because of the way we have represented life, death, and (Total) Life, the components of any form can be viewed as simulating or approximating the components of Life.

This way of viewing the omnipresence of the unconscious also suggests the futility of attempting to segregate the cognitive and the affective. If we associate cognition in the strict sense with the drawing of (conscious) differences, then it is clear that the cognitive is inseparable from the affective. The less differentiated unconscious is virtually synonymous with emotion. Moreover, every form can be viewed as arising from that relative lack of form which characterizes emotion or "affective cognition." Every distinction makes a difference, emotionally speaking. (Every distinction states a preference, G. Spencer Brown argues: "there can be no distinction without motive, and there can be no motive unless contents are seen to differ in value.") Conversely, every emotion makes a difference, cognitively speaking. There are always elements of asymmetry in predominantly symmetrical mental acts, always "cognitive" elements in emotion.

The psychic structure we have posited is not yet a unity, a self. The self, and perhaps the production of all forms, represents the effort to realize and express that unity. Our being can only be expressed in our doing, in the fashioning of objective forms which symbolize that being. This adds a depth psychological dimension to the Marxist idea of externalization of human activity, and the notion of seeing ourselves in that which we have created. In every form we see our two modes of being. We are always re-creating ourselves, in this sense. It is a kind of repetition compulsion, but we are saved from this living death by extending ourselves into ever richer, ever different and more differentiated forms. Our being can only be expressed as becoming. Alienation and anomie represent the two basic ways we fail to become what we are: being at the expense of becoming, becoming at the expense of being. To become what we are is to stamp our being on our becoming.

This does not exhaust the associated meanings. It may be that all thought reflects the most primitive distinction and relation between mother and child. Maybe this is why, as Simmel observes, that the categories of form and content (substance, matter) are of all categories the most difficult to do without: logically and emotionally, they represent the distinctions from which all subsequent distinctions derive. Separation from the Mother is by no means the only or immediate meaning of every division we think or experience, nor is each act of equalizing or union to be equated with fusion with the Mother. But this is likely the model and source of all subsequent division and equalization. Not only is it the earliest meaning, it pre-exists or perhaps coincides with the dawn of ordered time. (Freud suggested that the sense of time arises from the contrast of secondary and primary process.) If so, it continues to exist even when time ravages more differentiated meanings. Accordingly, it lends the emotional coloration of this fundamental ambivalence to each and every more differentiated cognition-emotion. As Simmel remarks, forms are inherently individual. As with the individual, the formless gives birth to the form.

This points the way to a promising way of viewing the relation between universals and particulars. Everything particular and distinct that we see or conceive represents a kind of explicate or unfolded order, it seems, whereas the universal of this particular is enfolded in an order which is "dense," non-Cartesian, undifferentiated, unconscious. To differentiate is to unfold. No doubt such intuitions led Leibnitz to his monadic universe of self-contained universes. Goethe returned again and again to similar images: the balance of putting out and gathering in, of unfolding and enfolding, was a dominant motif of his thought. In a similar vein is Schrödinger's notorious conception of the mind, as a blank screen on which the brain inscribes differentiated messages. The blankness may be the undifferentiated and therefore unconscious totality, and the differentiated messages appear against and emerge from this backdrop. In which case the mind is not located in ordered space nor successive time. Maybe this explains why no one has managed to locate it.

As for the various dualisms we have entertained thus far, most of these point us directly back to the primal ambivalence we have posited. The argument here suggests why this is so, but also why this ambivalence is basic to any such dualism, any distinction whatsoever.

Alienation and Anomie as Opposites

Given cultures and individuals find some oppositions salient and vexing, are cognizant of others which seem less important and less troublesome, and are ignorant of the rest. Even cultures which are by cross-cultural standards quite close to one another exhibit significant differences: for example, the American preoccupation with sex, the German obsession with authority. A number of these pairs have been encountered in connection with the "death problem." On the surface they exhibit much variety, but many can be seen as composed of one member suggesting the differentiating mode, the other pointing to the dedifferentiating mode. As we have suggested, when this is not obviously the case (in terms of the specific contents of the dualism) it is nevertheless true of its underlying structure and cognitive-affective content.

Without further ado, alienation and anomie can now be defined as two basic pathological or deadly relations between the differentiated and the dedifferentiated modes. Alienation, self-alienation, represents undue separation or segregation of the two modes, the lack of effective contact and communication. Whatever the proximate or ultimate cause, the unconscious is unable to soften, transform, make pliable and permeable the distinctions and boundaries maintained by the differentiated consciousness. Anomie represents the unmanageable intrusion of undifferentiated material into the differentiated conscious, the lack of an effective barrier between the two modes. These extremes generate one another. Both are pathological relative to that more beneficial relationship between the two modes, which arrests massive surges of less differentiated material while allowing mutually nourishing exchanges. Both represent barriers to taming, acceptance, and overcoming of ambivalence

All alienation is self-alienation. Even Marx briefly subscribed to this proposition, until his metaphysical commitments intruded. His insistence that there must be an "other man", who alienates me from myself led to an exclusively social view of the sources of alienation, a thoroughgoing neglect of ambivalence and a well-known series of seductive but simplistic propositions concerning the barriers to self-realization and creativity. If only social barriers and contradictions exist, we need not inquire further into the nature of the individual and species in order to diagnose and prescribe for man's basic maladies and conflicts. The social dimensions, influences, barriers are a vital part of any theory of alienation or anomie. On the other hand, lest alienation be equated with whatever the philistines, political elites or social scientists think it is, it must be given a firmer grounding in human nature and psychology than Marx gave it.

Similarly, conceptions of anomie and the social circumstances productive of subjective anomie must be more closely tied to our conception of what anomie means for the individual subject. Otherwise we create a gulf between anomie and anomia, the social condition and the psychological correlates. Merton has rightly complained of this gulf. Yet he divorces his own sociological view of anomie from any coherent set of propositions concerning what this means for individual psychology. Having left a perfectly open field, he then complains that a thousand flowers have bloomed, all calling themselves "anomia."

The presence of these maladies suggest that the process of unconscious compensation has somehow gone awry. Both suggest a conscious concentration on certain desires and fears (objects, goals, conceptions) to the exclusion of their unconscious opposites. One-sided cultural emphases both reflect and promote this myopia. Yet opposites are never completely excluded or extirpated; the struggle is for dominion, not survival. Their illicit, unacknowledged forms of expression tend to be disruptive, to become extreme in proportion to the conscious, opposite extreme. The personality becomes an armed camp, if not a battleground.

Alienation and anomie can also be expressed in terms of the two ways of representing Death discussed earlier. One version is associated with what is rigid, controlled, trapped, bounded, stuck, as conjured up by Sartre in his essay on slime. This Masculine Death arrests and impedes the process of differentiation, and should not be confused or equated with that process. Feminine Death involves chaos, confusion, isolation, and the like, rather than being stuck or confined or suffocated. It is the pathological form of dedifferentiation, produced by the rigid and vigorous resistance of the conscious faculties to the return to less differentiated states. These states arise from within or without, typically both. Alienation corresponds to Masculine Death; anomie, to Feminine Death.

This conception can be further explicated in terms of many of the dualisms we have encountered and emphasized. One of the most familiar refers to boundaries, their defense and penetration. Boundary defense or fortification, carried to extremes, is alienation. The wholesale violation and dissolution of boundaries amounts to anomie. Anomie is associated with the intrusion of the equalizing mode *and* the resistance of the differentiating mode, and therefore various states of fragmentation, confusion, disorientation, frenzy, uncertainty, the absence of firm distinctions and guidelines. Both are a far cry from the kind of semi-permeable boundaries which allow orderly intercourse without massive, unmanageable intrusions. Rigidity and chaos, and the respective versions of Death they represent—alienation and anomie—have much more in common than first meets the eye. Not only do they breed one another, but also, to dwell long enough in the distinction is to experience its virtual dissolution. If our conscious faculties do not allow us to see them as the same malady, if we must create the illusion of their passing over, then at very least they must be regarded as mutual breeding grounds.

Another pair with which alienation and anomie can be readily and helpfully associated are Rank's life fear and death fear. Rank's life fear is the fear of individuation and differentiation, of being different, separate, isolated, alone. To life fear corresponds the wish to belong, be secure, included, enclosed, equal, identical. Death fear is the fear of *loss* of individuality, freedom, mobility, and the like: the fear of fusion. Life fear, when sufficiently threatened by death fear, promotes the Death we have labeled Masculine: differentiation in a arrested, separated mode. Nothing ventured, nothing lost, except life itself, which is the process of progressive differentiation. This is alienation. Death fear is the fear of being stuck, limited, all-too finite: rendered immobile, trapped, suffocated, strangled. The attempt to avoid getting stuck with a firm fixed identity, stagnant circumstances, false certitude, confining social roles, finite perspectives, finitude itself, can lead to wholesale, escapist violation of boundaries and limits, and thus to identity diffusion, confusion, and uncertainty. These maladies are anomic in nature.

Life and death fear point directly to the problem of partialization and totalization, and on to the Durkheimian themes of the division of labor and the maladies of the infinite. Much like the neurotic, the alienated subject suffers from an inability to let finite actions and achievements symbolize for him the whole. He is "symbol poor." Both tend to *equate* the finite with the infinite, with the total. The alienated try to solve the problem of partialization and finitude by suspending choice. (This may include always "choosing" as others choose. Nor is mere motion to be equated with significant choice and change.) The anomic can also be said to avoid life, partialization, finitude, and choice. He does it in the opposite manner, using the multiplication of choices to avoid choice, commitment, attachment, entanglements. He may choose continually and frantically in order to avoid living with any particular choice. (We have argued that Marx and Marxist theory exhibit this tendency to a marked degree.) If the alienated see or experience individuation and partialization in terms of the feminine abyss that living life fully conjures up—being caught and swallowed up in its flow—the anomic see it as signifying being stuck or trapped or tied down with the finite, partial and flawed in a world of limitless possibilities which cannot be ignored. Madness, Voltaire suggested, is to think of too many things in succession too fast, or of one thing too exclusively.

The anomic proclaims that everything is or should be possible. The alienated responds that this is what he is afraid of. The anomic tends to flit from choice to choice, none of which can be taken seriously or savored. His world is awash with possibilities and missed opportunities; he is never at home with his choice of objects. He must cut his successive ties more or less chaotically, aggressively, at the loss of continuity and meaning. It is the anomic variation on Marx's "sense of having," wherein one never really possesses anything, whatever is acquired. Opting for everything, the enjoyment and significance of everything is reduced to nothing. Differences make less and less difference, partly because of the objective overgrowth and confusion of choices, opportunities, and guidelines, partly because of the rigid response of the surface faculties. Sometimes this leads to literal death, as in Durkheim's suicides of the successful. Anomie as well as alienation presents obstacles to genuine change, meaningful choice, and creativity. Or rather, anomie generates and attends alienation.

This is the neglected truth of an anomic society, as surely as anomie itself is neglected or seen as something else. With alienation the obstacles to meaningful change, the deathlike aspects, are often obvious. The alienated simulate death, while anomics caricature life. Both types are stuck. Both are lost, in a world rendered excessively alien and chaotic, and therefore rigid and unresponsive. If we stare long enough, we can catch fleeting glimpses of their essential unity. Once again: this is not to deny that the social order may itself be rigid or chaotic. It is simply to suggest the aspects of being human that are involved, that aggravate and perpetuate those conditions and lead us to thoroughly underestimate the prospects for significant change.

The problem of partialization is bound up with the maladies of the infinite and the finite. The former I associate with anomie, much as Durkheim did. The latter is a way of looking at alienation. Durkheim associated maladies of the infinite with prosperity's effect on the relatively prosperous, with dangerous and tragic illusions of omnipotence and absence of limits. Otherwise he left the idea undeveloped. Since Durkheim, diseases of the infinite have received little attention in anomie theory. Lacking a conception of what is human, they have no conception of what is pathological.

The extension and the generalization of these ideas are partly dependent on conceptual tools which were not at Durkheim's disposal, and partly dependent on perspectives he probably would not have found congenial. One of these, found in Nietzsche and further developed by Freud, is the tendency of close ambivalences to bloat the expression and the pursuit of those wishes and urges which are only in a slight majority. Conscious wishes are hotly pursued by their unconscious opposites. Matte Blanco's model of the unrepressed unconscious, the notion of infinite sets and the principle of symmetry, are helpful in spotting and tracking unconscious involvement in or "contamination" of the conscious. They offer a broader context as well as new analytical tools in analyzing displacement, projection, adualism, identification, romanticization, idealization, paleological reasoning, and unconscious mentation in general.

Alienation may be associated with depressed states and diseases of the finite, characterized by self-constriction, self-flagellation, self-starvation—though again, the oppression and constriction can be from without, all of it or in part. The individual seeks ways to express in oblique fashion those opposites, those sides of self that his condition and circumstances demand that he exclude or extirpate. The nation, group, reference group acquire the strength I do not possess, often to an infinite degree. Countless other valued people, objects, institutions are gathered into an infinite sets of successively greater width. Symmetry renders all the elements of a given set identical. Hence the incredible lengths to which individuals will adjust their perceptions and conceptions to conform to the reference group, or to one of its authoritative representatives. To the real power of a given individual, group, institution, whatever is added an infinity of projected powers.

As for anomie, infinite sets are associated with what Jung has called psychic inflation, mania or megalomania: the dangers and difficulties of trying to be too many places, too many people, too many different things at once; more than finite, more than human. Opposite attributes, unacceptable impulses and the like are not projected with as much frequency or force in this mode. Projections are called in. We attempt to live our fantasies, which is about as dangerous and self-defeating as ignoring them. Again, extremes begat extremes. This is not merely a matter of the inhospitability of the world to infinite aspirations: it is not merely a sociological point. If even slight setbacks can bring us crashing from God to worm, then it is because godlike states can be wearisome and frightening as well as invigorating and exhilarating. Rilke captures the point in a strikingly appropriate verse:

> And then, in this wearisome nowhere, all of a sudden,
> the ineffable spot where the pure too-little
> incomprehensibly changes,—springs round
> into that empty too-much!
> Where the many-digited sum solves into zero.[1]

The "pure too-little" of alienation generates the "empty too-much" of anomie. And conversely: the richness, as Sartre's character Roquentin complains, was lost in confusion. Finally it was "no more because it was too much."

Overcoming Alienation and Anomie

If we agree to return Nicholas de Cusa's *coincidentia oppositorum* to the psyche from which it was projected, if we hypothesize a fundamental human ambivalence based on dividing and equalizing modes, then the unbalanced extremes associated with these two modes have a strong claim to the labels of anomie and alienation. Each generates and depends on the other. Or rather it appears this way to the conscious. More likely there is a continuum, so that to speak of one and not the other is always a mistake, as it is with any dualism. Similarly for the many associated oppositions, the poles of which have no life apart from their relationship and their interaction. Ultimately this interaction is more important than whether we happen to be expressing this fundamental, apparently bi-polar malady in the language of alienation or anomie. To the degree that a person appears alienated to us, we can readily observe anomie in much the same degree. We see the subject fending off the wishes (or the opposite fears) behind the expressed, conscious fears (or the opposed wishes). If we equip ourselves with the appropriate spectacles, that is.

Once we do, we observe a marked tendency for extremes to be accompanied and followed by opposite extremes. Opposite fears and wishes become conscious and ascendent, or are increasingly expressed in other spheres of our lives, segregated in space and time. Most likely, these afflictions appear different only to our differentiating mode. In any event we must scramble to stay abreast of their tendency to pass over to one another, *as if* the postulated opposition were indeed mistaken. Paradoxically, the only way for us to do so is to constantly keep their opposition in mind. Mental traffic in opposites is the only way to convey the unity and the coincidence of opposites, to express the unity of the self (or any form).

On the positive side, the union of opposites suggests the union of conscious and unconscious, dividing and equating modes, and their psychological correlates. Much like the Tao, or Cusa's coincidentia oppositorum, this cannot be expressed without contradiction. (Except by means of symbols, which express a broader, less differentiated view of life.) Irrespective of our success in such a project, as an interpretation of human striving it has extraordinary reach. In some respects the proposition is practically trivial and commonplace. Few serious thinkers have suggested or implied that a coherent personality or world can be fashioned out of various conflicting bits and pieces, mutually indifferent if not antagonistic. No one seriously maintains that a personality consists of a pile of parts, even though many entertain theories which imply this is the case. This would violate our deepest intuitions of unity and continuity (perhaps immortality) of our personalities, and our observations of the terrible suffering of those who have lost such intuitions. On the other hand, we are slowly coming to understand the self as an achievement. Psychic unity, the essential continuity amidst our changes and opposing inclinations, the very sense of being, cannot be taken for granted.

Those who make such arguments explicit and pursue their implications, however, are a smaller tribe, at least in Western culture. Perhaps the most challenging modern statement on behalf of the coincidence of opposites on all levels of existence is found in Nietzsche.[2] Contrary to Normon O. Brown's contention, this is the essence of Nietzsche's mature synthesis of individuation/differentiation (the Apollonian) and dedifferentiation (the Dionysian). It coincides with his attempt to characterize life in terms of various degrees of the will to power. It also has much in common with Simmel's conception of life, death, and Life, as we shall see. In Nietzsche's case the result is a kind of dialectical monism—his infamous will to power—in which the basic force is both that which overcomes and that which must be overcome.

Nietzsche's treatment of the social and political dimensions of these maladies, while sometimes insightful and suggestive, suffers from a certain dyspeptic myopia. (Many of his political observations are "second hand and third rate," Walter Kaufmann observes.) The social conditions conducive to "overcoming" are neglected, and he often writes as if only genius and heroism can avail. His acquaintance with socialist thought and democratic theory was superficial, his treatment of them one-sided and prejudicial. He promotes the notion that only a few supremely gifted and courageous individuals can make of themselves a work of art, can by super-human effort immerse themselves in all the decadence, disillusionment, malaise, confusion, and conflict of the day, and yet overcome it to earn genuine modernity. Nietzsche did not speak directly of alienation (nor of anomie; he was no longer sane at the time Durkheim resurrected the concept). Yet he excelled in his penetrating accounts of these afflictions, and what overcoming them must involve for the individual. These are the crucial areas which both Marx and Durkheim slight. No theorist of alienation and anomie has seen more clearly their opposition, nor challenged it so consistently or persuasively. No doubt this is because none of them examined and challenged their own belief in opposites, and therefore themselves, so relentlessly.

This distinctive contribution is reflected, first of all, in his assessment of the juncture at which the West finds itself in mid-nineteenth century. The central fact of the modern world, for Nietzsche, is the decline or death of the Christian faith. In many respects his reaction resembles that of Burke or Durkheim more than that of Voltaire or Marx.

Much less may one suppose that many people know as yet what this event really means—and how much must collapse now that this faith has been undermined because it was built upon this faith, propped up by it, grown into it—for example, the whole of European morality. This long plenitude and sequence of breakdown, ruin, and cataclysm that is now impending . . . a gloom and an eclipse of the sun whose like has probably never yet occurred on earth. . . . [Y]et the initial consequences, consequences for ourselves, are quite the opposite of what one might expect: They are not at all sad and gloomy but rather like a new and indescribable light.[3]

No one is free to be a crab, he observes. He has only scorn for those who are led back to faith by their nostalgia, not their judgment. Nevertheless, his declaration of war against the "anemic Christian ideal" is a war for dominion, not for extermination. The latter way would merely repeat Christianity's violence against flesh and spirit. Besides, in the sphere of the spirit there is no extermination, only repression and the return of the repressed.

Far from being intoxicated by the liberalization and dissolution of the old order, he wonders whether the militant faith and ideals, the will requisite to institution building have been permanently destroyed:

The whole of the West no longer possesses the instincts out of which institutions grow, out of which a future grows: perhaps nothing antagonizes its "modern spirit" so much. One lives for the day, one lives very fast, one lives very irresponsibly: precisely this is called "freedom." That which makes an institution an institution is despised, hated, repudiated: one fears the danger of a new slavery the moment the word "authority" is even spoken out loud.[4]

Nor is science the answer, even though it has fallen heir to much of that confidence.

Science today is a hiding place for every kind of discontent, disbelief, gnawing worm, bad conscience—it is the unrest of the lack of ideals, the suffering from the lack of any great love, the discontent in the face of involuntary contentment.[5]

Science seeks the familiar in the unfamiliar. In the process it removes explanation from the realm of the humanly comforting and intelligible. It multiplies distinctions which seem to make no human difference, and thereby prepares for us a "sovereign ignorance."

Into this gaping spiritual wound rush the various germs of modernism and utilitarianism.

Even now one is ashamed of resting, and prolonged reflection almost gives people a bad conscience. . . . [J]ust as all forms are visibly perishing in the haste of the workers, the feeling for form itself, the ear and eye for the melody of movements are also perishing. The proof of this may be found in the universal demand for gross obviousness in all those situations in which human beings wish to be honest with one another for once .... [O]ne no longer has time or energy for ceremonies, for being obliging in an indirect way, for esprit in conversation, and for any otium at all.[6]

Beneath this restless striving, this anomic–aggressive rejection of forms, this inability to rest and reflect, Nietzsche detects motivations antithetical to truly modern aspirations. "Such a man's fundamental desire is that the war which he *is* should come to an end."[7] Beneath the anomie, the frenetic hubbub, he senses the desire for peace at any price, and for objects of devotion however cheap and tawdry.

Utilitarianism, in both its liberal democratic and socialist variants, is both symptom and cause of the weightlessness he feared and indicted:

Modern socialism wants to create the secular counterpart to Jesuitism: everyone a perfect instrument. But the purpose, the wherefore? has not yet been ascertained.[8]

Marx naively suggested to Bentham that the problem of human purpose is a matter of distinguishing between the nature of a dog and man, as if certainty and consensus on the subject of human nature had not been profoundly shaken already. And as for utilitarianism: is there any course of action, any moral argument, any public policy which cannot be supported by utilitarian arguments and assumptions?

At present men's sentiments on moral things run in such labyrinthic paths that, while we demonstrate morality to one man by virtue of its utility, we refute it to another on account of this utility.[9]

This proponent of strikingly modern views (and classical ideals) had little taste for "modernity." He doubted whether so-called moderns had much taste for it either. Modern man "has learned to digest many things; nay, almost everything; it is his ambition to do so. However ... *homo pomphagus* is not the finest type of the human race."[10] In terms reminiscent of Durkheim's discussion of anomie, he characterizes modern men as "greedy, unsatisfied, undisciplined, disgusted, and harrassed spirits." His Zarathustra taunts the "free" man:

Do you call yourself free? I want to hear your ruling ideas, and not that you have escaped from a yoke.

Are you such a man as ought to escape a yoke?

There are many who threw off their final worth when they threw off their bondage.

Free from what? Zarathustra does not care about that. But your eye should clearly tell me: free *for* what?

Can you furnish yourself with your own good and evil and hang up your

own will above yourself as a law? Can you be judge of yourself and
avenger of your law?
It is terrible to be alone with the judge and avenger of one's own law. It is
to be like a star thrown forth into empty space and into the icy breath of
solitude.[11]

To be really modern is to work one's way through, not around, the
positions and perspectives which brought us to such a pass. We *are* all
these things, these conflicts and contradictions, traditional and critical,
regressive and progressive, however much we consciously cling to one
pole or another. Those who consider themselves strictly modern, in
search of nothing save release, escape, "freedom" will soon enough
reveal that one foot remains mired in the muck of the past. They are
liable to get the second foot stuck in the effort to extricate the first. This
escapist pursuit of the free, the new, the modern betrays the
conservative desire to have an end of it, to locate a peaceful, permanent,
bounded place of rest, an alienated solution to an anomic state.

Thus it is entirely appropriate, as well as ironic, that this paralleled
champion of the "free spirit" evokes so powerfully the sense of loss and
disorientation in setting forth on such a radically new tack:

> Horizon: infinity—We have left the land and taken to our ship. We have
> burned our bridges—more, we have burned our land behind us. Now,
> little ship, take care. The ocean lies all around you; true, it is not always
> roaring, and sometimes it lies there as if it were silken and golden and a
> gentle favourable dream. But there will be times when you will know
> that it is infinite and there is nothing more terrible than
> infinity . . . . [A]las, if homesickness for land should assail you, as if there
> were more freedom there—and there is no longer any "land."[12]

To be genuinely adrift, with the horizons themselves receding, is
frightful. "There is nothing more terrible than infinity." This helps
explain the curiously unserious quality of so many of our most
advanced cultural specimens. They have not really burned their
bridges, much less set sail. Often they continue to receive money from
home. This is why so many of the avant garde, for all their calculated
eccentricities, bear such strong resemblance to one another, particularly
in their obvious willingness to seek out any old port in a storm. Anomie
leads to alienation. But then the new culture depends on remnants of the
old to keep its fires going. Alienation leads to anomie.

The Free, the Strong, the Envious

Nietzsche's "free spirit" is perpetually, perhaps eternally, engaged in a
certain kind of assault on all oppositions, and particularly those we have
associated with alienation and anomie. Alienation and anomie are

intimately tied to his doctrine of the will to power, his critique of Christian asceticism and *ressentiment,* and his denunciation of "free thinkers" and the doctrine of *laisser aller.*

Nietzsche admits that his "will to power" could actually be labeled "freedom" (Kaufmann argues it is "an Eros"). He avoided "freedom" for the same reason that Freud insisted on speaking of sex instead of love. Their unwillingness to make concessions to slimy moralists and the compulsively squeamish is admirable, but the distance from freedom to will to power, and from sex to love, is considerable, at least as these terms are commonly understood. As Nietzsche takes his analysis farther and farther from the conventional connotations of power, his efforts to see all phenomena in terms of power become increasingly ingenious, artificial, implausible. We can neither neologize all our new insights nor manipulate old concepts at will, even if the will in question is the will to power. Once Nietzsche is reduced to describing various forms of gross weakness (in the physical or political sense) as so many manifestations of will to power, the very cognitive and linguistic limitations that he otherwise exposed and denounced so effectively begin to constrain his own account. He is trying to characterize all of life's manifestations, but applying any concept to it, will to power or whatever, cleaves it in two. The Tao has no name, and for good reason.

Power is not power that yieldeth when resistance meets, that is not exercised on external objects and revealed in their altered course. Nietzsche sometimes seems to confuse power with will to power, and both with power as power over oneself: self-mastery or self-overcoming. The third is usually his intended meaning. An added difficulty is Nietzsche's penchant for portraying the struggle for self-mastery in terms of war, cruelty, violence, and other terms suggesting external social conflict. The evidence that he did not mean to glorify brute force is conclusive, however careless his language at times.

> Deification of success is truly commensurate with human meanness .... [T]o find in history the realization of the good and the just is blasphemy against the good and the just.... [W]hat is *strong* wins: that is the universal law. If only it were not so often precisely what is stupid and beastly.[14]

Neither necessity nor desire is the "demon of man". It is love of power: "the demon waits and waits and will be satisfied". He was dedicated to making us more conscious of the presence and influence of this demon, better equipped to fashion artful sublimations. The gods within us, he observed, are *reason* and *experience.* The relentless critic of the naivete of the Enlightenment was in some ways the champion of its ideals.

Suffice to say that he advocates a refined, subtle, sublimated power, power above all over oneself: self-control, in a sense as far removed from Christian asceticism as from debauchery and libertinism. He vents spleen and venom on both these extremes, together with seekers and holders of conventional power: "realists," Machiavellians, Lasswell's *homo politicus*. Often the latter wish to acquire the *feeling* of power, and therefore

> seize upon any means, and look upon nothing as too petty which can foster this feeling. He who already possesses power, however, has grown fastidious and refined in his tastes; few things can be found to satisfy him.[15]

The truly powerful, the confident and self assured, do not press their advantage at the expense of the weaker. This would be bad taste, and contrary to their nature.

> *Striving for Gentleness*—When a vigorous nature has not an inclination towards cruelty, and is not always preoccupied with itself, it involuntarily strives after gentleness—this is its distinctive characteristic. Weak natures, on the other hand, have a tendency towards harsh judgments.[16]

The highest degree of power is ascribed to the power over opposites, not power over others. "Who will prove to be the strongest . . . ? The most moderate." And those who have the old-fashioned virtues of intellectual integrity and courage, the unquenchable desire to know themselves. It is not merely the courage of one's convictions that is required, but the courage to question one's convictions.

Of greater value than the specific doctrine of the will to power is the notion of man overcoming himself. This applies to any salient opposition, but Nietzsche repeatedly returns to the oppositions we have associated with differentiated and dedifferentiated, conscious and unconscious modes. The maladies the Nietzschean "free spirit" must avoid are asceticism and its accompanying *ressentiment* on the right hand, and libertinism and the doctrine of *laisser aller* on the left. These are variants of alienation and anomie, the fundamental false opposites. He mercilessly exposes the illicit link between piety and debauchery. He grants that piety may well have been the only means up until now for man to beautify himself. He admits that it is *Christian* honesty that ultimately exposes the nihilistic core of its runaway asceticism, its controls out of control, crimes against the spirit and flesh. Nietzsche openly admired the spirit of discipline and the willingness to deny oneself seen in exemplary Christians like Christ and Saint Augustine, even as he pilloried the purposes and the psychological counterfeiting with which it was entangled, the lengths to which fanatics against the flesh took this discipline, the confusion of self-immolation with sublimation. If anything, his scorn for "free thinkers" and "anarchists" was greater than his scorn for ascetic moralities. Free for what?—Zarathustra asks. Few so-called moderns were giving the question serious thought. Few appreciated the stakes riding on the answer. Those who babbled most of freedom were precisely those "for whom no reins would be strict enough," who might have lost their last stitch of value when they threw off the yoke.

To Nietzsche, what is so galling about Christianity is not so much the discipline it demands, but the methods by which it insists upon achieving self-control: the psychological dishonesty it reflects and fosters, the violence and envy which are frequent concomitants. Slave morality begins by training the value-positing eye outwards, finding what is negative, deplorable, sinful, evil (and exciting, fascinating, attractive as well). The Christian doctrine of good and evil has made the world "overfull of things to hate": "we begin by unlearning to love others, and we end by finding nothing lovable in ourselves."[17] "In every ascetic morality", he asserts, "man worships a part of himself as God and for that he needs to diabolize the other part."[18] "Whoever despises himself still respects himself as one who despises."[19] While the "ascetic imposes on himself what the barbarian imposes on others," they are first cousins. Attempting to extirpate that aspect of ourselves we have banned and diabolized, cutting it off from consciousness, we generously attribute it to others. Forbidden impulses receive oblique expression, and the superstitious ascetic is titillated even as he hunts down and condemns the offending, exciting party.

Nietzsche repeatedly expressed and demonstrated appreciation for his antipodes. By contrast, the ascetic wants to stamp them out, as if his world would not be intolerably bleak and boring without symbols of the Satanic to kick around, or as if he could permanently avoid facing his own devils. What is merely suggestive of these forbidden impulses is made equal to them, to other objects, and still others. The ascetic has weak eyes, a strong propensity not just to seek out the similar but to level, tear down, to render crappy what is different and better. In this mode, there is little that cannot be seen as similar, worthy of leveling. The ascetic imbued with *ressentiment* has the weakest eyes of all, and the keenest nose for threatening differences. At times the total destruction of the offending party may seem to be the only way out.

Interestingly, we can readily discuss many of the same phenomena in seemingly opposite terms: as the exaggerated drive for distinction. As Nietzsche himself observed, the desire for distinction often coincides with the desire to subject and level one's neighbor. This amounts to saying that the same syndrome can be thought of as alienation (wherein we try to get others down into the hole we're in) or anomie (wherein the only point is to distinguish ourselves, but distinctions become increasingly pointless).

Ressentiment can therefore be viewed as an aggressive form of alienation or anomie or both, associated with those who have not been able to retaliate directly and effectively for their oppression and subordination. To the envious, what is other becomes infinitely threatening, great, exciting, special. The envious are continually subjected to Hegel's "sorrow of finitude." What remains inside is infinitely small, empty, barren, lifeless. Insofar as he retains an identification with what is forbidden, he must search out and destroy whatever hints of the diabolical.

The apostle Paul, who epitomized for Nietzsche the ascetic riddled with ressentiment—Paul the cripple, whom Nietzsche suspected of wanting everyone to break a leg for Jesus—saw these matters differently. Knowledge puffeth up, he warned the Corinthians. The striving for infinite knowledge, the assault on boundaries, the assumption of prerogatives heretofore reserved for God (or His agents, prophets, spokesmen, interpreters) may puff up infinitely. In this respect their perspectives dovetail. But Paul's brand of balance and restraint was no longer available by Nietzsche's time. Unlike crabs, human beings must push forward. If this takes us step by step toward prerogatives heretofore reserved for God, then so be it.

So Nietzsche's argument does not bring back to Paul. To be sure, we must respect and acquire the will to ignorance: "a great, firm dome of ignorance must encompass you." Wisdom sets limits on knowledge, he points out. Ignorance is its helpmate. But this is his advice to "free spirits," not those individuals who readily accept permanent bounds, who confuse the roles they play with life itself. The advice issues from first-hand acquaintance with the terrors of questioning everything at once. He who would question all received wisdom must proceed piecemeal, bracketing an infinity of other questions. On the conscious level, we think approximately one thought at a time, however many undifferentiated thoughts it may contain and later spawn.

> Brief habits—I love brief habits and consider them an inestimable means for getting to know many things and states . . . . [M]y nature is designed entirely for brief habits . . . . from the lowest to the highest. I always believe that here is something that will give me lasting satisfaction . . . . But one day its time is up . . . . [E]nduring habits I hate . . . and most intolerable, to be sure, and the terrible par excellence would be for me a life entirely devoid of habits, a life that would demand perpetual improvisation. That would be my exile and my Siberia.[20]

Overcoming oppositions is steady work, a long march, and endless endeavor. Those who attempt to question everything at once may collapse in anomic confusion, followed by or virtually coinciding with alienated rigidity or apathy. In either condition they effectively challenge nothing.

"The libertinage, the principle of *laisser aller* should not be confused with the will to power (which is the counter principle)."[21] Nor does he advocate reversion to instinct, which would simply be "one catastrophe more." While Nietzsche would be the last to underestimate the importance of drives, his notion of how much guidance they provide is very nearly that of Durkheim. (Their impact on behavior, their paired aspect, the wisdom of ignoring or trying to extirpate them are different matters.) We have seen his appreciation of past Christian piety in this regard. "All ideals are dangerous: because they debase and brand the actual; all are poisons, but indispensible as temporary cures."[22] The bad conscience is a disease, "no doubt of that." But he adds that it is a disease in the sense that pregnancy is a disease.

Nietzsche stressed self-discipline like few before him and pitifully few since. The affinity with Durkheim and the conservative sociological tradition is noteworthy and rarely noted. Yet his message, the point of self-discipline and self-denial, is quite different.

> At bottom I abhor those moralities which say: "Do not do this! Renounce! Overcome yourself." But I am well disposed toward those moralities which goad me to do something and do it again.... [W]hen one lives like that, one thing after another that simply does not belong to such a life drops off... eyes riveted to goal, not forward, sideward, backward, downward. What we do should determine what we forego; by doing we forego—But I do not wish to strive with open eyes for my own impoverishment; I do not like negative virtues—virtues whose very essence it is to negate and deny oneself something.[23]

The "no" of noble moralities is an afterthought, the side effect of pursuing what is excellent, fine. It is in this light that his otherwise conservative emphasis on discipline and constraint should be understood: "the essential and invaluable element in every morality is that it is protracted constraint."[24] He who cannot obey himself will be commanded, for protracted obedience in one direction is "the essential thing 'in heaven and upon earth.'" Hence his formula for happiness: "A Yes, a No, a straight line, a *goal*".[25]

The way *back* to the Yes and the No passes through the idea of overcoming ambivalences and the related idea of reason, defined as a kind of balance among contradictory drives and emotions. In our terms, reason consists of or is predicated upon a certain balance or felicitious relationship between conscious and unconscious, the dividing and equalizing modes. The unconscious is made conscious, the symmetrical translated into asymmetrical terms, but at a rate that is possible to tolerate and express. This is in sharp contrast to with the greedy omnivores called "modern men," who are awash in possibilities and realize few, whose condition resembles the stagflation of their economy. The futile effort to ignore or extinguish passions is not only abandoned, it is condemned. Instead, passions are shaped, sublimated and refined, receiving symbolic and spiritualized expression.

> All passions have a phase when they are merely disastrous, when they drag down their victim with the weight of stupidity—and a later, much later phase when they wed the spirit, when they "spiritualize" themselves.[26]

Reason is a matter of the economy of passions, whereas the ascetic moralities attempt to dam and dry up "the torrents of the soul":

> The same means in the fight against a craving—castration, extirpation—is instinctively chosen by those who are too weak willed, too degenerate, to be able to impose moderation on themselves.[27]

Immoderation is weakness, a low degree of the will to power. The self-consciously modern have begun to experiment with giving up the internal fight, with the glorification and deification of craving. Rather than confronting ambivalence, they flee and deny it. These are the people "who become slaves as soon as they serve." For them Nietzsche prescribes some bitter traditional medicine:

> Your desires are greater than your understanding, and your vanity is even greater than your desires—to people of your type a great deal of Christian practice and a little Schopenhauerian pessimism may be strongly recommended.[28]

His own view he sums up as follows: "domination of the passions, not their weakening or extirpation! The greater the dominating power of a will, the more freedom may the passions be allowed."[29]

Once we look carefully at what people do and aspire to, the overcoming or reconciliation of opposites appears as everyone's project. The basic maladies to which we are prone, the ways we fall short, the false opposites on which we insist upon crucifying ourselves, speak eloquently of this aspiration and the human obstacles to its achievement. Here as everywhere, life dominates logic.

Undifferentiated Unconscious: Anticipations and Adumbrations

Despite obvious differences in terminology and focus, Nietzsche saw the connection of alienation and anomie in a manner remarkably similar to the theory advanced here. The primitive opposition of making different and making equal dominates and energizes his epistomologic-al speculations, critique of logic and language, analysis of ressentiment, notion of eternal recurrance, synthesis of the Dionysian and the Apollonian, and so on and on.

Yet it would appear that Nietzsche's polemic against leveling in all its guises, on behalf of difference and distinction, is in some respects uncompromising. This casts doubt on his appreciation of the necessary interpenetration and cooperation of the two modes. It calls into question his doctrine of psychic ambivalence and his dialectical understanding of alienation and anomie. Many of his more memorable aphorisms seem to support such a judgment, together with the general tenor of both his epistemological speculations in *Will to Power* and his psycho-political analyses in *Geneology of Morals*. He appears to violate his own off-stated stipulation that all distinctions must be retained but struggled against. For these reasons Nietzsche's adumbration of our account of alienation and anomie must be complemented by a look at arguments in which the notion of the unrepressed unconscious seems to be rejected. In the main these apparently contradictory arguments actually amount to keen intuitions of some the major features and effects of this structural view of the psyche.

We do not think in terms of difference alone, though the absence of difference cannot be conscious. Nor do we find the sense of anything, including ourselves and society, in terms of mere difference. Since non-differentiation pervades and underlies what is distinguished and divided, Nietzsche's polemics praising difference and scorning equality seem to sponsor the anomie chaos and fragmentation which he repeatedly denounces.

Witness the following:

> Fundamentally, all our *actions* are altogether incomparably personal, unique, and infinitely individual; there is no doubt of that. But as soon as we translate them into consciousness they no longer seem to be.... [C]onsciousness belongs to man's social or herd nature.[30]

Certainly it is the undifferentiated unconscious which would seem to foster man's "herd nature," not the differentiating faculties. What Nietzsche has in mind, however, is the ultimate function or impact of unconscious mentation, working in tandem and harmony with the conscious. The paradoxical result of unconscious mentation is to break down and "equalize" those ossified and isolated conceptions, previously differentiated similarities, themselves associated with our "social or herd nature." This amounts to setting them in motion as well. Then, in conjunction with the differentiated mode, they produce newly differentiated similarities, breathing life into new forms. Sooner or later the newly distinguished equations become conventional wisdom, stale generalities, bloodless cliches, lifeless forms. But Nietzsche correctly divined the net impact of the unconscious when it is working in creative harmony with conscious faculties, and he did so in a way perfectly compatible with our structural view of the psyche. The same line of argument accounts for his contention that advances of knowledge always consist in making what is unconscious conscious.

Another troublesome contention characterizes his critique of logic and language: their alleged alienating powers, the conservative needs they reflect and cater to. He fails to note that to see things as equal is to posit other things as different from that we have equalized. Any mental production (including his "will to power") is always both equalizing and dividing, in motivation as well as effect. His concern is that concepts and forms provide a haven for inertia, security needs, passivity and the like. By his own postulates, however, he would have done better to assign individuals or groups some combination of the tendency to equalize and the tendency to make different, more or less as Simmel did. A partial explanation is that Nietzsche was simply pointing to those tendencies prominent in certain uses of logic and habits of mind. There is, for example, the *ressentiment* of certain logicians and academics, whose profession consists of forcing their opponents to prove they are not idiots.

In all events these difficulties are balanced by his oft-stated belief that life miscarries when either mode is carried to an extreme, and his inspired and unflagging efforts to indicate how and why this occurs. For example, there is his dogged critique of the emotions in their raw and unruly form. Until mutual balance is achieved, reason is impossible. Instead we have the "mob of the senses." Reliance on feelings puts us in bondage to the thoughts and ideas of our grandfathers. Their effect is leveling. In like manner the careless advocate of spontaneity inadvertently delivers us over to the herd, to what is common and conventional. The result is anything but freedom, fluidity of thought, uniqueness of style. This is not at all what he means by "going with the flow."

Feelings as such are "terrible," "torrential." Nietzsche calls attention to their refusal to assume small, nearly zero values, much as Matte Blanco does. He emphasizes their "envious," monopolizing quality: all past philosophical systems, he asserts, are one-sided expressions of single drives philosophizing on their own behalf. Above all, emotions are leveling in the cognitive sense: individuals and distinct situations and perceptions get thrown into a class with others. Everything in the class is made identical. This class is identified with another, larger class within which everything is made identical. And so on, unless checked by the dividing mode.

At the heart of his account of equalizing and making different are those emotions and patterns of thought connected with Christian asceticism and modernistic abandon. Pity and envy accompany asceticism, and are the greatest of levelizers and homogenizers. Carried to extremes, the equalizing mode is not merely sloppy, it robs the sufferer of the uniqueness of his suffering. Individious and vengeful distinctions are always latent in and never far from this sharing of suffering. Pity draws a distinction between the sufferer and the benefactor, even as it appears to do the opposite. *Ressentiment* is the leveling sentiment par excellence. But this destructive leveling, the lynx-eyed gaze of the terrible sympathizers and simplifiers, is not at all incompatible with the positing of sharp, rigid, invidious distinctions. These apparently opposite extremes co-exist nicely.

Of course one particular opposition or class of oppositions is singled out for special attention: good and evil. Every distinction states a preference, and there is probably no such thing as pure or mere difference. In this light, good and evil symbolize our tendency to pose rigid and false opposites, whatever their specific "content," and to deny our ambivalence toward the distinction itself as well as specific poles. We opt for one and deny or repress the other. As Nietzsche points out, the real attraction and fascination is therefore the evil, that which we most emphatically are not. Relegated to undifferentiated status, it tends to consume us. To which the conscious faculties, not wishing to be eaten and dissolved, react with further resistance and rigidity. The opposition of good and evil is tantamount, then, to the denial of the unconscious, the mode which softens and makes permeable all such overdrawn boundaries. By the same token it represents alienation, the generic tendency to take refuge from life and change and difference by imprisoning ourselves behind rigid forms, boundaries, distinctions. To the many meanings of beyond good and evil, then, this adds another: beyond good and evil as beyond alienation.

What is literally beyond good and evil in Nietzsche's account is the distinction between good and bad. We must not destroy the difference altogether, lest we substitute for alienation the anomie which he simultaneously deplored because he intuited their essential identity. From the chaos attendant upon the total destruction of such distinctions to a new alienated order of brittle rigid forms is but a short step in space and time. Only our ordered conceptions of space and time prevent our seeing their coincidence in both.

A particularly potent motive for crushing evil is to retaliate for the crucifixion the righteous experience at their own hands as a result of being righteous. For this reason things to hate and to envy, differences to level, are forever popping up. Pollution phobia makes a sewer of the unconscious, which otherwise would have the power to cleanse and refreshen, and it periodically overflows to render their world disgusting. Nietzsche brilliantly dissected this alternation of distinction-making with a vengeance followed by distinction-destroying with a vengeance. Not only did he deplore the extreme myopia of weak eyes for the similar, he also deplored the excessively keen eyes for the different. To be sure, in some contexts Nietzsche slanders equality and sharing without qualification. Yet elsewhere he makes it clear he is not against sharing as such. The question is what can be shared, and with whom. The answer is critically dependent on whether sharing and the equalizing mode are somehow combined with the generation and appreciation of difference.

Nietzsche repeatedly appealed to the "good Europeans." This community was not altogether mythical, and it shared some beliefs or orientations in which he believed deeply. Rather than dismissing sharing, compassion, gentleness, or kindness, he suggests that we should seek to share what is uplifting, what makes us more graceful, high-spirited, different in positive ways. Distinction is not so much the point of the activity as a by-product of giving expression to one's being. "Share not suffering but joy." This can be thought of in terms of overcoming the difference between distinctions and no distinctions among men: distinctions exist, and serve as guides to what is worthy of our efforts; they point to what is superior in life, but are not themselves the point of life. No doubt it is what Simmel had in mind in suggesting that there must surely be forms of individualism beyond the individualism of equality and the individualism of difference. It can even be interpreted as a kind of a liberal community: what is shared is an appreciation of what is different, unique, uplifting, high-spirited, species-advancing: "sharing" in the unique accomplishments of the excellent, extraordinary, incomparable. This is the appropriate context in which to place his assertion that "all contact is bad contact except with one's equals", a contention which is more humane than it seems.

Numerous other subjects are treated in much the same terms: for example, the psychoanalytic concepts of projection, adualism, displacement, identification. In addition, he makes clear our reliance on continual periodic regression to less differentiated modes. "Between two thoughts many affects play their game, but they are too quick to be caught." Reversions to dedifferentiation are difficult to catch not simply because they are fast and fleeting but often all but "blank," because of the cancelling out of so many conflicting thoughts and images. Yet this periodic "regression" can be the antithesis of regressive, and is essential to the continuity and coherence of otherwise fragmented, discontinuous, and meaningless significations. The threat of anomie exists between every thought and every word of every line. (And when those conscious faculties go to sleep—they sleep most of the time, day as well as night—what is it that assures us that the person who awakes is the same one who went to sleep?) It is the acceptance of rhythmic, periodic dissolution of difference which prevents anomic fragmentation and incoherence.

His critique of naive notions of precision, clarity, and certainty serves to round out these comments. Precision can be antagonistic to "far-seeing providentiality." The latter is "led by a deeper instinct." Here he anticipates Ehrenzweig's idea of undifferentiated scanning, with its superior ability to handle a multitude of future possibilities. In a similar vein are his repeated criticisms of the rush to judgment, often found in tandem with "great imperatives" in the conscious. The surface of consciousness should be kept clear of all great imperatives, he suggests: consciousness *is* a surface, he adds. He labors incessantly to invent stylistic and conceptual devices to derail himself and us from our predetermined, conventional course of thought or action, from the greedy rush to appropriate. In this he anticipates Ehrenzweig's discussion of the importance of combating the art student's headlong rush to a premature solution. He affirms the importance of a higher economy and a "democratic" mode which can hold in suspension multiple alternatives, treating the various possibilities and alternatives in an outrageously evenhanded fashion. If creativity were a matter of establishing "great imperatives," pushing us along predetermined paths, it would not be creativity. As in psychoanalytic therapy, militant truths and great imperatives are often part of the problem.

These are some of the many areas in which his treatment of equality and difference anticipate the themes of ambivalence, the unrepressed unconscious, and alienation and anomie set forth here. Nietzsche does not directly associate dedifferentiation with the unconscious, but he does attribute to it qualities and capacities such that it readily translates into these terms. In a sense, *not* associating undifferentiation with the unconscious is fortuitous. Every thought production, examined closely and thoroughly, reveals the presence of every level of mentation from the most highly differentiated to the minimum of differentiation, that near-zero point in which everything is equated to everything else. This is true no matter what proportion of the two modes is immediately perceived and preferred. Even the association of undifferentiation with the unconscious can be misleading if we forget that it pervades differentiated, conscious modes at all times. And conversely. To pin it down spatially, to a precise location, may be self-deception, however human.

The point of these remarks is that Nietzsche was preoccupied with alienation, anomie, and their basis in human ambivalence. He clearly associates those discontents we have christened alienation and anomie with extreme forms of dividing and equalizing modes. What this suggests is that, aside from many specific anticipations of Freud, the fundamental link between the two is in fact the unrepressed undifferentiated unconscious, which to a remarkable extent dovetails with Nietzsche's understanding of the unconscious, ambivalence, the will to power, and life as that which must overcome itself.

It is fascinating to recall Freud's lifelong contention that this unconscious is in fact the true psychic reality, and then to observe his obvious reluctance to stare for long into such a abyss. For his attitude toward Nietzsche was much the same: he stopped reading Nietzsche, he claims, because he feared his own originality would suffer. Fear of death, of fusion, Rank might say. Perhaps in both cases his embattled individuality and originality would not have suffered at all, but have been enhanced immeasurably.

10

Lifeless Form, Formless Life

> No Pleasure sated him, no great
> bestowment,
> He reeled from form to form, it
> did not last.
>
> *Goethe*

> Life . . . can manifest itself only in particular forms; yet, owing to its
> essential restlessness, life constantly struggles against its own products,
> which have become fixed and do not move along with it. This process
> manifests itself as the displacement of an old form by a new one. This
> constant change in the content of culture, even of whole cultural styles, is
> the sign of the infinite fruitfulness of life. At the same time, it marks the
> deep contradiction between life's eternal flux and the objective validity
> and authenticity of the forms through which it proceeds. It moves
> constantly between death and resurrection-between resurrection and
> death.
>
> *Simmel*

The social theory of Georg Simmel, the least known and appreciated of
the major turn-of-the-century sociologists, closely parallels the account
of alienation and anomie offered in this study.[1] In part this is explained
by his intellectual affinity with Nietzsche. His special contribution is to
help us extend the idea of human ambivalence to the analysis of social
forms, and to generalize our view of alienation and anomie in the
process.

Simmel's perspectives have already been put to use: his account of
eighteenth and nineteenth century conceptions of freedom and
individualism, for example. He wonders whether we have seen the last
such conception or if some kind of synthesis of the two is possible. In
fact his preoccupation with overcoming the difference between
equality and difference is the guiding thread that runs through his
otherwise heterogeneous writings. It leads straight to the dualisms at

the heart of his formal method and the conception of ambivalence articulated in this study. By no means are these dualisms of relevance only to his work. In Marx we encounter an unacknowledged and uneasy mixture of eighteenth and nineteenth century individualism. Similarly with Durkheim, though again the mixture is different. Durkheim pictures a society whose conscience collective contains the tenets of moral individualism and whose primary integrative institution is the division of labor. The first aspect approximates the individualism of equality; the second, the individualism of difference or uniqueness. The difference is that Simmel deliberately confronts these contradictions and ambivalences, continually challenges their sovereignty, and constantly searches for social forms which reconcile individual differences and social equality.

Simmel also anticipates certain Freudian themes in ways akin to those suggested and pursued in this study. This is in large part attributable to Nietzsche's influence. Here we have modified Freud's account by resurrecting the unrepressed unconscious; ambivalence as between conscious and unconscious, dividing and equalizing modes; and the "death problem" as involving the exaggerated extremes of these modes. Simmel's dualisms are closely akin. Sometimes he refers to them as "heuristic principles." Elsewhere he simply asserts their empirical importance, or refers to general human tendencies or characteristics. The salient point is that throughout his work there is a lively appreciation of psychic and social conflict as essential to personality, consensus, peace, sociation. He stresses the necessity of attractive and repulsive forces in society and the individual in virtually the same words used by Freud in claiming that the hypothesis of life and death instincts is actually a familiar idea.

Furthermore the notion of basic ambivalence as a split between differentiated conscious and dedifferentiated unconscious, two basic modes of being, while not expressed in this way, is central. In particular it is reflected in his preoccupation with boundaries which mark and maintain differences. As Simmel puts it: we *are* our boundaries. We are also the reaching out across them. We are "too ready to see one or the other faction as our essential being." The Nietzschean influence is also pronounced in his concern with creativity, with emphasis on "overcoming" in life and ethics. Life itself is "form-giving creativity." For Nietzsche it is the will to power which not only dissolves but realizes form, which bounds and crosses bounds. For Simmel it is simply life, or Life. Thus, Life can only express itself in forms, but it refuses to be permanently dammed up and defined by given forms. Given the difficulties Nietzsche encounters in attempting to see all of life as manifestations of will to power, Simmel's label is perhaps more prudent if less evocative.

Central to this inventory of affinities is his treatment of those individual and social discontents we have labeled anomie and alienation.[2] The idea of anomie and alienation as opposites is suggested by his constant use of dualisms which virtually coincide with the polarities we have associated with anomie and alienation, and his keen sense of the way each is continually passing over to the other. He repeatedly states the suspicion voiced earlier: we must think in dualistic terms simply because the calculating intellect lacks a paradigm for the unity of opposites.

Life: Form and Content

Simmel's remarks on man as a social animal serve to introduce to his conception of life as both content and form, and his manner of posing and dealing with dualisms. Man finds himself both within sociation and confronted by it, both the "within" and the "without" defining the "fully homogeneous position of man as social animal." His existence is not partly social and partly individual (as Durkheim would have it). Instead it

> belongs to the fundamental, decisive, and irreducible category of a unity which we cannot designate other than as a synthesis . . . of two logically contradictory characterizations of man.[3]

The contradictory characterizations are (social) equalization and individual differentiation. The contradiction is confronted squarely, and he refuses to settle for misleading and escapist characterizations in terms of segregated spheres of the self. Neither does he pretend that the two views are logically compatible.

This view of man as simultaneously social and individual reflects Simmel's insistence that strictly sociological categories are not the only ones "with which we may contemplate the contents of human experience." In addition to the analysis and judgements of man in terms of sociological categories, there is individual man, the man "without," that stranger to society which everyone also is. There is also the perspective of humanity, or of Nietzsche's world-historical individual, not to be judged by the utilitarian standards of the day but by the advancement of the species over time. There are also cultural phenomena that develop according to their own inherent principles. We can analyze science, art, logic and anything else that belongs to objective culture in terms of its objective content and its laws of development. In this way, Simmel inserts a conceptual wedge between the development and cultivation of individuals and the progress of objective culture. In so doing he suggests that we err in limiting the causes of alienation and anomie to those which are centered on production or organizations. Indirectly he suggests that both discontents are as individual and human as they are social. Both, he implies, are both.

The world seems somehow more deserving of existence, he writes, when we shape it to our purposes. There is a continuous "struggle with objects as extensions of the subject and . . . objects independent of the subject and capable of resisting him."[4] Simmel, like Nietzsche, unlike Marx, sees that struggle as "unending." The transcendence of life, in the form of forms, is immanent in life itself: life expresses itself as something outside the flow of life. This is its defining characteristic: to transcend itself and create that which is objective, permanent, lifeless, dead. To make a religion or fetish of immanence therefore, is to encourage a hopeless and tragic enterprise. There is significant agreement with Marx, however, in Simmel's attitude toward the division of labor. By means of the division of labor, the object first isolates and alienates itself from the working subject. Simmel shares Marx's low opinion of the contribution of specialized tasks to the worker's self-development or "subjective culture." Both appeal to a conception of man as multifaceted and potentially multitalented, though Simmel is prone to stress his potential uniqueness as well. and thus to regard this development as thoroughly problematic, if not tragic.

At this point their analysis of alienation and its causes diverges. Simmel is somewhat more interested in culture, cultural objects, and their autonomy vis à vis the individual and his subjective culture—as opposed to social alienation in various forms, or the production, domination, and exploitation of cultural objects by capitalist interests. In part this is because he wishes to correct the overemphasis on social alienation. Hence his preoccupation with the sheer volume of cultural objects. In principle they tend to infinity, at least as long as societies retain their memories. Finite man can neither ignore nor fully assimilate this "overgrowth of objective culture." Simmel sees culture and social institutions alike as part of that larger panorama of the creation and destruction of form.

As we have seen, Simmel often makes us of the metaphor of distance in his analyses of social phenomena. Nietzsche's critique of precision probably influenced him here. He argues that an accurate view from any given distance has its own justification and standards of accuracy.

Distance can be expressed in terms of degrees of differentiation, the extent to which details and distinctions blend into major features of the landscape.[5] At the large distance from which he views the culture and cultural alienation, he misses many specific sources of alienation and anomie. The the same token, he highlights oppressive aspects of the growth of culture which are related to universal human tendencies as well as the overall trajectory of modern societies.

Simmel asserts that form is that basic category to which we inevitably appeal in conceptualizing the manifestations of life. Unlike Kant's forms, Simmel's are not merely conceptual. If conceptual forms make experience possible, intelligible social forms make sociation and society itself possible. He contends that

> There is perhaps no necessity of thought which is so hard to cast off as the analysis of things into content and form, even though this analysis has neither logical force not the force of sensibly given data. In countless modifications, under this and other names, this division cuts across our image of the world. It is one of the organizers and flexible instruments with which the mind gives structure to the mass of all that is, a mass which, in its immediate unity, is structureless.[6]

Forms are as simple as a single distinction or as complicated as Hegelian metaphysics, giant bureaucracies or the metropolis. They include the social "structures" of English anthropology and the cognitive structures of Levi-Strauss. They also include the kinds of social phenomena that are either smaller in scale or cut across various social institutions: domination, secrecy, competition, sociality, the adventure, friendship, and myriad others.

There is no denying the Protean quality of his idea of form. He prefers to allow it the freedom to be itself. The opposed aspect of life, formless content, is even more difficult to pin down. But there is a striking resemblence between Simmel's distinction and the basic ambivalence we have posited between conscious and unconscious, dividing and equalizing modes. His accounts of social forms, seemingly so diverse and disparate, always revolve about differentiation versus nondifferentiation, individuation versus (social) equalization, dividing versus equalizing. Simmel does not tie the differentiated and dedifferentiated modes to his dualism of form and content, and does not explore the connection between formless content and what is unconscious, as a result of its undifferentiated nature. But the affinity with these ideas is unmistakable and remarkable.[7]

In most contexts Simmel associates life with the absence of forms and death with forms. Clinging to forms amounts to alienation. The absense or confusion of forms—or formless "content," which he properly associates with the chaotic proliferation of forms—represents anomie. Alienation is implicitly defined, therefore, as the undue separation of the differentiated conscious and the undifferentiated unconscious. Anomie is seen as the confusion and chaotic collision of the two modes.

Speaking of our tendency to separate Life into positive and negative pairs and to relegate the negative to the status of non–being, he argues that

> The highest conception indicated in respect to these contrasting pairs appears to me different . . . . [W]e must sense the pulse of a central vitality even in that which, if seen from the standpoint of a particular ideal, ought not to be at all and is merely something negative; we must allow the total meaning of our existence to flow out of both parties.[8]

Simmel conceives of life in terms of this coincidence of opposites, even though this is a vantage point humans try in vain to achieve:

> Perhaps it is not given to us to attain, much less always to maintain, the height from which all phenomena can felt as making up the unity of life, even though from an objective or value standpoint, they appear to oppose one another as pluses and minuses, contradictions, and mutual eliminations. We are too inclined to think and feel that our essential being, our true, ultimate significance, is identical with one of these factions.[9]

He repeatedly returns to the distinction between a dualizing, differentiating mode and an attitude which "lets the whole really be the whole, . . . alive in each of these contrasts and their juncture." His conception of dualisms and their overcoming, anomie and alienation, dovetails with our account. His discussion of boundaries reflects both concerns. Man must have boundaries. Since he must, man *is* his boundaries. Man is also the transcending of boundaries and limits. Echoing Vico, he suggests that "man is the limited being who has no limit."

This division of man into an infinite and finite aspects is also encountered in Hegel, Marx, Feuerbach, Nietzsche even Durkheim. Simmel's view all but coincides with the view developed here. In effect he divides man into a limited, differentiated, partial, and bounded aspect, and an undifferentiated totality as the infinite aspect. Then he suggests that these seemingly different and separate aspects might not actually be different or opposed at all. Putting it in Matte Blanco's terms: the nature of man is such that there is an infinite, generalizing part, the symmetrical unconscious, associated with the formation and use of symbols, and a restricting (asymmetrical) part, leading to differentiated, asymmetrical thinking.

In the absense of form we have a kind of Heraclitic flux which "lacks a definite, persistent something, which does not contain the boundary over which a reaching out is to occur."[10] For asymmetrical being, this is felt as the loss of identity and the threat of annihilation. Be this as it may:

> Although the boundary is necessary, every single determinate boundary can be stepped over.... [T]he boundary is unconditional... but no particular boundary is unconditional.... [W]e are bounded in every direction, we are bounded in no direction.... [J]ust as the boundary partakes both of "this side" and "that side," so the unified act of life includes both the state of being bounded and the transcending of the boundary.... [E]very limit is..... transcended but of course only as a result of the fact that it is set, that there exists something to transcend.[11]

Even this view has a touch of megalomania. Man may not be able to alter the laws of gravitational attraction; our inability to think except by means of difference is itself a kind of barrier. Nevertheless, Simmel's position differs significantly from Hegel's aspiration for "something else–namely, infinity." Simmel understands that infinity is not a "something," no more than "freedom" or "success," which are also spoken of in this way, and which no doubt betray the same conservative desire to have a rest from it and an end to it. That is precisely the problem. He often refers to forms and limits as the opposite of life. Yet life, he points out repeatedly, can only express itself in finite, differentiated forms, in a deathlike guise. Alienation and anomie, each in its way, represent the tragic attempt to have it otherwise. Alienation dams up and constricts the flow of life. Anomie overflows the banks. Because we are limited beings who are also unlimited, we are forever vulnerable to alienation. Because we are unlimited beings who are also limited, we are also vulnerable to anomie. Man's fate, Rilke suggests, is to forever reside between rock and river.

This helps explain Simmel's penchant for formulations that sacrifice logical rigor to the simultaneous affirmation of opposite truths.

> Perhaps the ties between individuals are quite homogeneous... but we cannot grasp their homogeneity. The calculating intellect often lacks a paradigm for this unity.... [P]rocesses within individuals are... of same kind.... So called mixed feelings may be entirely self-consistent.[12]

This recalls Matte Blanco's argument that there is a great deal of symmetry at the base of our asymmetrical logical systems, irrespective of what primitive (undefined) terms we begin with. There is indivisible oneness amidst our divided reality, a boundless totality infusing our bounded selves, timeless spaceless eternity pervading the temporal and spatial discontinuities of history, place, experience, and ego. (The action of symmetry tends to dissolve space and time, since both depend on asymmetrical coordinates which symmetry renders identical.) Simmel places human truths ahead of logical imperatives which would prohibit their airing. Nor are the impediments merely or strictly logical. We must expect rigid "pollution behavior" in response to attempts to contradict going distinctions, to challenge the "fundamental faith of the metaphysicians."

His attitude toward realizing in life the unity beyond our dualisms is generally pessimistic. Yet he is aware that certain spheres of life partake or hint of such a unity. The most familiar is personal love. Under ideal and rare circumstances, the essential unity and compatibility of the social and individual is affirmed. Simmel also points to other spheres like work, art, law, and religion, which offer partial and fleeting examples.[13] The task of confronting and reconciling opposites is never-ending, a long march, as in Nietzsche. But this "highest level of spiritual cultivation" can at least be approximated, even if the unity we achieve cannot be conceptualized. The effort to do so is what Life, and Simmel's life work, are all about.

Fashion and Conflict

Simmel's analysis of fashion is offered against a backdrop of decline in the "great, permanent convictions." This helps explain why fashion exercises such a powerful influence:

> For this reason fashion... has become much broader and animated... for man requires an ephemeral tyrant the moment he has rid himself of the absolute and permanent one. The frequent change of fashion represents a tremendous subjugation of the individual and in that respect forms one of the essential complements of the increased social and political freedom.[14]

He not only appeals to historical trends but also to trans-historical forms and human "givens."

> The essential forms of life in the history of our race invariably show the effort to combine the interest in duration, unity, and similarity with that in change, specialization, and peculiarity.[15]

These pairs are variations on differentiation/nondifferentiation or individualization/equalization, as he himself suggests. Already we have the characteristic features of his approach: the prominence of dualisms; forms, seen as attempts to embody and unify or overcome these dualisms; appeals to human nature, or universal forms suggestive of human nature.

"No institution, no law, no estate of life, can uniformly satisfy the full demands of the two opposing principles."[16] The only realization possible is the "constantly changing approximation, in ever retracted attempts and ever revived hopes.... [T]his constitutes the whole wealth of our development."[17] Fashion, any form, speaks to a fundamental ambivalence: the need to be different and outstanding and unique on the one hand; the need to belong, to imitate, to be equal or to fuse on the other. Being fashionable, insofar as it serves the need to be different, defeats its own purpose precisely to the extent that more strive for and achieve it. The more fashionable company there is, the less fashionable and distinctive the company. Once something is really in we may find that we want out. Faced with equality, we crave difference. And conversely. Hence the ambiguity of fashion: intended to distinguish the individual, it simultaneously involves conformity and enslavement to the trendy.

Fashion is rooted in the "psychological tendency toward imitation." In his studiously ironic manner, he suggests that imitation

> affords the pregnant possibility of continually extending the greatest creation of the human spirit.... [W]henever we imitate, we transfer not only the demand for creative activity but also the responsibility for the action from ourselves to another. Thus the individual is freed from the worry of choosing and appears simply as a creature of the group, as a vessel for the social contents.[18]

Imitation is one of the "fundamental tendencies of our character": "that which contents itself with similarity, with uniformity, with the adaptation of the special to the general, and accentuates the constant element in change."[19] On the other side are dividing "tendencies," desires for change and contrast. Fashion involves and appeals to both kinds of needs, as does any form. It is

> one of the many forms of life by the aid of which we seek to combine in uniform spheres of activity the tendency towards social equalization with the desire for individual differentiation and change.[20]

Simmel proceeds to analyze the formal characteristics of fashion, the motivations of those who would be fashionable (or unfashionable) at any cost, and the general irrelevance of aesthetic standards in determining what is fashionable.

In this context Simmel offers a sober estimate of the possibilities of creating forms which manage to serve both kinds of needs simultaneously. To those who imagine that implacable opposition to fashion (conformity, convention, imitation) suffices to set them free, Simmel gives little encouragement. (Opposition to fashion is itself a familiar modern fashion.) He also observes that fashion is not the worst of the forms that play on these needs.

Like fashion, conflict is "designed" to resolve divergent dualisms: "it is a way of achieving some kind of unity, even if it be through the annihilation of the conflicting parties."[22] If it does not literally "aim at peace," it often results in a social equilibrium less ridden with tension and less subject to explosion and disruption. The analogy to attaining a better personal equilibrium or balance of conflicting needs is close:

> The individual does not attain the unity of the personality exclusively by an exhaustive harmonization, according to logical, objective, religious, or ethical norms, of the contents of personality. On the contrary, contradiction and conflict not only precede this unity but are operative in it at every moment of its existence. Just so, there probably exists no social unit in which convergent and divergent currents among its members are not inseparably interwoven.[23]

Conflict as sociation is a favorite Simmelian theme, and he delights in demonstrating how apparent opposites like conflict and consensus are forever proving more complementary than competitive. In "Metropolis and Mental Life", for example, he points to the blase attitude and slight antipathy as significant forms of sociation in urban settings.

In this connection Simmel calls attention to a distinction of signal importance in the discussion of social conflict and unity. We tend to confuse two meanings of unity, he contends:

> We designate as "unity" the consensus and concord of interacting individuals, as against their discords, separations and disharmonies. But we also call "unity" the total group-synthesis of persons, energies, and forms, that is, the ultimate wholeness of that group, a wholeness which covers both strictly-speaking unitary relations and dualistic relations.[24]

The application to the usual sociological conception of consensus is immediate. Simmel's hunch is that the attempt to suppress conflict is usually more dangerous and destructive than its encouragement.

Conflict alone does not suffice to constitute a relationship, much less to unify a society. But neither does consensus, if by consensus we understand its opposite. His most interesting passages concern those elements of unity that lie beneath the surface of conflict—whether in social institutions, groups, or intimate relationships—and perhaps beyond our ability to conceptualize.

> Perhaps the ties between individuals are indeed often quite homogeneous, but our mind cannot grasp their homogeneity. The very relations that are rich and live on many different contents are apt to make us most aware of this mysterious homogeneity; and what we have to do is represent it as the co-efficiency of several cohesive forces which restrict and modify one another, resulting in the picture which objective reality attains by a much simpler and much more consistent route. Yet we cannot follow it with our mind even though we would.[25]

As for individual unity,

> probably much of what we are forced to represent to ourselves as mixed feelings, as composites of many drives, as the competition of opposite sensations, is entirely self-consistent. But the calculating intellect often lacks a paradigm for this unity.[26]

Erotic relationships are particularly revealing in this respect:

> How often do they not strike us as woven together of love and respect, or disrespect; of love and the felt harmony of the individuals and, at the same time, their consciousness of supplementing each other through opposite traits; of love and an urge to dominate or the need for dependence. But what the observer or the participant himself thus divides into two intermingling trends may in reality be only one.[27]

In connection with these forms, and a host of others, Simmel demonstrates that there are perfectly valid and most fruitful ways of regarding the individual which are not exclusively from the point of view of society, its forms, institutions, and structured differences. This is a valuable service, and one obvious key to the neglect he has suffered, or in some respects enjoyed. Ambivalence is channeled socially, culturally, linguistically, symbolically, individually. In this sense it varies over time and space. Ambivalence itself, like life and death, is apparently here to stay. Maybe this is because the fundamental ambivalence is between life and death.

Alienation and Anomie, Cultural and Social

Simmel's understanding of alienation and anomie is best seen in connection with his account of the overgrowth of objective culture. He begins by drawing the distinction between subjective culture, the degree of development or cultivation of the individual; and objective culture, the sum total of all the results of man's form-giving creativity. The "overarching goal is . . . the extent to which psychic life processes make use of objective goods and accomplishments."[28] The movement toward personal perfection is "somehow latent in the individual's natural structural potential . . . even though this can only be realized through culture".[29] He takes for granted that the "personality as a whole" contains an "image of potentiality,"[30] and the "goal of perfection . . . guides unified development." In turn, this informs his idea of "cultivation": "when cultural traits develop that aspect of his soul which exists as its most indigenous drive."[31]

Social life has a peculiar feature so familiar it is rarely noticed or appreciated: personal development is pursued and achieved in a roundabout way. Typically, creation and utilization of forms are separate matters, and often uncoordinated. We can try to imagine a society whose cultural objects are of a number and quality such that most individuals can both create and assimilate it all, all forms redounding to the self-enhancement of most members of the society. A few passages in Marx conjure up such a society. But even at this unimaginably primitive stage there are elements of "roundaboutness." Another difficulty is that the ability to assimilate and use and profit from specified cultural objects varies with the individual. It is not simply a matter of ability or initiative. Individuality requires a unique complement of social institutions and cultural objects, just as it requires a unique complement of other individuals and groups. Simmel goes on to point out serious gaps between subjective culture and objective culture. Some are timeless, while others pertain to modern society.

Among the latter, one is rooted in the division of labor. No one has control over the processes and end product because of the many specialized stages in its production. The question is not merely whether the end product enhances one's subjective culture, but whether one has been allowed to put one's personal stamp on that product. Or rather: these amount to the same question. The difference with Marx is that Simmel sees that extreme specialization of task is "only a special form of this very general cultural predicament," the dissolution of the liason between subject and object.

The liason of subject and object is dissolved not simply as a result of the division of labor. No matter how they are produced or by whom, cultural objects are gathered together in meaningful constellations and are developed with respect to indigenous lines of development. This underlies the perennial poignant complaint of the student who wants to become a better or happier person as a result of pursuing this or that course of study. We have not yet managed to turn higher education into a supermarket, wherein individual packages and the total basket contains exactly what and only what the student consumer desires. It is also the case with the development of logic itself, which is not designed to satisfy the innermost longings of the heart. One no longer masters a body of knowledge for one's own purposes, even though a few may "develop" or "realize" themselves in the study of it. If lucky, we get to choose which such master will be followed. None of these masters is likely to care one whit for one's "natural structural potential," notwithstanding all the recent rhetoric about how this job and that corporation are designed and run with only your self-realization in mind. Wherever one looks in modern society, the autonomy of cultural contents and forms dominates the landscape. In the face of this overgrowth of objective culture, the choice is often between an irresponsible, tragic dilettantism or resignation to this nook or that niche: anomie or alienation.

The overgrowth of objective culture has another meaning for Simmel. It concerns the sheer number of cultural objects and artifacts, another facet of anomie neglected by Durkheim. Simmel points to the obvious limitations on our capacity to assimilate, master, use, and gain information about cultural objects. Yet in a modern society it is increasingly difficult to be unaware of many of these objects; it cannot be said that they are completely meaningless. Thus the misery. The mad dash to look over as much as possible creates less than ideal circumstances in which to sort wheat from chaff. Choices are hurried, skewed. There is pressure to choose and pressure to not choose, to stay loose. Another possibility always beckons. The individual's own form is threatened in the process: "How to protect the unity of form from the touch and temptation of all those things?"

As to the sources of this undesirable and unmanageable trajectory of Western societies, Simmel does not offer a definitive answer, though he squelches easy answers. He observes that the form-giving creativity of man, the ubiquitous and omnipresent movement from form to form, is a force for cultural diversity—not unity, as Marx seems to have assumed. Some forms do subsume or help integrate the previously segregated, perhaps producing temporary peace and relief, but in general his contention is sound. A second source of this infinitization of culture is the division of labor, a powerful engine behind more specialized products and specialized people. A third source is capitalism, and the capitalist market. Simmel generally concentrates on other factors like the division of labor, the characteristics of metropolitan life, ahistorical forms. This is of a piece with his focus on forms or protoforms rather than more institutionalized interactions. Yet if only for the gigantic strides in productivity it has achieved, capitalism looms large in the background. Moreover, it does not have the perfection of subjective culture in mind either, much less an egalitarian society. Simmel anticipates Galbraith in suggesting that "vast supplies of products . . . call forth an artifical demand that is senseless from the perspective of subject's culture."[32]

So it is a curious reversal of Marx that Simmel offers. Instead of genuine poverty and exploitation, the poverty Simmel exposes and stresses is poverty relative to the cultural riches (and a measure of material abundance). Unlike Durkheim, Simmel refers not to infinite aspirations as such, but to an actual infinitude of possibilities, to finite men unable to protect and define themselves vis à vis culture, unable to make use of all the possibilities and personal potentialities it represents. This plight, which Simmel regards as tragic, appears to have little to do with greed, or with the absence of restraints on emotions, or with the paucity of group life. It has everything to do with the historical, objective, overgrowth of culture, whatever combination of factors have entered into that process.

While he is aware that the attempt to assimilate objects on this scale is of a piece with the madness of production on this scale, he seems to lapse into the assumption that tragedy he depicts is somehow a natural response to an overgrown culture. But the frustration and rage which stem from not being able to use cultural objects to enhance subjective culture is not altogether different from experiencing the sorrow of finitude in the face of a single object: both reactions may involve and conceal infinite aspirations. The despair and misery *seem* reasonable, a natural result of confronting the object, of the actual historical overgrowth of objective culture. But surely there are other ways of perceiving and reacting to this wealth of cultural objects: more relaxed, less narcissistic, less greedy responses. If it is somehow natural to feel sorrow or helplessness in such circumstances as Hegel or Simmel depicts, neither has explained why. Neither has disentangled such responses from the biases peculiar to the psychology of their own society, era, social strata.

In any event, however misleading to pin the predicament on the simple overgrowth of objective culture, Simmel has identified a deep difficulty, a source of anomie and alienation probably applicable to increasing numbers. The mass of cultural objects, to the increasingly well informed subject, is neither meaningful nor meaningless. The subject can neither ignore them, nor reject them without fuss nor trial, nor pain of loss. Nor can he manage to assimilate them to the purposes of his development. Those of us lucky enough to share in the material wealth may all become anomic dilettantes, periodically falling back on simplistic, alienated fashions and fads, and the alienated states these represent and promote. For the empty too much, we will inevitably substitute the pure too little.

Simmel was more sensitive to these tragic outcomes for individual and society because he was more sensitive to human, not exclusively sociological, ambivalence. His account of the peril and tragedy of formlessness rivals Durkheim's moving account of anomie. Unlike Durkheim, Simmel was not particularly patriotic, nor did he instinctively associate all manner of good things with social order, as such, certainly not when it was achieved through the suppression of difference and conflict. He was a cosmopolite and sophisticate. Yet he retained the appreciation of certain truths that, while revealed in the course of history—how else?—occur and recur. One is that when the individual frees himself of traditional chains, he will tend to seek out other chains, however ephemeral. Formlessness and anomie are not simply sloppy and unpleasant, nor merely tragic. They have the potential of destroying the kind of cultural guidance, group life, and social supports which alone can sustain individuality and individual development. The resulting tyrants need not be ephemeral.

Accordingly, Simmel sees fetishism as "only a special case of this general fate of the contents of culture." Simmel saw cultural alienation, the tyranny of a given object, or objects in a dialectical relationship to anomie. Nor is the problem always that of the tyranny of the object. It can also be the chaos (and therefore the tyranny) represented by an indigestible superabundance of cultural objects. The overload may involve or lead to the genuine deprivation of alienation, which represents the various ways we unnecessarily restrict ourselves (typically with the aid of those social structures and institutions or movements which benefit thereby) in the face of this chaos. In this light, it is impoverishment, not poverty, which is the problem. Marx was likewise concerned with impoverishment at least as much as poverty, but his attempt to see the problem exclusively in social and economic terms fails to convince. As Simmel implies, this oscillation is neither a matter of individual psychology or of society, but of both. (Or these are complementary ways of looking at the same phenomenon.) Thus when Simmel states that "everything appears as oppressive form" it means something different from analogous statements by Marx. Anomie itself is oppressive. He simultaneously suggests that those who make a religion or cult of immanence, who seek to reject form altogether, are vainly attempting to escape the human condition. That attempt is central to the problem itself, to its continual exacerbation.

Simmel goes so far as to wonder, in much the same way and words as Nietzsche, whether our appreciation of form itself, our understanding that life is difference and distance and form as well as unmediated intimacy and unreflective awareness, is dying. Nietzsche points to the universal demand for gross obviousness in all our social encounters. This is a piece with the sleazy secularization of the sacred: God becomes your co-pilot, Jesus your jogging mate.

This suggests a close connection between the overgrowth of cultural objects and forms, in principle tending toward infinity, and the rejection and effective absence of form. Too much and too little have much in common. In advanced circles (including the "youth culture" of the turn of the century, according to Simmel) life is increasingly regarded as nothing more than its expression. Nothing traditional is accepted, not at deep levels of emotions and conviction. Thought is "dissolved in and by the stream of life." Even language does not escape this treatment: the modern fascination with language and its distorting and confining effects on thought and emotion attests to his observation that we increasingly "perceive language as a strange natural force." The distinction between those who are actually bumping up against the limits of language and those who are merely bumping against their ignorance of it is progressively blurred, along with every other distinction.

Surrounded by greater opportunities, spread wider over the populace than ever before, we rarely experience this wealth, these greater possibilities for life and the cultivation of self, as happiness or an occasion for joy. Nietzsche contended that modern man, "this proud ape," is immeasurably dissatisfied with himself. Simmel concurs:

> The basic impulse behind continental culture is a negative one.... [W]e have been for some time now living without any shared ideal, even perhaps without any ideals at all.[33]

Nietzsche puts the point even more emphatically:

> What will not be built any more henceforth, and cannot be built any more, is—a society in the old sense of that word; to build that, everything is lacking, above all the material. All of us are no longer material for society.[34]

An expanding galaxy of anomic fools consider this progress, and "a long shadow falls between the will to destroy old forms and the desire to build new ones.... [T]he bridge between past and future of cultural forms seems demolished." Simmel warns: "we gaze into an abyss of unformed life beneath our feet." Small wonder that the cage of rigid form holds such attraction.

On first glance the overgrowth of objective culture might seem to be relevant to only a relatively small and elite minority. But once we replace Merton's consensus on success goals with Simmel's view of culture we realize that this outlook and concern has everything to do with anomie, including that aspect of anomie which Merton describes with such care in such one-dimensional fashion. To place social forms and institutions, Merton's "institutional means," in this cultural setting is to better understand how we turn poverty into impoverishment, replace moral commitments with demoralization, exchange principles for strategies, and transform virtue itself into just one more thing we bring to the market.

Of course Merton's central contention is that there is a cultural overemphasis on success goals. But he never really argues the point, nor can he. There is no standard outside the data, no view of anomie that differs decisively from the very cultural perspectives he probably wishes to indict, no view of the specifically and irremediably human that would justify his condemnation of this disjunction between goals and means. Overemphasis indeed: but compared to what? And supposing there were no such overemphasis, what then? Society could teach us nihilism itself, and provide abundant opportunities for its expression: but would alienation and anomie be things of the past?

Whither modern society? Simmel half-heartedly suggests that we may be entering a transitional period, leading to an era in which formlessness will be the dominant form of life. Or we may be in for some kind of cultural convulsion, conceivably both creative and cataclysmic. Others, including many sociologists, think reconstruction is impossible on any basis other than a religious one. Simmel believes neither will suffice, although the latter is a real and wretched possibility. For we are dealing in incompatibles, "the deepest internal contradictions of the spirit": "Life wishes to obtain something it cannot reach.... [I]t can only substitute one form for another."[35] Yet this is a proposition contradicted by the animating, organizing principle of all his work, including the very article in which he makes the assertion.

What is missing in Simmel is a sustained consideration of whether taking on the entire cultural world in this way is normal or necessary, and with it the question of a better relationship between form and life. Simmel's doggedly "dualistic" approach, his appeal to differentiation and equalization, clearly implies a critique of modern culture in terms of its oscillation between anomie and alienation. Positively, it suggests the self-overcoming, fundamentally akin to Nietzsche's will to power, that would keep it balanced and bounded. But in not extending these ideas to the *criticism* of modern culture he exhibits a reluctance which may itself reflect this malady; the inability to say no, decisively and pre-emptorily, to anything new that comes along. In so doing maybe he illustrates his own contention that our stock of shared limits, shared ideals, ideals at all, may have dwindled to nothing. In their absence, who can say no, and mean it?

It was the road back to the Yes *and* No that Nietzsche claimed to have discovered, a set of weights with which conquer the weightlessness of modern culture. Simmel's brilliantly delineates the social and cultural alienation and anomie from which Nietzsche must extricate himself. In the face of this plague of modern ideas and objects, Nietzsche recommends a kind of wise ignorance. Yet we learn precious little about that crucial brand of wisdom, save the necessity of acquiring it.

The reduction of complexity is not an adequate principle of selection or basis of priorities, even if we were so brash as to assume widespread agreement on its necessity. It smacks of pre-Faustian naivete. The alternative to limiting knowledge by wisdom is to do so by means of ignorance. In the modern setting this ignorant alternative is increasingly vulnerable to accumulating knowledge and improving communications. Both wisdom and ignorance are vulnerable in the post-Faustian world which Simmel depicts. And if ignorance has an advantage, based on knowing not it knows not, it is also true that ignorance breeds alienation.

But before we rush here and there seeking consolation and relief, exemplifying and aggravating the anomie and alienation which plague us, we do well to immerse ourselves in Simmel's subtle and sober account of these dilemmas, simultaneously social and human. This may yield altogether less comfort than we desire, but it will certainly help us distinguish among consolations.

11

Loose Ends, New Beginnings

> What must be said, may well be
> Said twice o'er.
>
> *Empedocles*

To assert that all alienation is self-alienation does not privilege individual over social sources, nor this social source over that. But it does imply the existence of a specifically human nature. The aspect of human nature stressed here, the source of standards by which we can be seen as alienated or anomic, is that we are constituted by a equalizing, symmetrical mode of thought and being, the undifferentiated unconscious; and a dividing, asymmetrical mode, the differentiated conscious. This, to paraphrase Durkheim, is the antinomy of which we are the realization; but it is not Durkheim's antinomy. On the individual level, alienation and anomie consist of two kinds of imbalance between the two basic modes. Irrespective of the ultimate source of these discontents, alienation consists of a preponderance of the differentiated mode, or separation from the undifferentiated mode; anomie amounts to an unassimilatable influx of less dedifferentiated material into the conscious. In part, alienation occurs as a protection against anomie, and conversely. This is not to deny external sources, but to suggest that what is external and what is internal is often difficult to distinguish.

This means that anomie and alienation have an objective existence which is both individual and social. Subjects are not necessarily fully conscious of their alienated or anomic state. Both discontents have social counterparts and causes whose focus and forms vary with historical circumstance and social setting. They must be conceptualized as opposites. Like all opposites, they readily pass over into one another, as if they weren't, as if our very belief in opposites were false. Their relationship is a pathological distortion of a potentially creative relationship embracing both modes. This universal human project is expressed by the idea of incorporating or overcoming modes of difference and equality, differentiated conscious and dedifferentiated unconscious, without denying or extirpating either. This amounts to a never-ending assault on overdrawn and underdrawn distinctions and the recognition that we establish difference by means of equality and equality by means of difference.

These modes of cognition and emotion were refined and elaborated in dialogue and disputation with the Freudian death instinct, ambivalence and the unconscious. The "death problem" was recast in terms of dedifferentiation and differentiation. In the process we stumbled upon two apparently opposed symbolic forms of death, often lumped together: Masculine Death, the death of rigidity; Feminine Death, the death of chaos. This amounts to a way of viewing alienation and anomie, though there are numerous other closely related binary pairs.

One of the most serviceable is Otto Rank's distinction between life fear and death fear. Life fear is the fear of being individuated, separated, isolated, alone, adrift, cut off. Death fear is the fear of being trapped, confined, finite, limited, stuck, stopped. Modes of alienation can be thought of as results of or responses to life fear. Anomie is seen as a result of death fear. It involves the attempt to avoid choices and finitude by moving, distancing, separating, fleeing. On the other side, life fear involves the fear of striking out as an individual, lest one wind up lost, separate, alone. In this light, alienation is the disease of the finite; anomie is the disease of the infinite.

While these distinctions, and indeed the distinction between alienation and anomie, are of first importance in sorting out fundamental social discontents, we will repeat the same kind of error which produces so much confusion in the literature we criticize if we allow a significant distinction to become a stark opposition. The fear of life, sufficiently exaggerated, passes over to the fear of death, and conversely. Probably the two fears were one in early infancy. In like manner the malady of infiniteness leads inevitably to getting trapped and stuck by the particular and the finite, and conversely. The rigidity of alienation and the chaos of anomie are not really so different. Both involve aggression, either in the maintenence of boundaries or the breaking of them. Rigidity is a form of chaos, as well as a producer of it. But chaos, and the compulsive need to break ties, to flee, to move on, is likewise a form of rigidity, a rigidity in motion. As with all oppositions, we posit and think we see opposites, while it is likely that there is only a continuum.

Alienation and anomie are therefore grounded in Freud's unrepressed or dedifferentiated unconscious, "the" psychic reality. The two modes of which they are pathological extremes suggest the related notion of unconscious compensation. This amounts to the effort to overcome oppositions, based on the fact that logic and language, in tandem with the limitations of the conscious, relegate the pole not preferred by consciousness to the undifferentiated and therefore unconscious state. The idea of overcoming oppositions, carried to the limit, is synonymous with the *Coincidentia Oppositorum*. We saw that Cusa attributes this quality or achievement to God, but that he also wishes to acquire it for himself. Once we get to Hegel, Feuerbach, Marx, and especially Nietzsche, this godlike aspiration is thoroughly humanized. Aspirations previously assigned or projected onto God become the property of man, if not his defining attribute. The requirement that opposites be continually confronted with their opposites is a force for moderation, though it should be carefully distinguished from smoothing over or ignoring opposition. Extreme positions suggest the denial of opposite tendencies, though on closer look the denial appears to be based on close ambivalence.

The historical setting yields only part of the explanation for such phenomena. Viewed in this manner, their changeless and recurring features are neglected. The infinite sets characteristic of the functioning of the undifferentiated unconscious describe and help explain the cognitive aspects of this extremist tendency. The salience of given oppositions varies over time and place; the problem of ambivalence, of opposition and emotional opposition itself, remains. Diseases of the infinite—self-glorification, self-deification, megalomania, neurotic ambition—involve the ascription of positive qualities to persons, events, and emotions, all of which are rendered equal (identical, from the point of view of the undifferentiated unconscious) to the individual himself. "I am all that." The opposite extreme is the conviction that I am nothing, or a despicable worm.

The idea of self-overcoming in no way insures the elimination of such possibilities, but does have the virtue of recognizing the nature, difficulty, and omnipresence of the struggle. Nor does it indicate the social arenas and contradictions in which these human polarities are at work, the social-cultural sublimations basic drives undergo. It simply suggests the kind of phenomenon and contradictions to look for, the associated maladies and symptoms, ways of tracing the logic of the illogical and spotting its manifestations. There is, one might say, a logic of the universal form which is ambivalence, or at least a logic of its illogic. The theory also suggests the positive conception of life implicit in this conception and critique of alienation and anomie.

Alienation for Marx is also an objective phenomenon. Alienated subjects are likely to be unaware of their condition. Marx introduces self-alienation only to attribute it to the effects of the tyranny of capital. Self-alienation is quickly transformed into alienation from the worker's "activity." The place of human nature and self-alienation is rendered ambiguous. The idea of a species nature or being, consisting of the best that is human, continues to play an indispensable if subterranean role in his overall perspective, especially in its underemphasized yet most significant ethical dimensions. And for good reason. A theory already awash in determinism and relativism might otherwise have no ideal point of reference. The subsequent analysis of capitalist economics, not to mention communist utopia, would be more or less pointless.

In addition to being out of place in a theory claims to dispense with ethics and stresses the historical–epochal nature of human needs and wants, Marx's furtive conception of human nature, insofar as it can be ferreted out, presents further difficulties. It reflects all–too–convenient confusion concerning whether species nature is a normative ideal or has some empirical content. There is also the significant confusion between symbolizing the universal in a particular life or society and actually attempting to live it. Marx follows Feuerbach in attributing only the best and most attractive qualities to species man and future Communist man. Marx's man is multifaceted and multitalented, productive, creative, dynamic, social, and all that. But in addition to the more attractive, active, creative, conscious qualities Marx finds in species being—those qualities which make alienation inhuman and despicable—there are the more conservative, passive, dependent, security-minded, order-prone qualities and their corresponding wishes and fears—those qualities which make alienation attractive and anomie frightening. For this reason, alienation cannot be conceived apart from anomie, nor can its overcoming.

Marx has no place for the concept of anomie, since he has no place for those human qualities which might make us eternally vulnerable to it. Yet he encourages those attitudes of release from constraint, hostility to dependence, expansion to infinity, opposition to sublimation and repression such that anomie is a likely product. Apparently the only way in which he could conceive of human beings, and especially his proletariat, as being subject to these maladies is to attribute them to pernicious social structures and determinants. This is a fine sentiment, but as a portrait of man it is a whitewash. Of course if social influences were *completely* eliminated . . . . [B]ut in that case man, by Marx's own sociological understanding, would not be man.

More than once Marx makes a point of asserting that alienated labor actually causes or produces private capital. However the relationship of alienated labor and capital evolved, the system was thereafter mutually sustained by coercion from the one side and submission and alienated participation on the other. This is consistent with the self-conscious effort in the Paris Manuscripts to present a dialectical view of man in society. But it is a Trojan horse deposited in the very center of his theory. The admission that the alienated proletariat could be viewed as genuine actors threatens his entire rosy view of man and species being, as Tucker has pointed out. In general Marx does not ascribe the qualities of an agent or actor to the empirical behavior of real, flawed human beings. We see a great deal of distaste, sometimes bordering on disgust, for real people: weak, all-too-human subjects; proletariat and anarchist as well as capitalist. When the subject is explicitly broached, however, it is affirmed that all men are in the grips of the system. In which case: how could men behave otherwise? But if they do have latitude: why do they behave *this* way?

As for sources of alienation other than private capital, there is the alienation embodied and symbolized by the capitalist division of labor. This contention could have been used as an entree to a more generalized view of the sources of alienation. Whether Marx saw this in terms of generalizing the concept or whether he was impressed by the centrality of the division of labor for English political economy is not clear. The addition of commodity fetishism in *Capital* tends to further muddy matters, and it adds little that is new to an analysis of the nature and causes of alienation. Nevertheless, underlying the analysis of alienation in all its Marxist guises, lending force and urgency and interest to Marx's whole career, is the concern for the development and emergence of a certain kind of society, a certain kind of man. Overcoming alienation remains the point of it all.

Despite these ambiguities and shortcomings, his view of alienation has much to recommend it when compared attempts of many modern authors (like Etzioni, Kariel, Fromm) to generalize the kinds and causes of alienation. Their cameras are badly out of focus. However, they do expose one of the central shortcomings of the Marxist view: the kinds, sources, and sites of alienation are not so few or simple. To limit alienation to or center it about capitalist institutions and the class society is neither theoretically sound nor empirically adequate. A host of distinguished thinkers realized this even in Marx's time. The separation of bureaucratic workers from products and processes may be as basic as the alienation of capitalist enterprise, and in a sense represents its generalization. Differential authority in Weber's "imperatively coordinated organizations" is perhaps as relevant to alienation as authority derived from the ownership of capital. The division of labor or the division of labor "properly so-called" is by no means unique to capitalism. Nor is fetishism limited to commodities, much less commodities under capitalism.

There is a more inclusive perspective, implicit in Nietzsche and especially Simmel. Here alienation is a constant threat, the normal pathology. Life ceaselessly transcends life in order to express itself in forms: social, cultural, intellectual. The forms which express life inevitably come to deny life, to impede its flow. In this light, Marx's implacable opposition to transcendence seems less mistaken than quixotic. It suggests the omnipresent possibility that life will be dammed up in forms: capitalist or bureaucratic institutions; social roles; current styles or fads or fashions in any field; ways of thinking of ourselves, as individuals or as a people; specialized tasks; language, logic, and so on. The rigidity of lifeless form represents the constant threat of alienation. The absense, or disorderly mixture, or chaotic fragmentation, or infinite proliferation of form is anomic. The obvious disadvantage of this admittedly abstract view is that the potentiality of alienation and anomie exists always and everywhere. We must not execute the theory, however, for bringing bad news.

To be a bit more specific: Simmel locates the possibility of alienation in the cultural as well as social sphere, which is not assumed to be a simple derivative of the economic; in bureaucracies, public and private; in the division of labor itself, irrespective of the social-institutional setting; in the capitalist enterprise, insofar as additional forms of constraint are involved; in protoforms, and even elementary social interactions, insofar as the interaction is dominated by unresponsive typifications. The crucial point is that subjects *are* actors when they act in ways opposite to the characteristics of Marx's idealized species. In eliminating ambivalence from our conception of man we forego indispensable analytical and psychoanalytic tools. It is the failure to address ubiquitous human ambivalence that causes so much mischief and myopia in Marx's account. Given that Marx was a man whose personal contradictions moved whole societies, it is most unfortunate that he handled his own ambivalences in such a shabby way.

Durkheim's difficulties are in some ways the mirror image of Marx's. There is no formal place for alienation in his theoretical system, with the slight exception of his promising but neglected category of fatalistic suicide. The concern itself can be seen throughout his work: e.g., in his treatment of the forced division of labor and his lively interest in periods of collective renewal. But of course it is anomie which is the very heart of his perspective. It is reflected in his conception of *homo duplex,* whose anarchistic tendencies cry out for constraint and control. Durkheim associates anomie with the "malady of infiniteness," wherein desires recognize no limits, no constraint, no discipline; and also with the disparity between what goals we are encouraged to entertain and what social institutions and other barriers and impedients enable us to achieve. Exclusive concentration on the second "disjunction" enables Merton and many others to think rather simplistically in terms of the reform of social institutions so as to match outcomes with expectations.

Durkheim's treatment of diseases of the infinite is hampered by his failure to affirm that society, the inexhaustible source of what is great and good in us, can likewise be the source of anomic striving and anomic goals. Perhaps this is more difficult for Durkheim to admit than to see. In any event it is a proposition that calls society and its cultural goals into account, and seems to get our alleged native egoism and anarchism off the hook. Whatever the reason, in this context Durkheim is less sociological and less radical than his own position implies and requires.

A similar problem concerns how to judge whether social behavior is inappropriate or abnormal. Disregarding his own conception of human nature, Durkheim suggested two standards: consistency with other societies in a similar stage of their development, and consistency with other institutions appropriate to the given society's stage of development. These standards raise rather more questions than they settle. Our ability to see a whole society as anomic gets mired in sociological relativism. The society may be desperately anomic, but as long as this is normal for societies at this stage of development, it is not anomic after all. Thus Durkheim's analysis turns timid, reflecting an anemic psychology. Neither standard provides that Archimedean point from which to offer the criticisms he seeks to offer. Hence his vulnerability at the hands of modern followers who identify with the very social strata and the values and behavior his theories indict.

Durkheim chafed under these aspects of the theoretical regime he established for sociology and for himself. They not only introduced a certain incompleteness to his treatment of anomie, but to his (muted and isolated) criticisms of alienation as well. As for not elaborating the opposition of anomie to alienation, here he may have been the victim of fear of paradox, though it is noteworthy that he did not flinch in repeatedly asserting his formula for liberty through dependence. These and other hints of a kind of dialectic of the emotions, the necessity of treating both alienation and anomie as though they were at bottom the same malady, went nowhere. George Simpson has speculated that

Durkheim would have been obligated and able to incorporate many elements of Freud's work. Whether or not Durkheim would have combined his social maladies with Freud's psycho–pathologies, the argument of this study suggests that significant steps in this direction are both necessary and possible. Nor, in the process, is it necessary to jettison the concern with alienation. In fact it is not possible, so long as we understand ambivalence as human, not exclusively sociological.

On this note we return to the social–scientific studies with which we began. Merton's paradigm of responses to anomie purports to be a straightforward extension of Durkheim's view of anomie. It errs by eliminating Durkheim's external standards, either *homo duplex* or the sociological comparisons of societies in similar stages, institutions within the same society, and so forth. It embraces the outlook and the values of the upper middle class strata that Durkheim was particularly concerned to criticize: it overlooks the anomie of affluence and the "malady of infiniteness." To do so radically disembowels Durkheim's conception of anomie. (Perhaps this is the point at which, for Merton and modern Durkheimians, Durkheim stops preaching and starts to meddling.) Durkheim, for all his alleged conservatism, verges on a radical critique of the basic commitments and cultural goals of the society. Merton's paradigm does not take radical threats and alternatives to society and culture seriously. Even if we limit our concern to those who don't make it, Merton and the social science of anomie mislead us as to why.

Most of these difficulties, to repeat a familiar refrain, stem from a neglect of individual ambivalence, and a resulting one-dimensional view of culture. Any cultural emphasis is bivalent in nature, and we can always detect individual ambivalence with respect to the dominant cultural goals. The absense of psychoanalytic perspectives contribute directly to the neglect of the anomie of affluence, megalomania, greed, pity, and the leveling syndrome of *ressentiment*. Nor can we grasp the dialectical relationship between the ascetic and the modernist, the new and old culture.

These difficulties can be brought to a head by asking where alienation fits into his analysis of anomie. His "adaptations to anomie" are among those states attributed to *alienation* in this study. Much like Berger, Merton could argue that alienation (as withdrawal, retreat, conformity) is a *response* to anomie. To my knowledge he does not. In fact, the relationship between the two is most mysterious. As an example of middle-range theorizing, it makes one almost nostalgic for Parson's Grand Theory, which at least attempts to incorporate psychoanalysis and to keep the larger questions in view.

Another way alienation and anomie have been transformed and rendered relatively innocuous involves virtually the opposite procedure from Merton's careful and limited selection of aspects of Durkheim's treatment of anomie. The procedure is to expand the concepts, to the point that everything qualifies. Alienation as the unresponsiveness of society is one of these; alienation as powerlessness is another. The latter is one of the five senses of alienation that Seeman has uncovered. His category of powerlessness is problematic, his use of Rotter's expectancies is equally so. In Rotter's terms, Seeman's idea of self-alienation is the expectancy that the individual will not have an external or extrinsic locus of control of his actions. The subject is no longer self-alienated when there exist no external barriers to doing whatever it is he wants to do. Surely this suggests the poverty or exhaustion of the liberal idea of freedom, and no doubt its view of the self as well.

At the outset I called attention to the atheoretical eclecticism, the thoroughgoing confusion of alienation and anomie, the subjectivization of the concepts, the general attempt to deradicalize and de-humanize both concepts, the neglect, distortion, one-dimensiona-lization, deradicalization of Marx, Durkheim, and other classic nineteenth century and turn-of-the-century contributors. These difficulties, as aggravated by difficulties in classical treatments of the subject as well, are intimately related to a neglect of human ambivalence and the view of man and society this implies. On the basis of the intervening arguments, perhaps these propositions have gained plausibility.

While my argument has leaned heavily on Nietzsche, Simmel, Marx, Durkheim, and Freud, they are not the only cultural resources which modern theorists of alienation and anomie have ignored or forgotten. Pascal is one of these. Nietzsche pillored him for wallowing in contradiction, and for using contradiction and ambivalence as arguments for faith. He also learned from him. Pascal captures much of the argument pursued here in the following:

> They have a secret instinct which impels them to seek amusement and occupation abroad, and which arises from the sense of their constant unhappiness. They have another secret instinct . . . happiness in rest, and not in stir. Thus they aim at rest through excitement.[1]

The measure of these opposite wishes for rest and quiet is the frenzy with which we pursue satisfaction and excitement abroad. The very anomie we exhibit suggests the presence of the conservative needs productive of alienation. "Everyone wants to *be* somebody," Goethe complained, "and no one wants to grow." The crucial question, which has merely been introduced here, is what a reconciliation of opposed needs—above all, the paired oppositions we have associated with conscious and unconscious, differentiation and dedifferentiation—means and implies for individual and social life. One thing is clear. Achieving what we want is predicated on knowing what else we want, above and beyond those inevitably simplistic and fetishistic selves we posit in order to take a rest from ourselves and to allay the anxieties of others. We must affirm the existence of that shadow self produced by our every attempt to specify and bound life, that companion who will neither leave us alone nor be caught and confined. Only then can we set about becoming what we are.

★　★　★　★　★

This account of anomie and alienation is one long brief on behalf of the proposition that social theory cannot do without a vision of human nature. Neither can we manage with one modified from epoch to epoch or sold to us in order to sell us other things. Those who claim to have escaped this loathsome reactionary practice are among the first to reveal their own poorly disguised, hastily considered, often inconsistent assumptions in this regard. The mere beginnings offered here have been developed in disputation and dialogue with Marx, Durkheim, Freud, Nietzsche, Simmel, and other luminaries. One must be grateful to these distinguished allies and antipodes. The argument itself, centered on human ambivalence and the consolation and compensation of opposites, requires it.

Someone has observed that man lords it over the lower primates (given their different posture and more colorful bottoms) because he fancies he has a less visible conclusion. In any event we are the never-finished animal. It has to do with expectations. Despite disclaimers to ourselves and to anyone who will listen, we rarely undertake to author a book, or anything of the sort, without a megalomanic rush of poorly defined aspirations and emotions. Once these are married to keen and clever conscious faculties, no doubt we will restore intellectual peace over a vast area in a most exciting and liberating way. Our subject is never merely the subject in view and at hand; its particulars always point far beyond themselves. Nor are we creatures merely finite and differentiated, limited to what we happen to know of ourselves. However finite our means, however mired in specific tasks and wedded to limited faculties, we insist on "something more . . . infinity" because "part of us" is already astraddle or beyond any boundary we encounter or posit. We ceaselessly gather together the seemingly disparate and heterogeneous, forging ever wider ever newer equalities, striving for distinctions which make more and more difference. A bit more effort and intelligence and will, and tomorrow we may put it all together. Tomorrow is all mortal man needs, though he always needs it.

Eventually we must return and report on our transcendent mountaintop experiences, translating the tablets. What survives are mere hints and scraps. Even here the distortion continues. Thoughts are formed or deformed or determined by the words close at hand. We say too much and we say too little. The law of noncontradiction wreaks its necessary violence. Whole worlds are forgotten or misplaced by our damnable inability to think more than one thought at a time. What at last remains is puny and paltry when not misleading: we feel "not one whit closer to the infinite." No conclusion is sufficiently inclusive to be conclusive. Other questions press forward. In the end we are left with a beginning, at best.

But is this not consistent with the task of reconciling opposites, the steady work it imposes, the argument advanced here from beginning to end? Well then, let us be content to hope it is an ending worthy of a beginning!

Notes

Chapter One

1. This designation includes those authors who refer to themselves as social scientists, who are interested in the empirical testing of hypotheses, and who typically seek to minimize normative or ideological components in their research. Excluded at this point are myriad Marxist treatments of alienation; philosophical inquiries and critiques; psychoanalytical perspectives, by and large; and a number of broader, more speculative accounts. (For example, the contributions of Bell, Lane, Schumpeter, Riesman, Rieff, Slater, de Grazia, Fromm). As the analysis of alienation and anomie is itself broadened in subsequent chapters, I touch on some of these more ambitious formulations.

2. Melvin Seeman, "On the Meaning of Alienation," *American Sociological Review* 24, no. 6 (1959), pp. 783-91.

3. Dwight Dean, "Alienation: Its Meaning and Measurement," *American Sociological Review* 26, no. 5 (1961), pp. 753-58.

4. Ada Finifter, ed., *Alienation and the Social System* (New York: John Wiley and Sons, 1972)p. 7.

5. Lewis Feuer, "What Is Alienation? The Career of a Concept," *New Politics* 1, no. 3 (Spring 1962).

6. "Factor analysis is used to demonstrate that there are empirical, as well as theoretical, grounds for considering political alienation as a multidimensional concept," *Alienation and the Social System*, p.190, note 7.

7. David Nachmias, "Modes and Types of Political Alienation," *British Journal of Sociology* 25, no. 4 (1974).

8. Kenneth Keniston, *The Uncommitted* (New York: Dell Publishing, 1965), pp. 453-58.

9. Gwynn Nettler, "A Measure of Alienation," *American Sociological Review* 22, no. 6 (1957), pp. 670-77.

10. Jan Hadja, "Alienation and Integration of Student Intellectuals," *American Sociological Review* 26, no. 5 (1961), pp. 758-77.

11. Michael Aiken and Jerald Hage, "Organizational Alienation: A Comparative Analysis," *American Sociological Review* 31, no. 4 (1966), pp. 497-507.

12. Morton Grodzins, *The Loyal and the Disloyal* (Chicago: University of Chicago Press, 1956), p. 134.

13. Murray B. Levin, *The Alienated Voter* (New York: Holt, Rinehart and Winston,

1960); John Horton, "The Dehumanization of Anomie and Alienation: A Problem in the Sociology of Knowledge," *British Journal of Sociology* 15 (1964), pp. 283-300; Wayne E. Thompson and John Horton, "Political Alienation as a Force in Political Action," *Social Forces* 38, no. 3 (1960), pp. 190-95; John Clark. "Measuring Alienation Within a Social System," *American Sociological Review* 24 (1959), pp. 849-52.

14. John Clark, "Measuring Alienation Within a Social System."

15. Ada Finifter, *Alienation and the Social System*, p. 8.

16. See "Expanding the Political Present," *American Political Science Review* 63, no. 3 (September, 1969).

17. Amitai Etzioni, *The Active Society* (New York: The Free Press, 1968); see especially Chap. 21, "Alienation, Inauthenticity, and Their Reduction."

18. Seeman, "On the Meaning of Alienation," p. 48.

19. Ibid., p. 54.

20. Alvin Gouldner, *The Coming Crisis of Western Sociology* (New York: Avon Books, 1970), p. 103.

21. Albert K. Cohen, "The Study of Social Disorganization and Deviant Behavior," in Robert K. Merton et al., eds., *Sociology Today* (New York: Basic Books, 1959), p. 464.

22. Robert Merton, *Social Theory and Social Structure* (New York: The Free Press, 1968); particularly chaps. 6 and 7.

23. Robert Merton, *Sociological Ambivalence* (New York: The Free Press, 1976); particularly chap. 1.

24. See the references cited in Marshall B. Clinard, ed., *Anomie and Deviant Behavior*. (New York: The Free Press, 1964); especially chap. 1; see also chap. 2, Edwin Lemert, "Social Structure, Social Control, and Deviation"; and "Annotated Bibliography of Theoretical Studies."

25. Ibid., p. 73.

26. Ibid., p. 80.

27. Robert Dubin, "Deviant Behavior and Social Structure," *American Sociological Review* 24, pp. 147-64; also pp. 299-300.

28. Albert K. Cohen, "Towards a Theory of Deviant Behavior: Continuities Continued," paper presented at the 1963 meeting of American Sociological Association, Los Angeles, California. Also see "The Study of Social Disorganization and Deviant Behavior," pp. 461-85.

29. Lemert, "Social Structure, Social Control, and Deviation."

30. Albert Cohen, *Delinquent Boys*. New York: The Free Press (1955).

31. Leo Srole. "Social Integration and Certain Corollaries: An Exploratory Study." *American Sociological Review* 21 (December 1956), pp. 709-716.

32. Ada Finifter, "Alienation and the Social System," pp. 55-56 and elsewhere.

33. Dorothy Meier and Wendell Bell. "Anomie and Differential Access to the Achievement of Life Goal." *American Sociological Review* 24 (1959), pp. 189-202.

34. Robert Merton. "Anomie, Anomia, and Social Interaction: Contexts of Deviant Behavior," in Clinard, ed., *Anomie and Deviant Behavior*, p. 213.

35. Emile Durkheim, "The Dualism of Human Nature and Its Social Conditions," in *Emile Durkheim: On Morality and Society*, ed. Robert N. Bellah (Chicago: University of Chicago Press, 1973).

36. The only classical sociologist to directly assault this tradition was Herman Schmalenbach, who made a strong case for a third sociological mode, communion. Communion is dialectically related to both community and society, and in some respects represents a synthesis of the two. The neglect of his path-breaking argument has been almost total. See Herman Schmalenbach, *On Society and Experience,* ed. Gunther Lüschen and Gregory P. Stony (Chicago: University of Chicago Press, 1977).

37. Daniel Bell has written of "cultural contradictions," as between the increasingly hedonistic and unrestrained "new culture"--closely related to the hyperliberalism we have encountered--and the old culture, centered on the discipline at the workplace, grounded in the Puritan ethic. In effect Bell pictures an anomic culture and a society which remains alienated in many sectors, especially in its places of employment. His argument bears some similarities to that of Simmel (see Chapter Ten), though Simmel is more prone to see anomie in the society and economy as well as in the culture. See Daniel Bell, *The Cultural Contradictions of Capitalism* (New York: Basic Books, 1976).

38. Ada Finifter, *Alienation and the Social System,* p. 56; see also Clinard, *Anomie and Deviant Behavior,* pp. 37-38. This idea, also suggested by Peter Berger, has great merit; but Finifter offers it in a haphazard, theoretically arbitrary fashion. Why alienation might be the subjective manifestation of anomie is a mystery. With so many permutations of possible relationships being tossed about, it is unlikely that felicitous formulations will not be stumbled upon occasionally. It is a question of knowing what one has stumbled upon.

39. Ada Finifter, *Alienation and the Social System,* p. 56.

40. Dorothy Meier and Wendell Bell, "Anomie and Differential Access to the Achievement of Life Goals," p. 190.

41. Igor S. Kon, "The Concept of Alienation in Modern Sociology," *Social Research* 34, no. 3 (1967), pp. 507-28.

42. Albert Cohen, "The Study of Social Disorganization and Deviant Behavior"; also *Delinquent Boys*. As Cohen's critique and Merton's response show, there seems to be no intermediate alternative betwen this questionable view of how deviants make fateful choices and the other pole toward which Cohen points, whereby our motivation is gaining acceptance at all times, at practically any cost.

43. See for example Melanie Klein, *Envy and Gratitude* (New York: Delta Publishing, 1975), particularly chaps. 10 and 12. Nietzsche and Scheler place the critique of ressentiment at the very center of their social and political theory, psychology, and epistemology. C. Wright Mills argues that lower-middle class ressentiment is the virtual heartland of alienation. Edgar Friedenberg sees it as an insuperable barrier to the goals of political liberalism.

44.   This practice mars the otherwise excellent account of cultural bipolarity by Daniel Bell. In this way ambivalence tends to be wished or assumed away. This produces the fateful assumption that anomie and alienation, which he properly treats as opposed

maladies, cannot simultaneously plague given individuals and groups. (Daniel Bell, *Cultural Contradictions of Capitalism* (New York: Basic Books, 1972)).

45.   Particularly relevant are *The Neurotic Personality of Our Time* (New York: W. W. Norton, 1937); and *Neurosis and Human Growth* (New York: W. W. Norton and Co., 1950).

46.   Parsons, *The Social System* (New York: Free Press, 1951), chap. 7.

Chapter Two

1.   See Steven Lukes, "Alienation and Anomie," in Peter Laslett and W. Runciman, eds., *Philosophy, Politics, and Society*, 3rd series (Oxford: Basil Blackwell, 1967). Reprinted in Ada W. Finifter, ed., *Alienation and the Social System* (New York: John Wiley & Sons, 1972).

2.   John Horton, "The Dehumanization of Anomie and Alienation," *British Journal of Sociology* 15 (1964), pp. 283-300. Reprinted in James E. Curtis and John W. Petras, eds., *Sociology of Knowledge* (New York: Praeger Publishers, 1970), pp. 586-605.

3.   Lukes, in Finifter, *Alienation and the Social System,* p. 25.

4.   Ibid., in Finifter, p. 25.

5.   Ibid., in Finifter, p. 26.

6.   Ibid., in Finifter, p. 26.

7.   Ibid., in Finifter, p. 26.

8.   Ibid., in Finifter, p. 27.

9.   Emile Durkheim, *Suicide,* trans. John A. Spaulding and George Simpson, ed. George Simpson (1897; rpt. New York: The Free Press, 1952), p. 250.

10.   Particularly relevant are Peter Berger and Thomas Luckmann, *The Social Construction of Reality* (Garden City, N.Y.: Doubleday, 1966); Berger, *The Sacred Canopy* (Garden City, N.Y.: Doubleday, 1969); "Reification and the Sociological Critique of Consciousness," (also with Thomas Luckmann), *New Left Review* 35 (1966), pp. 56-75.

11.   Berger and Luckmann, p. 17.

12.   Ibid., p. 18.

13.   Ibid., p. 33.

14.   Ibid., p. 51.

15.   Ibid., p. 52.

16.   Ibid., p. 53.

17.   Berger and Luckmann, *The Social Construction of Reality,* p. 49. Clifford Geertz makes much the same point: "One of the most significant facts about us may finally be that we all begin with the natural equipment to live a thousand kinds of life but end in the end only having lived one." In *The Interpretation of Cultures* (New York: Basic Books, 1973), p. 45.

18.   Bob Dylan's haunting account of the confrontation of the straight and hip worlds suggests the terror of the really new that even the sophisticated experience when their

categories prove inadequate to subduing and capturing experience. ("Ballad of a Thin Man," *Highway 61 Revisited*, Columbia Records, CL2389.)

19. *Mind, Self, and Society* is an overview of Mead's perspective. Charles W. Morris, ed. (Chicago: University of Chicago Press, 1934).

20. Berger and Luckmann, p. 132.

21. Ibid., p. 132.

22. Ibid., p. 134.

23. Ibid., p. 73.

24. See *Social Construction of Reality*, p. 73. Berger suggests this is essentially Durkheim's view of man as *homo duplex*.

25. Berger and Luckmann, p. 100.

26. Ibid., p. 101.

27. Berger and Luckmann, *Social Construction of Reality*, p. 102.

28. Berger, *The Sacred Canopy*, p. 20-25; Berger and Luckmann, *Social Construction of Reality*, p. 103.

29. Berger and Luckmann, p. 87.

30. Ibid., p. 94.

31. Igor Kon points out that Berger and Luckmann are "flatly against the psychologistic interpretation of alienation, observing that the typical form of alienated consciousness is by no means an anomie, but on the contrary, fetishization of social institutions, norms, and other products of human activity." Igor Kon, "The Concept of Alienation in Modern Sociology," *Social Research* 34 (1967), pp. 507-508.

32. Friedrich Nietzsche, *Beyond Good and Evil*, trans. by Walter Kaufmann (1886; rpt. New York: Random House, 1966), p. 163.

Chapter Three

1. Georg Simmel, *The Sociology of George Simmel*, trans. and ed. Kurt H. Wolff (New York: The Free Press, 1950), pp. 64-65.

2. Ibid., pp. 676-68.

3. See Louis Dumont, *From Mandeville to Marx: The Genesis and Triumph of Economic Ideology* (Chicago: University of Chicago Press, 1977), chap. 7.

4. These characteristics are gleaned from what Marx says or implies in the works most relevant to the question of human nature: the *Manuscripts of 1844*; the *German Ideology*; *Grundrisse*, and the like. The list substantially coincides with similar lists culled from Marx by Schaff, Avineri, Fromm, Ollman, Schacht, and others.

5. See Louis Dumont, *From Mandeville to Marx*, chaps. 7-8.

6. See Marshall Sahlins, *Culture and Practical Reason* (Chicago: University of Chicago Press, 1976), particularly chaps. 3 and 4.

7. Karl Marx, *Economic and Philosophic Manuscripts of 1944*, trans. by T. B. Bottomore,

in Erich Fromm's *Marx's Concept of Man* (New York: Frederick Ungar Publishing, 1963), p. 75. Compare with Nietzsche: "how ludicrous I find the sociologists, with their nonsensical optimism concerning the 'good man,' who is waiting to appear from behind the scenes if only one would abolish the old 'order' and set all the 'natural drives' free." *Will to Power,* trans. and ed. by Walter Kaufmann (New York: Random House, 1967), p. 389.

8.   Robert Tucker, *Philosophy and Myth in Karl Marx* (Cambridge: Cambridge University Press, 1972), p. 149.

9.   Karl Marx, *Economic and Philosophic Manuscripts of 1844,* p. 75.

10.   Karl Marx, *1844 Manuscripts,* p. 106.

11.   This is simply to suggest, with Tocqueville and Durkheim, that there can be a brand of cruelty in raising expectations to levels which are individually unrealistic and socially destabilizing. In a similar connection Nietzsche comments that we thereby risk creating a society where there are few outright winners, no identifiable successes, and races have no finish lines.

12.   For an interesting if flawed attempt to finesse the possibility of serious conflict in communist society, see Eugene Kamenka, *The Ethical Basis of Marxism* (London: Routledge and Kegan Paul, 1962.) His solution defines "goods" as "being able to work and cooperate coherently, while evils conflict not only with goods, but with each other." But this is solution by fiat: would that all "goods" were so well behaved. In fact it is an attempt to do without ethics.

13.   Bertell Ollman offers a vigorous but unconvincing argument that the division of labor and the exploitation of the worker by capital are reciprocal ways of describing the same reality. See Bertell Ollman, *Alienation* (Cambridge: Cambridge University Press, 1971), chap. 24.

14.   Richard Schacht, *Alienation* (Garden City, N.Y.: Doubleday, 1970), chap. 3.

15.   This view has also been put forward by Berger, Fromm, and members of the Frankfurt School.

16.   Karl Marx, *1844 Manuscripts,* pp. 95-96.

17.   See Robert Tucker, *Philosophy and Myth in Karl Marx,* chaps. 8-11.

18.   Ollman, *Alienation,* chap. 33.

19.   The following are especially relevant: *The Heart of Man: Its Genius for Good and Evil* (New York: Harper & Row, 1964), chap. 3; *The Crisis of Psychoanalysis* (New York: Holt, Rinehart, Winston, 1970), chap. 3: "Marx's Contribution to the Knowledge of Man"; and *Beyond the Chains of Illusion: My Encounter with Marx and Freud* (New York: Simon and Schuster, 1962).

20.   Erich Fromm, *The Crisis of Psychoanalysis,* pp. 49-55.

21.   Ibid., p. 55.

22.   Adam Schaff, *Marxism and the Human Individual,* p. 40. His particular concern in this passage is the relation between economic base and superstructure.

23.   "Reflections of a Youth on Choosing an Occupation," in *Writings of the Young Marx on Philosophy and Society,* trans. and ed. by Loyd D. Easton and Kurt H. Guddat (Garden City, New York: Doubleday and Company, 1967), pp. 35-39.

Chapter Four

1. Lewis Coser, "Durkheim's Conservatism and Its Implications for His Sociological Theory," in *Essays on Sociology and Philosophy*, by Emile Durkheim et al., ed. Kurt H. Wolff (New York: Harper & Row, 1964), pp. 211-32.

2. Lewis Coser, "Durkheim's Conservatism and Its Implications for His Sociological Theory," p. 217.

3. Weber's view of ethical commitments was virtually the opposite: that they inspire, energize, activate, differentiate. The notion that the effect of religion is always or primarily to unite and to pacify can only be described as far-fetched. For a Frenchman to put forward such a thesis is odd indeed. By the time of his last major work, *Elementary Forms of Religious Life*, Durkheim had begun to incorporate significant elements of this alternative view of religion and social action.

4. Emile Durkheim, "The Dualism of Human Nature and Its Social Conditions," in *Emile Durkheim: On Morality and Society*, ed. Robert Bellah (Chicago: University of Chicago Press, 1973); p. 150.

5. The basic source is his critique of Spencer in *Division of Labor in Society*, trans. Greorge Simpson (1893; rpt. New York: The Free Press, 1933), pp. 200-55. See also *Moral Education*, ed. Everett K. Wilson, trans. Everett K. Wilson and Herman Schburer (New York: The Free Press, 1973); and several of the articles in *Emile Durkheim: On Morality and Society*, ed. Robert N. Bellah.

6. *Emile Durkheim: Selected Writings*, ed. and trans. by Anthony Giddens (Cambridge: Cambridge University Press, 1972), p. 147.

7. Ibid., pp. 146-47.

8. *Emile Durkheim: On Morality and Society*, p. 45.

9. *Durkheim: On Morality and Society*, ed. Robert N. Bellah; from the article "Individualism and the Intellectuals," p. 48.

10. Ibid., pp. 48-49.

11. Ibid., p. 51.

12. Ibid., p. 51.

13. See Durkheim, "The Principles of 1789 and Sociology," in *On Morality and Society*, pp. 34-42. Simmel develops the contrast in "Individual and Society in Eighteenth- and Nineteenth-Century Views of Life," in *The Sociology of Georg Simmel*, trans. and ed. Kurt H. Wolff (New York: The Free Press, 1950), chapter 4, pp. 58-84.

14. "The Dualism of Human Nature and Its Social Conditions," in *On Morality and Society*, chap. 10, pp. 149-63.

15. Emile Durkheim, *Suicide*, trans. John A. Spaulding and George Simpson (1897; rpt. New York: The Free Press, 1952), p. 247.

16. Durkheim, *Suicide*, p. 247.

17. Durkheim, *Moral Education*, p. 35.

18.   Ibid., p. 42.

19.   Ibid., p. 43.

20.   Georges Friedmann has argued that if Durkheim were to study "the anatomy of work" today, he would find most workers in job situations which, by his own criteria, would be abnormal or anomic. (Georges Freidman, *The Anatomy of Work* (Glencoe, Ill.: The Free Press, 1961), chap. 5.)

21.   Emile Durkheim, *The Division of Labor* in *Society*, pp. 1-31.

22.   Emile Durkheim, *Suicide*; especially chaps. 3 and 5.

23.   Durkheim, *Moral Education*, p. 43.

24.   Durkheim, *Suicide*, Book 2.

25.   Durkheim, *Suicide*, p. 257.

26.   Durkheim, *Suicide*, p. 254.

27.   Durkheim, *Suicide*, p. 257.

28.   Avineri has commented that such a disjunction cannot amount to a serious problem, since the socially generated nature of needs insures that such a correspondence is theoretically possible. This seems to assume that the want generating and want fulfilling institutions of the society are identical.

29.   Emile Durkheim, *The Elementary Forms of Religious Life*, trans. Joseph Swain Ward (1912; rpt. New York: The Free Press, 1965).

30.   See "Principles of 1789 and Sociology," in *On Morality and Society*.

31.   Durkheim, *Division of Labor in Society*, p. 402.

32.   Durkheim, *Moral Education*; especially Part I.

33.   Ibid., p. 108.

34.   Ibid., p. 54.

35.   Ibid., p. 114.

36.   Ibid., chaps. 2-8. Steven Lukes has observed that the lack of discipline and lack of attachments to social groups correspond to the two pairs of suicide categories: anomie-fatalism are the opposites focused on discipline, while egoism-altruism are focused on group ties.

37.   Ibid., p. 109.

38.   Giddens suggests that this conception of liberty is virtually identical to that entertained by Marx. The point is overstated: the Marxist emphasis on freedom as escape and release and the abolition of transcendent social forms is more akin to the utilitarians and liberals. The emphasis on self-overcoming and self-governance is more suggestive of Kant or even Nietzsche than Marx. His attitude toward passion is most Kantian, i.e., punitive and paranoid: "Passion is not a manifestation of prejudice, but prejudice in its most conspicuous form." (*Moral Education*, p. 94). Those are the words of someone whose passionate defense of society and whose empathetic account of anomie are landmarks in social philosophy.

39.   One obvious parallel is between the two parts of the self in Durkheim's view—the

egoistic instinctual side and the social side—and the heteronomous and autonomous in Kantian ethics. Even so, Durkheim does not succeed in making clear the role of reason in social ethics, since social realities are clearly assigned a superordinate position. To read Rousseau as a conservative sociologist brings him closer to Durkheim's view. But the notion that Rousseau was accidentally a democrat, that the General Will can be jettisoned, is surely untenable. The other conspicuous difference has to do with the role of emotion and sentiment. With Kant, Durkheim insists they have no place in morality.

40. Durkheim, *Moral Education*, p. 72.

41. Ibid., p. 68.

42. Ibid., p. 124.

43. Ibid., see p. 124: "The ideal that morality draws for us is a remarkable mixture of subordination and power, of submission and autonomy."

44. Ibid., p. 162.

45. Ibid., p. 102.

46. Durkheim, "Individualism and the Intellectuals," p. 49.

47. Ibid., pp. 43-57.

48. Durkheim, *Selected Writings*, p. 215.

49. Durkheim, "Division of Labor in Society: Conclusion," *On Morality and Society*, p. 139.

50. Durkheim, *Moral Education*, p. 265.

51. Ibid., p. 270. Durkheim might well have attacked poetry for its assault on language, somewhat in the manner of Burke or de Maistre. Someone has suggested that poetry amounts to language in a state of crisis.

52. Ibid., p. 271. Immediately after these embarrassing remarks, Durkheim reminds the potential teachers he is addressing that an aesthetic training is not a moral education—a bit as though that were all he had said. The passage amounts to a moralistic condemnation of art and artists.

53. Ibid., p. 45.

54. Ibid., p. 152.

55. Ibid., p. 138. Hazlitt remarked that without the aid of prejudice and custom he wouldn't be able to find his way across the room.

56. Ibid., pp. 99-100.

57. In Steven Lukes, *Emile Durkheim: His Life and Work* (New York: Penguin Books, 1977).

Chapter Five

1. Sigmund Freud, *Totem and Taboo*, ed. James Strachey (1923; rpt. New York: W. W. Norton, 1960), p. 68.

2. Ibid., p. 32.

3. Ibid., p. 49.

4. Sigmund Freud, *The Igo and the Id,* ed. James Strachey (1923; rpt. New York: W. W. Norton, 1960), p. 32.

5. "Instincts and Their Vicissitudes," 1915, in *General Psychological Theory,* ed. Philip Rieff (New York: MacMillan, 1963), p. 101.

6. Freud, *New Introductory Lectures,* p. 99; see also "Instincts and Their Vicissitudes," p. 102.

7. Sigmund Freud, *New Introductory Lectures on Psychoanalysis,* ed. James Strachey (1933; rpt. New York: W. W. Norton, 1965), p. 99.

8. Ibid., p. 104–105.

9. Ibid., p. 124; see also p. 99.

10. Philip Rieff, *Freud: The Mind of a Moralist* (New York: Doubleday, 1959), pp. 247–48.

11. Ibid., p. 187.

12. "The Unconscious," in *General Psychological Theory,* p. 118; see also pp. 116–21.

13. Sigmund Freud, *An Outline of Psycho-Analysis,* ed. James Strachey (1940; rpt., New York: W. W. Norton and Co., 1949), p. 21.

14. "The Unconscious," in *General Psychological Theory,* pp. 134–35.

15. Ibid., p. 139.

16. Ibid., p. 139.

17. *New Introductory Lectures,* p. 103.

18. Sigmund Freud, *Beyond the Pleasure Principle,* ed. James Strachey (1920; rpt. New York: W. W. Norton, 1961), p. 14.

19. Emile Durkheim, *Moral Education,* ed. Everett K. Wilson, trans. Everett K. Wilson and Herbert Schburer (New York: The Free Press, 1973), pp. 44–46.

20. Freud, *Beyond the Pleasure Principle,* p. 30.

21. Ibid., p. 30.

22. Ibid., p. 32.

23. Freud, *An Outline of Psycho-Analysis,* p. 6.

24. Ibid., p. 5.

Chapter Six

1. R. E. Money-Kyrle, "An Inconclusive Contribution to the Theory of the Death Instinct," in *New Directions in Psycho-analysis,* ed. Melanie Klein, Paula Heinemann, and R. E. Money-Kyrle (New York: Basic Books, 1957); pp. 499–509.

2. Money-Kyrle, *New Directions in Psycho-analysis,* p. 503.

3. Ibid, p. 505.

4. Ibid, p. 508.

5. Liam Hudson, *Human Beings: the Psychology of Human Experience* (Garden City, N.Y.: Anchor Press/Doubleday, 1975), especially chap. 10. See also his *The Cult of the Fact* (New York: Harpers & Row, 1972).

6. Ibid., pp. 133–34.

7. Ibid., pp. 151–52.

8. Sigmund Freud, *Beyond the Pleasure Principle,* ed. James Strachey (1920; rpt. New York: W. W. Norton, 1961), p. 43.

9. *Human Beings,* p. 165.

10. Ibid., p. 197.

11. Hudson, *The Cult of the Fact,* p. 171.

12. Erich Fromm, *The Heart of Man: Its Genius for Good and Evil* (New York: Harper & Row, 1964), p. 38.

13. Erich Fromm, *The Heart of Man,* p. 39.

14. Friedrich Nietzsche, *Beyond Good and Evil,* ed. Walter Kaufmann (1886; rpt. New York: Random House, 1966), p. 90.

15. Rilke suggests this is so:

> Master, do you hear the New,
> droning and throbbing?
> Harbingers come
> those who exalt it.
>
> True, no hearing is whole
> in all the turmoil
> yet the machine-part
> now wants to be praised.

Rainer Maria Rilke, *Sonnets to Orpheus,* trans., M. D. Herter Norton (New York: W. W. Norton, 1942), p. 51.

16. Erich Fromm, *Heart of Man,* p. 46.

17. See Victor Turner, *The Ritual Process* (Ithaca, New York: Cornell University Press, 1977), chaps. 3–5.

18. Fromm, *The Heart of Man,* p. 50.

19. Norman O. Brown, *Life against Death* (Middletown, CT.: Wesleyan University Press, 1959).

20. Ibid., p. 52.

21. *Life Against Death,* p. 52.

22. Ibid., p. 84.

23. David Bakan, *The Duality of Human Existence* (Boston: Beacon Press, 1966), p. 15.

24. Ibid., chaps. 1–3.

25.　Ibid., p. 15. He applies his conception to Weber, who "succeeded in drawing attention to the agentic and helped define it"; to Satan, as the projection of the agentic; to the relationship of the sexes, in which men are alleged to be the cultural and possibly the biological carriers of the agentic virus. Finally he argues that Freud's postulate of a death instinct resulted from his premonition of his own cancer. He sees cancer as unmitigated agency. The equation of cancer with rampant egoism of the cells, with unmitigated agency, appears to be a seizure of literal-mindedness. As a symbol of the agentic it is most fitting.

26.　Otto Rank, *Truth and Reality* (1936; rpt. New York: W. W. Norton, 1978). See also *Will Therapy* (1936; rpt. New York: W. W. Norton, 1978); and *The Myth of the Birth of the Hero*, ed. Philip Freund (1932; rpt. New York: Random House, 1959).

27.　Otto Rank, *The Myth at the Birth of the Hero*, p. 267.

28.　Rank, *The Myth of the Birth of the Hero*, p. 271.

29.　Rank, *Will Therapy*, p. 126.

30.　Ibid., p. 147.

31.　Ibid., pp. 166–77.

32.　Ibid., p. 199. This procedure can amount to escapism when ambivalence is involved. Our argument suggests that logical contradictions and emotional conflict are intimately associated. Following James's advice is akin to the behavior of the patient in analysis who, having come face to face with a deep ambivalence, escapes and buries it with a torrent of seemingly relevant observations and distinctions. The unconscious intent and actual effect is to distance what is threatening and painful. All the while the patient is convinced that he is dealing with the conflict.

Chapter Seven

1.　Mary Douglas, *Purity and Danger* (London: Routledge & Kegan Paul Ltd., 1966).

2.　Liam Hudson reports that "convergent" personalities react similarly in the face of creative, open-ended questions such as "how many different uses can you think of for a barrel?" On one occasion he gave this quiz to a number of distinguished physicists: the question provoked noticeable agitation, anxiety, embarrassment, and discomfort; it yielded surprisingly few ideas for how to use barrels creatively. The answers were mostly pedestrian (i.e., barrels for beer). Hudson is careful to point out that both convergers and divergers have defenses, and that the unusually creative come from both groups. They differ, not in being defended or open, but in the defensive style or policy they employ. (Liam Hudson, *Contrary Imaginations* (New York: Schocken Books, 1966)).

3.　Mary Douglas, *Purity and Danger*, p. l6l.

4.　Ibid., p. l63.

5.　Ibid., p. l69.

6.　Jean Paul Sartre, *Being and Nothingness* (New York: Washington Square Press, 1966). *Nausea* is concerned with the same themes, although the treatment is not entirely consistent. (New York: New Directions Publishing, 1964). Nietzsche suggests that "if a psychologist today has good taste (others might say, integrity) it consists in resistance to the shamefully moralized way of speaking which has gradually made all modern judgments of men and things slimy."

7. Sartre, *Being and Nothingness*, p. 774.

8. Ibid., p. 776.

9. Ibid., p. 777.

10. Sartre, *Nausea*, p. 125.

11. Ibid., p. 128.

12. Ibid., pp. 130-31.

13. Ibid., p. 134.

14. See Georg Simmel, *On Individuality and Social Forms*, ed. with introduction by Donald N. Levine (Chicago: University of Chicago Press, 1971), pp. 72-73.

15. See Mircea Eliade, *The Two and the One* (Chicago: University of Chicago Press, 1962); especially chap. 2, "Mephistopheles and the Androgyne."

16. This suggests that there is already something queer about drawing the distinction. We can only do so in the differentiating mode. Given that we tend to visualize different modes as separate spatial spheres, we fail to grasp their interpenetration. (Even "interpenetration" must be visualized in Cartesian space.) The fact that every differentiation is itself composed of a division and an equalization also suggests the difficulty in dividing the two modes, as does the fact that any dedifferentiated state has differentiated elements.

17. The exaggerations and extremes of behavior seem related to the closeness of the ambivalence, to the fact that the minority tendency is especially strong and threatening. Masculine Death, or alienation, is associated with rigidity. But by the same token, rigidity and boundary distance are associated with a *lack* of internal and external differentiations—as if fighting against a powerful equalizing tendency. Similarly, Feminine Death is associated with chaos (as opposed to fusion) because of the strong reaction of the conscious faculties. The dedifferentiating impulse to create ever greater areas of equality is resisted. It is this which creates fragmentation and destroys continuity, even as it multiplies parts or fragments. In this view, therefore, alienation is associated with differentiating tendencies which are only in a slight majority, and anomie with dedifferentiating tendencies in a slight majority. This helps explain why the two forms of Death resemble each other so, why rigidity and chaos are fundamentally akin.

This may seem to suggest that those who have clear majorities of one side or another are not alienated, since they are able to segregate and split off into secondary niches and roles those impulses in the small minority. On the other hand, ambivalence in these proportions may represent alienation, or anomie, in a quiescent mode, so that whenever the opposed sides of the poorly integrated self are forced—by life, not by logic or reflection—to confront one another the ambivalence becomes close, and extremes and exaggerations ensue. Once contrary impulses are confronted, they will *seem* equal. Certainly they are equal in the sense of posing equal threats to the integrity of the personality. This may help explain the privileged position of close ambivalence in explaining alienation and anomie.

18. Erwin Schrödinger, *What is Life? Mind and Matter* (Cambridge: Cambridge University Press, 1944).

19.   Ibid., p. 73.

Chapter Eight

1.   See Silvano Arieti, *The Intrapsychic Self* (New York: Basic Books, 1975), p. 10.

2.   Ibid., chap. 7 and pp. 274–77; his analysis of paleologic is based on the work of E. Von Domarus. See *Language and Thought in Schizophrenia,* ed. J. S. Kasanin (New York: W. W. Norton, 1939); "The Specific Laws of Logic in Schizophrenia."

3.   Ibid., p. 125.

4.   Anton Ehrenzweig, *The Hidden Order of Art* (Berkeley and Los Angeles: University of California Press, 1971). These terms (differentiation, undifferentiation, and so on) are awkward, though in analytic terms they do represent an improvement over more evocative polarities like Apollonian and Dionysian. When I wish to emphasize the activity associated with the modes, I have employed differentiating and dedifferentiating. The condition or state is referred to as differentiation and dedifferentiation. Another difficulty concerns the choice of undifferentiated or dedifferentiated. Strictly speaking, the (totally) undifferentiated state amounts to mental death; there is no pure state of undifferentiation (nor of differentiation). When Matte Blanco (see below, p. 231) uses the term undifferentiation, he has in mind the *dominant* structural aspect of the unconscious. This is consistent with our use of the term differentiation, given that it is never pure either.

    A further element of potential confusion concerns the use of unrepressed or structural unconscious for undifferentiated unconscious. They refer to essentially the same phenomena, though they highlight different facets of the model. I also employ a number of binary pairs which correspond closely to the modes as described and labeled in the model. These include asymmetry and symmetry, difference and equality, dividing and equalizing (or making equal); form and formlessness; structured and unstructured, among others. All of these refer to the two basic modes, and for most of our purposes are interchangeable.

    A final terminological difficulty involves the notion of "making equal" or "equalizing". This is clearly the view "from above", from the standpoint of the differentiating conscious, and in the strict sense equality is understood as equality in certain respects. But "making identical" suggests a peculiar combination of perspectives. I have generally settled for making equal and equalizing, with the understanding that unconscious mentation does not merely make equal, nor make identical. Rather, it sees or understands identity.

5.   Ibid., p. 19.

6.   Ibid., pp. 4–5.

7.   Ibid., p. 41.

8.   A congruent argument, grounded in gestalt perspectives rather than psychoanalysis, is offered by Rudolf Arnheim in *Visual Thinking* (Berkeley: University of California Press, 1969), especially chap. 7.

9.   Geza Roheim, *The Gates at the Dream* (New York: International Universities Press, 1952), Part I.

10. Ignacio Matte Blanco, *The Unconscious as Infinite Sets* (London: Duckworth, 1975).

11. See Sigmund Freud, *An Outline of Psychoanalysis*, ed. James Strachey (1940; rpt. New York: W. W. Norton, 1949), p. 2. Freud maintains that "Space may be a projection of the psychical apparatus." As Matte Blanco points out, it is questionable whether psychic phenomena can be represented in a space of only three dimensions.

12. Matte Blanco, p. 35.

13. The unrepressed, structural view is based on the repression of opposites. This is consistent with Freud's idea of repression. In some respects we may be looking at the same phenomena from two different points of view. Certainly the mere notion that what is unconscious is unacceptable to conscious cognition does little to distinguish the repression of opposites from the repression of other objectionable material. Opposites are objectionable (as well as attractive), and it is not simply a matter of logic but of emotions as well.

14. Ibid., p. 70.

15. Ibid., chap. 2.

16. Ibid., p. 38.

17. Ibid., p. 38; also pp. 37-47.

18. The "social" (as opposed to social-structural) character of unconscious mentation is of the greatest significance to social and political theory, given that it suggests a basis for sympathy and fellow-feeling prior to these social structures and ideological orientations which express, suppress, channel, and narrow such feelings. ("The effect of differentiation is to make vain the hope of direct, immediate fellow-feeling among men." (Chang Chung-yuan, *Creativity and Taoism* (New York: Harper & Row, 1962), p. 23).) In the process, the undifferentiated unconscious challenges the virtual monopoly of social structural understandings of human nature, including those models of the unconscious which in various ways render it "social" only in the sense of accommodating linguistic, social and cultural structures and strictures. Matte Blancho's dedifferentiating unconscious is not irrevocably tied to the system of differences which constitutes language. (In fact, his model makes it clear that a system of mere differences is no system at all.) The idea of *relations*, which are personal and idiosyncratic and not necessarily expressible as concepts, combats this linguistic hegemony. In this connection see "Primary Process, Secondary Process, and Language," Hans W. Loewald, in *Psychoanalysis and Language*, ed. Joseph H. Smith (New Haven: Yale University Press, 1978), pp. 235-270.

19. Ibid., p. 42.

20. Ibid., p. 317.

21. Ibid., p. 319.

22. Ibid., p. 349.

23. Ibid., p. 350.

24. Ibid., p. 351.

25. Ibid., p. 352.

26. Ibid., p. 353.

27. Ibid., p. 353.

28. Ibid., p. 353.

29. Ibid., p. 354. "Homogeneous-heterogeneous" and "totality-part" express the "same psychological experiences, seen from another angle."

30. Ibid., pp. 357-58.

31. Ibid., p. 360.

32. Ibid., p. 361.

33. Ibid., p. 362.

34. Ibid., p. 363. Goethe suggested that "men cannot dwell for long in a conscious state, or in consciousness. He must again take refuge in the unconscious, for that is where life is rooted." (*Wisdom and Experience,* trans. and ed. by Hermann J. Weigand (New York: Pantheon, 1969), p. 134.

35. Ibid., p. 131. It is not clear what he has in mind, given that instincts cannot be known except in their symbolic representations. Presumably we think about instincts as we think of anything else—i.e., as his model describes.

36. It is likely that the partitioning itself, the use of models and analogies based on Cartesian space, is the root difficulty. Relations among phenomena have the effect of condensing space, rendering it "homospatial." Yet Freud considered Cartesian spatial representation one of the advantages of his tripartite model: "We assume that mental life is the function of an apparatus to which we ascribe the characteristics of being extended in space and being made up of several portions." (*An Outline of Psycho-analysis,* ed. James Strachey (1940; rpt. New York: W. W. Norton, 1949), p. 2.)

37. Mircea Eliade, *The Two and the One* (Chicago: University of Chicago Press, 1962).

38. Chang Chung-yuan, *Creativity and Taoism* (New York: Harper & Row, 1963), p. 30.

39. Ibid., p. 47.

40. Ibid., p. 35.

41. Ibid., p. 35.

42. Ibid., p. 35.

43. Nicholas de Cusa, *Vision of God,* trans. Emma Gurney Salter (New York: Ungar, 1960).

44. Ibid., p. 39.

45. Ibid., p. 36.

46. Nicholas de Cusa, p. 44.

47. See C. G. Jung, *Psychology and the East,* trans. R. F. C. Hall (Princeton, N.J.: Princeton University Press, 1978); and *Psychology and Transference,* trans. R. F. C. Hall (Princeton, N.J.: Princeton University Press, 1954).

Chapter Nine

1. Rainer Maria Rilke, *Duino Elegies,* trans. J. B. Leishman and Stephen Spender (New

York: W. W. Norton, 1967), p. 53.

2. Perhaps the most comprehensive account is his *Beyond Good and Evil, trans.* Walter Kaufmann (1886; rpt. New York: Random House, 1966).

3. Friedrich Nietzche, *The Gay Science,* trans. Walter Kaufmann (1887; rpt. New York: Random House, 1974), p. 279.

4. Friedrich Nietzche, *Twilight of the Idols,* in *The Portable Nietzsche,* trans. Walter Kaufmann (New York: Random House, 1964), p. 543.

5. Friedrich Nietzsche, *The Geneology of Morals,* trans. Walter Kaufmann (New York: Random House, 1969), p. 153.

6. Nietzsche, *The Gay Science,* p. 259.

8. Friedrich Nietzsche, *The Will to Power,* trans. Walter Kaufmann (New York: Random House, 1967), p. 398.

9. Friedrich Nietzsche, *Dawn* (1881; rpt. Cambridge: Cambridge University Press, 1982), no. 230.

10. *Dawn,* no. 171.

11. Nietzsche, *Thus Spake Zarathustra,* in *The Portable Nietzsche,* "Of the Way of the Creator."

12. Nietzsche, *The Gay Science,* p. 180.

13. See *Will to Power,* Book Three.

14. Nietzsche, *Dawn,* no. 277.

15. Ibid., no. 348.

16. Ibid., no. 238.

17. Will to Power, p. 193.

18. Friedrich Nietzsche, *A Nietzsche Reader,* ed. R. J. Hollingdale (New York: Penguin, 1977), p. 215.

19. *Beyond Good and Evil,* p. 81.

20. *Gay Science,* pp. 236-37.

21. *Will to Power,* p.490.

22. Ibid., p. 130.

23. *Gay Science,* p. 244.

24. *Beyond Good and Evil,* pp. 100-102.

25. *Twilight of the Idols,* p. 473.

26. Ibid., p. 486.

27. Ibid., p. 487.

28. *Dawn,* p. 166.

29. *Will to Power,* p. 492. "The wisest man would be the one richest in contradictions, who has, as it were, antennae for all types of men—as well as his great moments of grand

harmony" (*Will to Power*, p. 150).

30.   *Gay Science*, p. 299.

Chapter Ten

1.   See Georg Simmel, *On Individuality and Social Forms,* ed. with introduction by Donald N. Levine (Chicago: University of Chicago Press, 1971), p. 17.

2.   The poverty of our linguistic resources in this respect reflects the predominantly dualistic intellectual history of Western culture. A few of these third areas or middle paths have been identified and discussed, however, and each discipline tends to have its particular versions. What is extraordinary is the degree to which discussions of these phenomena involving or suggesting the overcoming of basic oppositions have been segregated from one another. Examples include Eros, as I have interpreted it; love, as sometimes understood; Simmel's "sociability"; Simmel's "adventure"; play; art; certain conceptions of the self, especially those grounded in psychoanalysis; friendship (as in Nietzsche's *Thus Spake Zarathustra*); and Schmalenbach's communion (Bund), a kind of synthesis of difference and equality, conscious and unconscious modes, Gesellschaft and Gemeinschaft.

   The neglect of these modes, particularly Schmalenbach's communion, is surely significant. As a rule both the word and the idea are missing from mainstream sociology and political science, and this helps account for the many sterile and non-terminating disputes in these fields (consensus versus conflict models, reason versus desire in ethics, values versus interest in explaining social order, liberal versus collectivistic perspective, and the like). When these modes are not neglected, they are often confused with symbiosis, fusion, mere aggregation, "consensus," or other matters which do not involve or suggest overcoming, as such.

   This is true of the classical sociologists as well; their attempt to do without a conception of human nature is the root difficulty, Simmel represents an exception of sorts, and none of the classical sociologists were entirely comfortable with the dualisms they inherited or formulated. Weber's fascination with charisma, for example, is suggestive of this concern with the reconciliation of opposites. At stake is the reconciliation of opposite sides of the self, as well as the analysis and resolution of social contradictions.

3.   Ibid., "How Is Society Possible?", pp. 17-18.

4.   "Whatever I create and however much I love it--soon I must oppose it and my love; thus my will wills it." (Nietzsche, *Thus Spake Zarathustra,* in *The Portable Nietzsche,* ed. Walter Kaufmann (New York: Viking, 1954), p. 227.)

5.   "Distance" is related to questions of differentiation, clarity, precision, and certainty. Nietzsche criticizes those who "regard the indistinct idea as a lower kind of idea than the distinct," pointing out that "becoming obscure is a matter of perspective of consciousness" (*Will to Power*, p. 285). Elsewhere he points out that the degree of precision and certainty we agree upon or prefer is a question of values.

6.   Ibid., Levine, p. xxxii. Simmel's outlook might be labeled a dialectical dualism, the dualism of form and content. In many ways this resembles Nietzsche's will to power, a dialectical monism in which the will to power is both form and content. The strong resemblance reminds us that the dialectical quality is often more important than the

monistic or dualistic aspect. In effect, monism reflects a a tendency to see as much as possible as equal (a tendency Nietzsche criticized severely in some contexts). Yet its dialectical quality represents the contribution of the differentiated modes. Conversely, Simmel's dualistic outlook begins at the differentiated pole, and is rendered dialectical by the undifferentiated mode.

7.   One particular interpretation suggests a strong parallel with the model of the psyche we have entertained. Recall that Simmel speaks of (Total) Life as the non-logical union of life and death, in which life can either be differentiation and form or dedifferentiation and formlessness, though he prefers the latter. This means that Life can also be thought of as the overcoming of form and content. If Life equals life and death, which in turn equals form and contents—and if we associate (as Simmel usually does) form with differentiation with death, then his "contents" of life can be interpreted as dedifferentiated, and therefore unconscious. That is, life's "contents" can be thought of as the undifferentiated unconscious. Simmel's analysis of forms can be read accordingly.

8.   Simmel, "Conflict," p. 72.

9.   Ibid., p. 73.

10.   Simmel, "The Transcendent Character of Life," p. 363.

11.   Ibid., p. 355.

12.   Simmel, "Conflict," p. 77.

13.   He admits that "if we wished to postulate a goal adequate to life, it could not coincide with any category of conscious life; it would rather have to explain all of them as a means to itself." (*Will to Power,* trans. Walter Kaufmann (New York: Random House, 1967), p. 376.)) The will to power is not a goal, as such. Elsewhere he suggests that it is a generic category, i.e., willing in general. (*Will to Power,* p. 356.) This parallels our argument that primal ambivalence is a kind of generic opposition, involved in any specific ambivalence. "Will to power" would then be, in our terms, expressed as a formed element—the differentiated faculties—and a formless element, the unconscious. Or in terms of process: forming and rendering formless. In fact, the will to power manifests itself in these two basic ways: the overcoming, and that which is overcome. Overcoming is predicated on dedifferentiation.

14.   Simmel, "Fashion," p. 318.

15.   Ibid., pp. 294-95.

16.   Ibid., p. 295.

17.   Ibid., p. 295.

18.   Ibid., p. 295.

19.   Ibid., p. 295.

20.   Ibid., p. 295.

21.   This is so, but one wonders if he misses something. When the very purpose of being included is to exclude, we need not be surprised that life crashes into life this way. Whether other forms can better express or accommodate both the desire to make equal and to make different is another matter.

22.   Simmel, "Conflict," p. 70.

23.   Ibid., pp. 71-72.

24. Ibid., p. 73.

25. Ibid., p. 77.

26. Ibid., pp. 77-78.

27. Ibid., pp. 78-79.

28. Simmel, "Subjective Culture," p. 234.

29. Ibid., p. 228.

30. Ibid., p. 229.

31. Ibid., p. 229.

32. Ibid., p. 337.

33. Simmel, "The Conflict in Modern Culture," p. 381.

34. Friedrich, Nietzsche, *The Gay Science,* trans. Walter Kaufmann (1887; rpt. New York: Random House, 1964), p. 304.

35. Simmel, "The Conflict in Modern Culture," p. 393.

Chapter Eleven

1. Blaise Pascal, *Pensees and the Provincial Letters* (New York: Random House, 1941), pp. 50-51.

Indices

Index of Names

Subject Index

not exclusively social, 86, 186, 194, 202, 205; overcoming, 48, 91–92, 173–74, 204; punishment, 60–61, 99–100, 123, 166; realization, 16, 28, 44, 46, 49, 57–58, 81, 85, 123, 194–95; reflected, 33; social, 33, 86, 109; as symbolic union of conscious and unconscious, 159–60; total, 33. *See also* Individualism; Personality

Servility, 43, 54, 74. *See also* Alienation, Marx's theory of

Sexual instincts, 102–3. *See also* Instincts; Love

Significant others, 33

Slime, 128–31

Social: character, 52; class, 19, 52; cohesion, 16, 67–68, 74; constraint, 28, 45, 64, 68–69, 73–74; contradictions, 45, 58; facts, 68, 74, 81; forms, 159; functions, 49; interaction, 50, 69, 207; institutions, 35, 73; justice, 70, 72, 80–81; order, 16–17, 35, 39–40, 67, 74, 81, 88, 96, 197; relations, 47–48, 62–64; stability, 93; structure, 114, 188; theory, 91, 106, 159. *See also* Culture; Society

Socialism, 15–16, 68, 83, 86

Socialization, 14, 31–34, 39–40, 83–86, 100. *See also* Self; Social; Society

Society, 43, 45, 51, 61–65, 68, 71–76, 78, 85, 92, 188, 200. *See also* Community

Sociological: method, 80; relativism, 14–16, 157, 208; release, 43 (*see also* Freedom, as absence of constraint); tradition, 8, 176

Sociology, 7, 9, 12, 14, 43, 46. *See also* Functionalism; Sociological Space: cognition of, 141, 148–51, 156, 161, 180. *See also* Time; Timelessness

Species man. See Man, species

Species needs, 26, 50

Species powers, 26, 44, 47, 50

Spontaneity, 45, 47, 80, 92, 179

Srole scale, 11–12, 17. *See also* Anomie, confused with alienation, subjective

Structural model of psyche. *See* Dedifferentiation; Unconscious

Sublimation, 119, 145, 172. *See also* Ambivalence, overcoming of; Repression

Subordination, 54, 57

Suicide, 13, 17, 20; altruistic, 77; anomic, 13, 77; egoistic, 13, 17, 77; fatalistic, 77. *See also* Anomie

Superego, 23, 150. *See also* Tripartite model of psyche

Symbolic universes, 33–34, 38. *See also* Anomie, Berger's view of

Symbolism, 46, 75, 109, 123, 127–31, 154–55. *See also* Opposites, coexistence of, overcoming of; Unconscious

Symmetry, 147–51, 160, 166, 190–91. *See also* Asymmetry; Dedifferentiation

Sympathy, 70, 110. *See also* Infinite sets; Love

Taboo, 97, *See also* Ambivalence; Opposites, coexistence of

Tantric yoga, 152. *See also* Opposites, overcoming of

Taoism, 152, 167, 172. See Coincidentia oppositorum; Middle Way; Opposites, overcoming of

Thanatos. *See* Death, as instinctual

Third French Republic, 73

Time: cognition of, 143, 146–50, 156, 180

Timelessness, 101–2, 143; *See also* Dedifferentiation

Total Life. *See* Life

Totalization, 122, 154–55. *See also* Partialization

Unconscious, 65, 95–97, 100–102; cognition, 137, 178; compensation, 151, 155–57, 204; culture, as, 5; as dedifferentiated, 108, 125, 137, 141–42, 147–49, 158–59, 178–79, 183, 202; depth of, 141–42; as equalizing aspect of man, 152–53; equations established by, 137, 144–45; as establishing part-whole equivalence, 143; as god within, 153; as governed by Principle of Symmetry, 144–45; as the id, 101, 142; motility of cathexes, 101, 143; and paleologic, 101, 36–37; as primary process, 101–2; and repression of ambivalence, 98, 159; scanning, 138–39; "social" aspect of, 145; social, 58–59; as system Ucs, 101–2, 147, 151; as true psychic reality, 149. *See also* Consciousness; Dedifferentiation; Infinite sets; Instincts; Opposites

Undifferentiation, 108, 117, 130, 133. *See also* Dedifferentiation

Universals: and particulars, 75, 161. *See also* Coincidentia oppositorum; Creativity

Utilitarianism, 8, 12, 17–18, 26, 68–70, 82–85, 87, 89, 170; and neo-utilitarianism, 6, 21. *See also* Egoism; Instrumentalism

Welfare state, 14

Will therapy, 123. *See also* Ambivalence, overcoming of

Will to power, 168, 172–77, 185–86, 200; as Eros, 172; as freedom, 172. *See also* Life; Opposites; Self, overcoming

Work, 45, 47, 53, 56, 60–61, 75–76, 80–82; ethic, 16–17